Casebook of Indigenous Business Practices in Africa

The book 'Casebook of Indigenous Business Practices in Africa' has been long-awaited and stands out as one of the few publications that examines the origin and impact of African culture on successful business practices. This book provides a comprehensive depiction of the cultural characteristics, challenges, and orientations that have shaped successful African business practices. It articulates the enduring degree of timeless accomplishments identified across different segments, despite the interjection of Western approaches. Therefore, I highly recommend this book not only to scholars, but also to anyone who wishes to gain a deeper appreciation and understanding of Africa's dynamic indigenous business methods.

Dr. Clara Agomuonso, Chief Operations Officer, FirstBank Democratic Republic of Congo (DRC)

Casebook of Indigenous Business Practices in Africa: Trade, Production and Financial Services – Volume 2

EDITED BY

OGECHI ADEOLA

Lagos Business School, Pan-Atlantic University, Nigeria;
University of Kigali, Rwanda

United Kingdom – North America – Japan – India – Malaysia – China

Emerald Publishing Limited
Howard House, Wagon Lane, Bingley BD16 1WA, UK

First edition 2023

Reprints and permissions service
Contact: permissions@emeraldinsight.com

British Library Cataloguing in Publication Data
A catalogue record for this book is available from the British Library

ISBN: 978-1-80455-763-1 (Print)
ISBN: 978-1-80455-762-4 (Online)
ISBN: 978-1-80455-764-8 (Epub)

Printed and bound by CPI Group (UK) Ltd, Croydon, CR0 4YY

INVESTOR IN PEOPLE

To Dayo and Tochi Adeola, *the strokes of many pens are insufficient to describe my deep appreciation for your love, support and encouragement as I envisioned and then embarked on this journey of documenting indigenous business practices for posterity and a sustainable future in Africa.* Daalu! E se!

Table of Contents

About the Contributors

Ifedapo Adeleye is a Professor of the Practice at Georgetown University, USA. He has undertaken research on the banking industry in Africa in the areas of internationalisation strategy and human capital management, and recently guest-edited a special issue of *Africa Journal of Management* on financial institutions management. He received his PhD in Management from The University of Manchester, UK, and an MS in International Economics Banking and Finance from Cardiff University, UK.

Ogechi Adeola is a Professor of Marketing and the Head of Department of Operations, Marketing and Information Systems at the Lagos Business, Pan-Atlantic University, Nigeria. In addition, she serves as a member of the Governing Board of University of Kigali, Rwanda. Adeola's multi-dimensional research focuses on advancing knowledge across the intersection of marketing, entrepreneurship, tourism, and gender. Her co-authored articles won Best Paper Awards at international conferences for four consecutive years (2016–2019). She is a 2016 Visiting International Fellow, Open University Business School, UK, a 2017 Paul R. Lawrence Fellow, USA, and a recipient of the 2022 Female Achievers Recognition Award in Nigeria. She is the Editor of the 2020 book, 'Indigenous African Enterprise – the Igbo Traditional Business School (I-TBS)', published by Emerald Publishing Limited.

Adedeji Adewusi currently works as a Researcher at Lagos Business School Sustainability Centre, Pan-Atlantic University (formerly Pan-African University), and a research fellow at the Institut Français de Recherche en Afrique/French Institute for Research in Africa. Adedeji is a recipient of the LAPO Institute and International Centre for Tax and Development (ICTD) UK research grants. He holds bachelor's and master's degrees in Sociology. Adedeji's primary research interest revolves around indigenous entrepreneurship, informal economy, governance and their connection with the Sustainable Development Goals. He has published in both local and international journal outlets.

Isaiah Adisa is a management researcher and consultant based in Nigeria. He has co-edited book(s) and several other book chapters and journal articles in recognised outlets. His research interests cuts across human resources management, organizational behaviour, marketing, and gender studies. His consultancy experience spans education, IT and health sector. Isaiah was part of the Sector Master Plan Strategy (a team member of Tourism and Hospitality Industries Thematic Group -THITG) for the Nigeria Economic Summit Group. He is currently a Research Assistant at the Lagos Business School, Pan- Atlantic University, Nigeria.

Emeka Raphael Agu currently works as a Research Assistant at Lagos Business School, Pan-Atlantic University, Nigeria. As a Research fellow, he has worked with several faculty members in teaching and research-related activities and has published academic papers in top scholarly journals. His research interests include strategic management, public policy and leadership.

Olayinka Akanle (PhD) is a Lecturer and Senior Research Associate in the Department of Sociology, University of Ibadan, Nigeria, and University of Johannesburg, South Africa, respectively. Olayinka is an analytically ingenious development sociologist with interests covering research clusters of international migration and diaspora, gender, family and sexuality, child and youth, governance and environment, epistemology and knowledge production, conflict, crime and security, health and medicine. Olayinka has authored, edited and co-edited several journal articles and academic books.

Deogratias Bugandwa Mungu Akonkwa holds a PhD in Economics and Management from the Solvay Brussel School of Economics and Management, ULB, and an advanced Masters in Management Sciences from Louvain School of Management (UCLouvain, Belgium). He also has a Certificate in Governance and Management of Microfinance Institutions (Boulder Institute of Microfinance – ILO/Turin); and in Statistics and Data analysis. He has extensive experience in the governance/management of higher education and microfinance institutions. He is also a teacher-researcher and an expert in financial inclusion, gender and women autonomisation, data analysis, market studies, project evaluation and the conduct of high-level scientific studies. He has published and acted as a reviewer for international journals.

Didier Van Caillie holds a PhD in Business Administration (ULiège) and is a Full Professor of Management Control Systems and Performance Management at the University of Liège in Belgium (HEC-Liège). Since 1997, he has been chief of the Service of Diagnosis and Control of the Firm attached to the University of Liège. His research is focussed on the study of the design of management control systems and safety, risk and performance management systems of various types of firms such as high-tech industrial SMEs (specifically, in high-tech spin-offs) and in not-for-profit organisations such as Healthcare institutions, etc. In 2001, he founded the Research Center on Corporate Performance. He has published in peer-reviewed journals and attended international conferences on Management Control and Business Process Management. He is also an Administrator or Independent Administrator in many organisations and small firms.

Edidiong Esara is a case writer at Lagos Business School (LBS), Pan Atlantic University, Nigeria. Before joining LBS in January 2021, he was PR head of Ritman University for five years and winner of that institution's ambassadorial honour, after being a newspaper editor. He studied Mass Communication, winning the University of Nigeria's 2010 award for the best graduating student in

Reporting, plus two other laurels. A passionate teacher and writer, he has mentored young writers to award-winning status.

Prince Gyimah is a Lecturer in Accounting at Akenten Appiah-Menka University of Skills Training and Entrepreneurial Development and a PhD candidate at Kwame Nkrumah University of Science and Technology, Ghana. His research scholarships include sustainable development goals, small businesses, rural entrepreneurship, accounting, finance and general business management.

Oserere Ibelegbu is a Management Scholar Academy-Research Assistant at Lagos Business School, Pan-Atlantic University, Nigeria. She obtained a master's degree in Information Science and a bachelor's degree in Economics, both from the University of Ibadan, Nigeria. She has academic publications (journal and book chapter contributions in the areas of, consumer behaviour, customer service and service quality, digital technologies, informal economy, corporate social responsibility (CSR) and tourism, among others). Her current area of interest spans customers' reactions or responses to emerging technologies such as AI-induced service robots.

Patricia Isabirye has over 15 years' experience working in the non-profit and private sector in the East and Horn of Africa. She has a PhD in Leadership and a Master's in Leadership in Emerging Countries from the College of Business and Economics at the University of Johannesburg, an MSc in Development Studies from Aalborg University, Denmark and a Bachelor's degree in Mass Communication from Makerere University, Uganda. Patricia is currently the Chief of Staff of Adeso and a Research Associate with the University of Johannesburg. Patricia has authored and co-authored scholarly articles and book chapters and presented at global conferences.

Ishmael Obaeko Iwara is a Post-Doctoral Scholar at the Graduate School of Business and Leadership, University of KwaZulu-Natal in South Africa. Iwara's research interests are Afrocentric entrepreneurship models and pathways, social entrepreneurship and entrepreneurial university, as well as rural and regional economic development. He is a rated scholar by the National Research Foundation of South Africa and has been involved in various research initiatives. His research leadership history among others includes being a Chapter Coordinator of an EDTEA-funded project on social entrepreneurship, manager of an NRF-funded project on social entrepreneurship and innovation, Co-applicant of a Swedish bank-funded project on informal credit systems and entrepreneurial development – SASUF, as well as co-principal investigator of an internally funded project on social cohesion.

Abdul Karim Kafoir is a Sierra Leonean, who currently works as the Assistant Head of the Legal Unit at LAPO-SL Microfinance Company Limited. He also lectures Business Administration, SMEs and IP Strategy and Law at the College of Travel and Tourism Studies. He holds an MBA from the Institute of Public Administration and Management, USL and obtained a master's degree in Intellectual Property from Africa University, Zimbabwe. Kafoir holds degrees in

Law and History and Political Science from Fourah Bay College, University of Sierra Leone, and a Diploma in IP Management Strategies from the National Institute of Small Micro Enterprises, Hyderabad.

Marcellin Chirimwami Luvuga is a PhD Student in Management Sciences at the Catholic University of Bukavu (UCB, Democratic Republic of the Congo). He holds an advanced Masters in Management Sciences from the same university and a Master's degree in Financial Management from the State University of Bukavu (UOB). He is specialising in Small and Medium Entreprises' Control and Management Practices and is a consultant on fiscality of organisations in the DRCongo.

Mohammed Majeed is a Lecturer (PhD) at Tamale Technical University, Tamale-Ghana. His current research interest includes branding, hospitality and tourism, and social media in service organisations. Majeed holds a Doctor of Business Administration (DBA), MPhil and MBA Marketing, Postgraduate Diploma, HND Marketing. He lectures part-time in many Ghanaian public universities and is a reviewer for many journals in management, hospitality and marketing. Majeed has also published in reputed journals such as *Journal of Hospitality and Tourism Insights* (Emerald) and *Cogent Business & Management* (Taylor & Francis).

Felix Adamu Nandonde is a Senior Lecturer in Marketing at Sokoine University of Agriculture (SUA), Tanzania, with more than 26 publications and has co-edited a book titled *Supermarket Retailing in Africa* published by Routledge. He holds a PhD in Business Economics, Aalborg University, Denmark, an MSc in Food Marketing, Newcastle University upon Tyne, UK, and a BBA in Marketing, Mzumbe University, Tanzania. He worked with the National Bank of Commerce (NBC) in 1997 and the Ministry of Livestock and Fisheries in Tanzania from 2018 to 2020.

Belinda Nwosu (FIH) is a faculty member of the Organisational Behaviour and HRM department at Lagos Business School. Her main research interests centre around tourism in emerging economies and the human person in business contexts. To date, she has explored gender, HR leadership, sustainable HRM and governance in tourism; employee work ethic and behaviour and service climate. She has several journal and book chapter publications, including the first comprehensive study on human capital development in the hotel industry in Nigeria.

Babalola Josiah Olajubu (MBPsS) is a psychologist and the head of the psychology unit at the American University of Nigeria. His research cuts across areas of personality, consumer behaviour, Afrocentric business practices and savings culture. Most of his research is conducted using a mixed-method research approach.

Lillian Zippora Omosa (PhD) is the director of Afripreneur Consulting Services, a research and education firm specializing in financial inclusion. She has carried out research on the financial literacy of Micro, Small, and Medium women-owned enterprises in Kenya. Lillian is an accountant, financial strategist, researcher, and university lecturer experienced in leading and executing educational programmes, including developing and implementing financial literacy and governance and leadership training programmes. Her background includes decades of experience in the financial management of projects funded by global funds, the World Bank and USAID, specifically in the financial management of contracts and grants. Current research interests include financial literacy, financial inclusion, Africana Womanism, culturally relevant business practices and participatory action research methods.

Adiza Sadik is an Associate Professor of Hospitality at Tamale Technical University, the Department of Hospitality and Tourism Management (HTM). She obtained her PhD in Hospitality Management from Sheffield Hallam University in the United Kingdom. Sadik is currently the Dean of the Institute of International Programmes and Institutional Linkages (IPIL). Her research interest includes Hospitality and Tourism, Food Technology, Employability, Enterprise and Entrepreneurship, and Gender-related areas.

List of Contributors

Ifedapo Adeleye	Georgetown University, USA
Ogechi Adeola	Lagos Business School, Pan-Atlantic University, Nigeria; University of Kigali, Rwanda
Adedeji Adewusi	University of Ibadan, Nigeria
Isaiah Adisa	Lagos Business School, Pan-Atlantic University, Nigeria
Emeka Raphael Agu	Lagos Business School, Pan-Atlantic University, Nigeria
Olayinka Akanle	University of Ibadan, Nigeria
Edidiong Esara	Lagos Business School, Pan-Atlantic University, Nigeria
Prince Gyimah	Akenten Appiah-Menka University of Skills Training and Entrepreneurial Development, Ghana
Oserere Ibelegbu	Lagos Business School, Pan-Atlantic University, Nigeria
Patricia Isabirye	University of Johannesburg, South Africa
Ishmael Obaeko Iwara	University of KwaZulu-Natal, South Africa
Abdul Karim Kafoir	College of Travel and Tourism Studies, Sierra Leone
Marcellin Chirimwami Luvuga	State University of Bukavu, Congo
Mohammed Majeed	Tamale Technical University, Ghana
Deogratias Bugandwa Mungu Akonkwa	Catholic University of Bukavu, Congo
Felix Adamu Nandonde	Sokoine University of Agriculture, Tanzania

Belinda Nwosu	Lagos Business School, Pan-Atlantic University, Nigeria
Babalola Josiah Olajubu	American University of Nigeria, Nigeria
Lillian Zippora Omosa	Afripreneur Consulting Services, USA and Kenya
Adiza Sadik	Tamale Technical University, Ghana
Didier Van Caillie	Liège University, Belgium

Preface

Indigenous knowledge, long embedded in Africa's business practices, has been attracting interest in recent years as a valuable resource towards the growth and advancement of the African economy. The continent's long history of entrepreneurial trade, production and financial services is evident in cultural and economic clusters and social networks. Africa's diverse history and culture differ not only across regions but also among nations in the same region and even between communities in the same country. The social networks of indigenous business ideas, educational systems and financial management through which identities are established are held together by the culture and customs of each ethnic community. Within this diversity of cultures and traditions are some fundamental commonalities, such as principles of brotherhood, humanity and community support. If properly harnessed, these forms of social capital can propel economic growth and sustainability in the continent. Ubuntu is a primary example of a traditional African concept that embodies these important attributes.

This second part of a two-volume edited book explores Africa's indigenous knowledge and business practices in production, trade and financial services that drive the development of the continent. Case studies provide insights into unique indigenous business methods that can be adopted, innovated or incorporated into modern-day business systems. The importance of indigenous African practices as workable business applications tools is presented to business actors, financial institutions, foreign enterprises, regional governments, policymakers and other stakeholders, based on case study findings reported in these chapters:

Indigenous Black Soap (Ọṣẹ Dúdú) in Southwest Nigeria
Preparation for Business Negotiation at the Livestock Auction Market in Tanzania: The Case of Maasai Livestock Traders
Sustainability of Indigenous Butchery Business in Ghana
What is Peculiar in the Sustainability Practices of Indigenous Female Business Owners in Uganda?
Control/Management Practices and Performance of Small Congolese Enterprises
The Ecosystem of Indigenous Savings and Credit Associations in Sierra Leone
Structure of Indigenous Savings Groups in Nigeria: Cases and Implications for Business Actors

Exploring the Financial Literacy of a Chama Women's Group in Rural Western Kenya
Rotating Stokvel Model for Entrepreneurial Success in South Africa: Validation of Constructs From a Case Study
Internationalisation of Indigenous Agribusiness in Africa: The Case of JR Farms in Rwanda and Zambia

African and foreign scholars will discover how some of the continent's unique indigenous business models have been incorporated into the curricula of business schools in Africa and around the world. New or expanding enterprises aiming to enter or grow in the African market will find useful reference guides for developing sustainable businesses that appreciate and comply with cultural practices, enabling them to create unique value for consumers. The book also identifies the role of business actors in developing indigenous business orientations while offering carefully considered suggestions for all stakeholders – government, educational institutions, entrepreneurs and researchers. The significant contribution of each chapter is to advance knowledge about the economic and social value of indigenous practices in Africa. However, any progress that can be made towards achieving this goal must begin with a clear conviction among Africans that indigenous practices embedded in their culture are valuable and should be leveraged.

Acknowledgement

The editor acknowledges all the authors who embarked on this journey with her to document the indigenous processes, practices and business heritage across Africa, for posterity and to portray the uniqueness of the continent's indigenous enterprises. Thank you for this critical step towards establishing Africa-centric business models through the identification of traditional prototypes and sustainable practices embedded in culture, norms and values.

Chapter 1

Introduction to Casebook on Indigenous Business Practices in Africa – Volume II Trade, Production, and Financial Services

Ogechi Adeola

Abstract

Africa's history of trade, production and financial services that propelled the continent's economic systems existed long before an era of colonisation commonly recognised as beginning in the nineteenth century. By the time the decolonisation of a majority of African countries was achieved in the mid-twentieth century, the African economic identity had been, to a great extent, relegated by Westernised methods and orientations. Today, Indigenous practices are once again resurfacing in Africa's ongoing search for sustainable development, with increasing calls to resuscitate and incorporate these age-long business orientations. This introductory chapter provides readers with a synopsis of all the themes of this second of a two-volume edited book with a focus on the philosophies and practices of Indigenous businesses, which, if successfully explored and scaled up, would make significant contributions to Africa's economic infrastructure.

Keywords: Africa; production; trade; financial services; Indigenous business; casebook

Introduction

The value of Indigenous knowledge cannot be overestimated. Indigenous peoples' interactions with their natural, social, cultural or economic resources provide knowledge that is capable of promoting sustainable growth (Tharakan, 2015). Recent calls for Indigenous solutions to Africa's myriad challenges have prompted researchers, educators, and business leaders to revisit and explore Indigenous practices that have the potential to propel the continent's social and economic

Casebook of Indigenous Business Practices in Africa, 1–14
Copyright © 2023 Ogechi Adeola
Published under exclusive licence by Emerald Publishing Limited
doi:10.1108/978-1-80455-762-420231002

development, particularly within less-developed nations (Adeola, Uzo, & Adewusi, 2020; Aluko, 2018; Olutayo, Akanle, & Fadina, 2017; Tharakan, 2015).

Despite existential proof of the potential of Indigenous practices in providing solutions to many societal challenges, there is still a perception that these Indigenous methods are inferior, especially in comparison to Western ideologies (Briggs, 2005; Moyo, 2009; Moyo & Moyo, 2017). As a result, most Indigenous business knowledge related to production and financial practices on the continent has been gradually phased out, with very little remaining. Western practices have left an indelible footprint on the continent of Africa, drastically disrupting Indigenous businesses, production and financial services, contributing to the slow pace of growth on the continent. Oluwabamide (2015) identifies the lack of adequate research on the awareness and importance of Indigenous practices as one of the many reasons for Africa's Westernisation.

Against this backdrop, this book aims to fill a vacuum in the research regarding the use of Indigenous African practices, especially as they relate to trade, production and finance, in solving socio-cultural challenges prevalent in Indigenous cultures across the continent. The use and appreciation of these practices are essential for all stakeholders, especially business enterprises, in pursuit of the continent's goal of being among the top economies in the world.

An array of seasoned African authors and professionals, with diverse research interests and academic and practice backgrounds on the continent, have contributed to this book. They provide perspectives on Africa's Indigenous trade, production, and financial services practices. The authors engage in discussions about both existing and innovative practices, igniting new ideas and insights on how to amplify Africa's Indigenous traditions and enterprises.

This volume advocates for technocrats, business enterprises, scholars, researchers, educators, legislators and other stakeholders to harness Indigenous knowledge and commit to deliberate analyses of made-in-Africa methods, adopting research methods unique to the continent's resources and cultures rather than treading the research paths marked by Western methodologies. It should be noted, however, that this book does not seek to dismiss or overlook the merits of Western methods of investigation, a proven training ground for many African economic and social advisors. Rather it seeks to challenge those at the helm of affairs in Africa to promote research into Indigenous practices and methodologies, endeavours that will contribute to the growth and development of the continent.

Research into Africa's Indigenous practices will involve not only sifting through extant literature to consolidate prior research but also performing qualitative exploration across Africa's four regions to identify current practices and variances to ensure universality. In this regard, the authors have employed a variety of data-gathering approaches to capture the various features of Indigenous production, finance and trade practices in Africa, and in their bid to ensure their research is representative and captures Africa's unique characteristics, provided a qualitative exploration of Indigenous business models.

This volume begins with a look at the influence of Africa's cultural and Indigenous knowledge on the adoption of Indigenous business practices. Next, there is a discussion on the theory of Indigenous knowledge systems in Africa. The chapter concludes with a synopsis of the book's contributions.

Culture and Indigenous Knowledge in Africa

Unquestionably, culture plays a central role in the application of Indigenous knowledge to Africa's trade, production, and financial services. Culture is a way of life that describes the identity, values, life orientation and distinct characteristics of a set of people. Research on South Africa (Bray & Els, 2007; Mangaliso, 2001), Botswana (Hanson, 2008), Kenya (Jackson, Amaeshi, & Yavuz, 2008), Mauritius (Zafar, 2011), Nigeria (Igwe, 2022) and other African countries has shown that Indigenous African practices are capable of being efficient, innovative, enterprising and forward-thinking. Unfortunately, an emphasis on Western methodologies has suppressed Indigenous cultures rather than appreciating their economic and social value. Traditional Indigenous cultural values are often undermined and labeled as insignificant, wrong-headed, primitive, conservative and unscientific compared to the modern values of Europeans and their associates (Igwe, 2010).

The diverse Indigenous knowledge practices found among Africa's business management, education, finance, health and manufacturing sectors reflect the continent's cultural diversity. This is why it is important to look at Africa as not only a continent with many countries but also a home for many cultures (Ovadje, 2016; Oyewunmi et al., 2021). According to Igwe (2022), even within the same African culture, differences exist in some business practices, education systems and financial systems. As a result, no single culture or Indigenous knowledge practice is universally applicable to all African countries; each culture has value and can boost the continent's economy when properly harnessed. The African continent is blessed with abundant Indigenous knowledge and is unarguably resource-rich, given its abundant human and natural resources. However, the ample Indigenous knowledge and practices are not commonly known or even acknowledged. Western research dominates global management scholarship (Boshoff, Adeola, Hinson, & Heinonen, 2022; Tsui, 2004).

The quest for solutions to Africa's numerous challenges should be sourced from within, rather than 'depending on' Western methodologies. As Indigenous knowledge is culturally relevant, promoting any one method of investigation as universal is very limiting (Mkabela, 2005). Western concepts and methods are often inadequate, and in some cases, completely misaligned, when it comes to comprehensively understanding different social-cultural issues in Africa. As Asante (1987, p. 168) suggests, true universality can only be achieved when we acknowledge and appreciate the truth derived from specific cultural experiences. Some African scholars (Mkabela, 2005; Mpofu, 2011; Bame Nsamenang, 2006; Ntumngia, 2009; Pence & Nsamenang, 2008; Tanyaniwa & Chikwanha, 2011) are re-evaluating Western theories to incorporate African realities, asserting that Africa's Indigenous knowledge can enrich current Western knowledge. Indigenous knowledge has ground-breaking potential because it offers an understanding of how cultural influences are a valuable and endless source of information (Bray & Els, 2007).

Africa's development initiatives will entail Indigenous approaches that differ from Western practices, a growth pattern that can be observed when most developed economies worldwide find value in their Indigenous traditions (Bray & Els, 2007). It is now imperative for Africa to adopt a mindset of thinking globally while acting locally. In essence, Africa should strive to find solutions to its challenges from within the continent, leveraging its own resources, knowledge, and expertise.

The Theory of Indigenous Knowledge Systems in Africa

World Bank (1998) defines Indigenous knowledge as 'local knowledge specific to each culture and society'. It is a 'form' of knowledge passed down over generations to define a community's experiences and traditional interactions with its environment. Indigenous knowledge encompasses virtually every field of human endeavour. It varies significantly from community to community but serves as a common advantage in its ability to address challenges and solve problems unique to each community (Briggs, 2005). Contrary to popular opinion, Hoppers (2002) states that Indigenous knowledge is not static but rather innovative as it evolves over the years in response to changes. Wane (2002) also highlights the dynamic nature of Indigenous knowledge by pointing out that Indigenous forms of knowledge evolve over time, an important aspect of cultural change. According to Wane, learning old knowledge leads to discovering new knowledge, making Indigenous knowledge more dynamic. Barnhardt and Kawagley (2005) 'discussed' the persistence and validity of Indigenous knowledge:

> Indigenous peoples throughout the world have sustained their unique world views and associated knowledge systems for millennia, even while undergoing major social upheavals as a result of transformative forces beyond their control. Many of the core values, beliefs, and practices associated with those worldviews have survived and are beginning to be recognized as being just as valid for today's generations as they were for generations past. t. The depth of Indigenous knowledge rooted in the long inhabitation of a particular place offers lessons that can benefit everyone, from educator to scientist, as we search for a more satisfying and sustainable way to live on this planet. (p. 9)

Indigenous knowledge was defined by Masango (2010) as 'the sum total of all beliefs and skills founded on past experiences and opinions that people hold and use', and by Olaide and Omolere (2013) as 'an essential component of global knowledge'. Indigenous knowledge derives from deep, comprehensive and shared beliefs and rules about physical resources, social norms, health, ecosystems, cultures and the sources of livelihood of people who interact with the environment

(Olaide & Omolere, 2013). These definitions express recurring themes of 'people' who hold a 'belief or knowledge' over a 'lengthy period of time' in a specific 'geographical location'. Knowledge associated with specific cultures and locations has been repeatedly argued to have the potential to not only stimulate development but also sustainable development.

Indigenous knowledge defines the history, identity and social and economic values associated with specific people. For James D. Wolfensohn, President of the World Bank, 'Indigenous knowledge is an integral part of the culture and history of a local community. We need to learn from local communities to enrich the development process' (Gorjestani, 2004, p. 265).

Some Indigenous concepts, philosophies and systems described in this book include the Ubuntu Philosophy, Ethno-finance/Ethno-Manufacturing System, Indigenous Production and Trade in Africa, and Indigenous Practices and Philosophies in Financial Services. A brief description of each follows:

i. *The Ubuntu Philosophy*

   The Ubuntu business philosophy of South Africa, a classic example of Indigenous knowledge, corroborates the insights from World Bank President, James D. Wolfensohn (stated above) on the role of Indigenous knowledge in enriching the development process. Ubuntu, the most prominent of African philosophies, originated in the pre-colonial era but resonates with current day-to-day life (Mangaliso, 2001) and is the foundation of the emerging concept of African Management (West, 2014). Ubuntu philosophy is premised on Afro-centric kinship values, emphasising compassion for humans, oneness and group cohesion (Boshoff et al., 2022; Chigangaidze, 2021). Ubuntu is etymologically referred to with the description 'I am, because you are'. The core values and orientations associated with Ubuntu are that individuals' existence lies in brotherhood. This ideology is reflected in their business models as they act on the ideals of helping others, making sure others thrive and acting on the Ubuntu philosophy that one's achievement is linked to the achievement of others – a social contract of mutual cooperation. Therefore, Ubuntu has provided a social and economic orientation that is capable of driving financial practices in the continent, if well implemented. The rotating Stokvel enterprise discussed below demonstrates aspects of this philosophy.

ii. *Ethno-Finance and Ethno-Manufacturing*

   Africa is a continent of 54 countries with diverse cultures and various regional economic blocs. Africa's Indigenous financial and manufacturing systems are as diverse as the continent's cultures (Yülek & Yeda, 2018). People manage their finances through various age-long systems and engage in manufacturing that aligns with the practices and customs of their locality (Bray & Els, 2007). This cannot be over-emphasised in an emerging global knowledge economy where a country's ability to build and mobilise knowledge capital is just as crucial for long-term development as the availability of physical and financial capital (Gregersen & Johnson, 2009).

Incorporating finance (e.g. savings and lending) into the definition of Indigenous knowledge will result in Indigenous financial knowledge systems. Financial knowledge systems, or ethno-finance, and manufacturing, or ethno-manufacturing, are classified as sub-systems of Indigenous knowledge systems (Bray & Els, 2007). These systems have transformative potential because they provide a comprehensive understanding of cultural processes and legitimate and limitless sources of information (Bray & Els, 2007). The information gained through ethno-finance/-manufacturing will enable Indigenous people to become a part of a new knowledge economy that will act as a crucial driving force in the future and help boost Africa's economy. Unfortunately, the vital features of these concepts have not been adequately harnessed because of insufficient research documentation and the presence of Western cultural influences. Bray and Els (2007) argue that proper documentation and incorporation of ethno-finance/manufacturing as a subsystem of Indigenous knowledge will attract a wide range of limitless possibilities in Africa's economic outlook.

iii. *Indigenous Production and Trade in Africa*

Africa's prospering Indigenous production occupations and trade practices, sources of livelihood for tribes and communities, have been in existence for a long period of time. Africa is notable for food production, with different tribes and countries actively involved in the agricultural sector. For instance, in Senegal, West Africa, farming is the country's primary economic activity; 77.5% of the population are farmers who depend on and cultivate peanuts (*Arachis hypogaea*) and cotton (*Gossypium barbadense*) (Faye, 2020). In Senegal, cash crops are grown for export, while pearl millet (*Pennisetum glaucum*), sorghum (*Sorghum bicolor*), maize (*Zea mays*) and cowpea (*Vigna unguiculata*) as food crops (Faye, 2020).

In the Southern Africa region, there is a significant investment in goat rearing, with an estimated 70% of goats maintained under traditional management systems (Monau, Raphaka, Zvinorova-Chimboza, & Gondwe, 2020). Though challenged with poor infrastructure and a lack of defined marketing channels with multiple breeding objectives, this practice still provides a source of sustainable living, financial stability and resources in poor households, and holds a vital place in the African culture (Monau et al., 2020). Similarly, there are several African countries, including South Africa, Kenya and Ghana, that have become market leaders in vegetable exports.

Another Indigenous production model is black soap making in Ghana and Nigeria. Popularly called *Ọṣẹ dúdú*; the black soap originated in Nigeria (Adewusi & Akanle, 2020). *Ọṣẹ dúdú*, an age-long Yoruba trade product in West Africa, offers health and economic benefits. *Ọṣẹ dúdú* production and trade among the Yorubas have gradually diminished and been substituted with foreign brands (Adewusi & Akanle, 2020), but the production-to-trade network among the Yorubas is an Indigenous model that needs to be revisited because of its proven social and economic success.

iv. *Indigenous Practices and Philosophies in Financial Services*
Origin: African people have historically demonstrated their management practices and philosophies with epoch-making initiatives such as the massive engineering of pyramids in early civilisations in the Mali and Songhai Empires (Oghojafor, Alaneme, & Kuye, 2013). Researchers have found evidence of double-entry bookkeeping in ancient Egypt (Farag, 2009). Pre-colonial East and West Africa conducted trade that for centuries was a centrepiece of the societal fabric, complete with Indigenous currencies and market systems (Stiansen & Guyer, 1999). History clearly shows that monetisation of the African economic system began far before the advent of Europeans (Adebayo, 1994).

The pre-colonial market in Africa had a basic production system determined by the essential values rooted in the social structure (e.g. redistribution, prestige and gift exchange) (Turyahikayo-Rugyema, 1976). Markets in Africa originated from barter, followed by a progression from a monetised exchange to commercialisation involving long-distance trade in the nineteenth century. Some of the features of these Indigenous African trade and production systems were the use of trade finance, trade credit, currency, wealth accumulation and redistribution (Ojera, 2018). Instead of the Western financial management practice of viewing a firm as the unit of analysis, the Indigenous production units merged around family work, communal work and village work with no cash involved (Eze, 1995). Indigenous African businesses were informal and focussed on village, communal or family welfare. These African practices, unlike Western practices, are not codified but orally transmitted across generations through storytelling and communal interactions (Afro-Centric Alliance, 2001).

Compared to the pre-colonial era, contemporary financial management in Africa has a number of ills: inefficiency (Mutenheri, 2003), poor access to finance (Afrikstart, 2016), weak legal regulations, poor investor protection and information accessibility (Uyar & Kuzey, 2014). Yet, studies such as Eze (1995) have opined that colonialism disrupted the Indigenous systems in Africa, and thus fuelled what may be termed 'colonised African management'. In response, Oghojafor et al. (2013) argued that although African management practices had survived through tortuous colonialism, economic exploitation and cultural annihilation such that trade finance, wealth accumulation and redistribution continue as modern financial practices in Africa, they are severely tinted with Western paradigms.

This question needs a research-based response: Can the solutions to problems arising in the implementation of contemporary financial management across the continent be found in Indigenous African philosophy? For example, the response to inadequate finance for SMEs may be found in the Ubuntu philosophy, based on Indigenous African solidarity finance systems such as communal financial institutions (Ojera, 2018). Communal financial institutions found across Africa include Etibe, Esusu, and Osusu (Nigeria), Chama and Harambees (Kenya), Xitiques (Mozambique), Susu (Ghana), Chilemba and Dajanggi (Cameroon), Gamiayah (Egypt), Ungalebo and

Stokvel (South Africa), Chilimba (Zambia) and Chiperegani (Malawi). These examples demonstrate that pooling funds to support initiatives is well-ingrained in the African philosophy (Afrikstart, 2016). Case studies have found examples of these Indigenous financial practices across the continent:

Practices: There are notable and successful Indigenous financial practices across Africa. For instance, Indigenous savings associations are ubiquitous and important to the growth of the informal economy but have not been sufficiently harnessed by enterprises despite the opportunities they provide for investment, social cohesion and livelihood to the associations' members. Indigenous savings groups existed in Africa even before the introduction of formal banking institutions (Adeola et al., 2022). Known by different names, these groups exist in Africa as ROSCAs (rotating savings and credit associations) and accumulating savings and credit associations (ASCAs) and cooperative societies, which, in some cases, are not regulated. In Nigeria, Table 1 outlines the various names of ROSCAs across ethnic groups in the country.

In Sierra Leone, traditional savings plans, or 'Osusu', and credit associations are largely unions with common economic goals. Individual savings plans become a resource to meet members' financial needs, including asset acquisition, emergency expenses or starting a business. These Indigenous financial practices help foster inclusive growth, particularly in the informal sector.

In South Africa, the rotating Stokvel enterprise, a traditional credit association, has helped many businesses establish financial stability with savings plans created to support entrepreneurs (Iwara et al., 2021). The benefits of the rotating Stokvel enterprise for business financing among business actors in Africa are discussed in this book.

Table 1. ROSCAs Across Nigeria's Ethnic Groups.

Name	Tribe	Region
Esusu	Yoruba	South-western Nigeria
Isusu, oha, ogbo	Igbo	South-eastern Nigeria
Etibe	Ibibio	South-South Nigeria
Oku	Kalabari	South-South Nigeria
Asun	Ishan	South-South Nigeria
Etoto	Ibibio	South-South Nigeria
Osusu	Edo	South-South Nigeria
Adashi	Hausa	Northern Nigeria
Dashi	Nupe	North Central Nigeria

Source: Adeola et al. (2022, p. 196).

The Somalis business model in Kenya, East Africa, is another example of Indigenous financial practice. The rapid expansive growth of the Somali business community in many parts of the world has ignited varied debates. The Kenyan Somali community is made up of inhabitants of the north-eastern region that cuts across the three counties of Wajir, Garissa and Mandera, bordering Somalia and Ethiopia (Kinoti et al., 2022). The well-established Somali communities in all cities and urban centres throughout the area engage in a variety of economic activities, including informal value transfer systems (IVTS). Volume 1 of this edited work discussed this business model extensively.

The Structure of the Book and Summary of Chapters

This book is divided into 3 parts with 12 chapters, each of which focusses on a different aspect of Africa's Indigenous practices:

Part 1: Indigenous Trade Practices and Production
Part 2: Indigenous Financial Practices
Part 3: Conclusions and Recommendations

Part 1: Indigenous Trade Practices and Production
Chapter 2: Challenges of Indigenous Black Soap (Ọṣẹ Dúdú) Entrepreneurs in South-West Nigeria. Olayinka Akanle and Adewusi Adedeji describe the developmental benefits of Ọṣẹ dúdú production, sale and consumption. Several important benefits are associated with Ọṣẹ dúdú: It is a major Indigenous resource used in the South-western part of Nigeria for both body ornamentation and a medical complement. The soap plays an important role in the Yoruba people's system of Indigenous knowledge. It is a source of income and a crucial tool for social and economic development in Nigeria. The chapter authors conclude by pointing out some of the challenges faced by black soap (Ọṣẹ dúdú) entrepreneurs (e.g. lack of funds, product awareness and support) and suggest solutions to overcome those challenges.

Chapter 3: Preparation for Business Negotiation at the Livestock Auction Market in Tanzania: The Case of Maasai Livestock Traders. Felix Nandonde discusses in detail how preparation for business negotiation is conducted between Maasai livestock traders at the livestock auction market in Tanzania. The Maasai people's economy and way of life are connected with their cattle herds in the Great Rift Valley of southern Kenya and northern Tanzania. It makes them one of the continent's most vibrant Indigenous communities in the livestock trade. The people depend on their cattle to fulfil their most fundamental needs, including food, clothing and shelter. The livestock trade is the most important form of cash in the Maasai community.

Chapter 4: Sustainability of Indigenous Butchery Business in Ghana – Mohammed Majeed, Prince Gyimah and Adiza Sadik. The study explores the sustainability practices among Indigenous butchery businesses in a developing country, and in this context, Ghana. Qualitative interview data are employed to understand the start-up procedures, sustainable factors, benefits, opportunities, challenges and strategies that advance the sustainability of butchery businesses.

Chapter 5: What is Peculiar in the Sustainability Practices of Indigenous Female Business Owners in Uganda? Patricia Isabirye explores women's participation in Uganda's strong entrepreneurship culture. Uganda is one of only seven countries in the world to attain gender parity in terms of the number of women motivated to pursue entrepreneurial activities. Uganda's female business owners and the participation rate in economic activities are likewise high in comparison to other sub-Saharan African countries. The chapter author discusses Uganda's unique means of sustaining entrepreneurial business practices and what has made those practices flourish.

Chapter 6: Informality, Control/Management Practices, and Performance of Small Congolese Enterprises: A Focus on SMEs in the City of Bukavu. Marcellin Cirimwami Luvuga, Deogratias Bugandwa Mungu Akonkwa and Didier Van Caillie examine the role of informal management practices in order to ascertain how these practices may contribute to the financial success of Congolese SMEs. Applying the contingency theory, the multi-site case study focuses on the management practices of four SMEs in Bukavu, Congo.

Part 2: Indigenous Financial Practices

Chapter 7: The Ecosystem of Indigenous Savings and Credit Associations in Sierra Leone: Entrepreneurial Success or Nightmare? In this chapter, Abdul Karim Kafoir and Emeka Raphael Agu give an account of Sierra Leone's Indigenous financial practices, the ethical concerns related to those practices, and the manner in which they support entrepreneurs. Sierra Leone's major Indigenous financial processes supply credit in two ways: Osusu (rotating savings) and credit associations. Association members use these sources to save for medical expenses, bundu society, bride price or school expenses. In addition, they execute credit discipline by claiming any part of a defaulter's assets.

Chapter 8: Structure of Indigenous Savings Groups in Nigeria: Cases and Implications for Business Actors. Ogechi Adeola, Ifedapo Adeleye, Oserere Ibelegbu, Babalola Josiah Olajubu and Isaiah Adisa, through qualitative case analysis, examine the structure of Indigenous savings groups, which could either be unstructured, semi-structured or structured. The authors note that even though the savings groups have similar orientations and goals, they are unique in relation to their operating structures. Relative themes that cut across the cases discussed are highlighted, and plausible recommendations for upscaling and adopting Indigenous savings groups in Nigeria and Africa are provided. The authors conclude that the role of government and other business actors in facilitating Indigenous savings groups is highly crucial to experiencing a boom in the overall informal economy.

Chapter 9: The Financial Literacy of Chama Women's Groups in Rural Western Kenya. Lillian Zippora Omosa describes the age-old Indigenous financial practices and financial literacy of Chama women's groups in rural Western Kenya. Chama, a popular practice in Kenya, operates through a systematic gathering of funds from members and lending mechanisms offered to group members in a merry-go-round manner. The pooled money is lent to meet household necessities and support livelihoods. Members repay the loans within an agreed-upon cycle.

Chapter 10: Rotating Stokvel Model for Entrepreneurial Success in South Africa. Ishmael Obaeko Iwara and Ogechi Adeola describe the Stokvel model, a kind of credit union in which a group of people agree to contribute a set amount of money to a common pool on a weekly, biweekly or monthly basis. The authors assess the applicability of the model, especially among entrepreneurs in Limpopo Province of South Africa. They validate the model's construct through a study of Stokvel members in the Province.

Part 3: Conclusions and Recommendations

Chapter 11: Internationalisation of Indigenous Agribusiness in Africa: The Case of JR Farms in Rwanda and Zambia – Belinda Nwosu and Edidiong Esara. This chapter focusses on the internationalisation pathways for Indigenous businesses in Africa by taking a cue from JR Farms. Authors suggested that Indigenous businesses in Africa should leverage the opportunities in Africa-to-Africa internationalisation and position their businesses beyond the scope of their home countries.

Chapter 12: Advancing Africa's Indigenous Business Practices: Recommendations for Educators and Business Actors. The author, Ogechi Adeola, highlights the important recommendations made in each chapter and raises pertinent questions about the next course of action to be undertaken to advance the discourse on Indigenous practices in the African continent.

Conclusion

The authors' qualitative case studies provide plausible recommendations for business actors, educators and government agencies to pursue research into African Indigenous knowledge sustainability and awareness. Financial actors will be introduced to the value propositions of ethno-finance and ethno-manufacturing as a tool for fighting poverty in Africa. An exploration of Indigenous African philosophies such as Ubuntu can propel business growth and success as companies collaborate across tribes and regions. Educators, finance actors, governments and non-governmental organisations, and enterprise stakeholders are offered much-needed directions to initiate methods that appeal to various African localities, boost the economy and sustain the continent's age-old Indigenous culture.

References

Adebayo, A. G. (1994). Money, credit, and banking in pre-colonial Africa: The Yoruba experience. *Anthropos, 89*(4/6), 379–400.

Adeola, O., Uzo, U., & Adewusi, A. (2020). Indigenous financial practices of Igbo micro-entrepreneurs in lagos. In *Indigenous African enterprise.* Bingley: Emerald Publishing Limited.

Adeola, O., Adeleye, I., Muhammed, G., Olajubu, B. J., Oji, C., & Ibelegbu, O. (2022). Savings groups in Nigeria. In *Transforming Africa* (pp. 193–216). Bingley: Emerald Publishing Limited.

Adewusi, A. O., & Akanle, O. (2020). Ọṣẹ Dúdú: Exploring the benefits of Yoruba indigenous black soap in Southwest, Nigeria. *The International Indigenous Policy Journal, 11*(1), 1–20.

Afrikstart. (2016). *Crowdfunding in Africa fundraising goes digital in Africa: The emergence of Africa-based crowdfunding platforms.* Retrieved from http://afrikstart. com/report/wpcontent/uploads/2016/09/Afrikstart-Crowdfunding-In-Africa-Report.pdf

Afro-Centric Alliance. (2001). Indigenizing organizational change: Localization in Tanzania and Malawi. *Journal of Managerial Psychology, 16*(1), 5978.

Aluko, Y. A. (2018). Women's use of indigenous knowledge for environmental security and sustainable development in Southwest Nigeria. *International Indigenous Policy Journal, 9*(3).

Asante, S. K. (1987). Over a hundred years of a national legal system in Ghana. *Journal of African Law, 31*(1–2), 70–92.

Bame Nsamenang, A. (2006). Human ontogenesis: An Indigenous African view on development and intelligence. *International Journal of psychology, 41*(4), 293–297.

Barnhardt, R., & Oscar Kawagley, A. (2005). Indigenous knowledge systems and Alaska Native ways of knowing. *Anthropology & Education Quarterly, 36*(1), 8–23.

Boshoff, C., Adeola, O., Hinson, R. E., & Heinonen, K. (2022). Viewpoint: Plotting a way forward for service research in and out of Africa. *Journal of Services Marketing, 36*(4), 450–460.

Bray, R. J. C., & Els, G. (2007). Unpacking 'ethno-finance': An introduction to indigenous 'financial' knowledge systems. *South African Journal of Information Management, 9*(1), 1–12.

Briggs, J. (2005). The use of indigenous knowledge in development: Problems and challenges. *Progress in Development Studies, 5*(2), 99–114.

Chigangaidze, R. K. (2021). An exposition of humanistic-existential social work in light of ubuntu philosophy: Towards theorizing ubuntu in social work practice. *Journal of Religion & Spirituality in Social Work: Social Thought, 40*(2), 146–165.

Eze, N. (1995). *Human resource management in Africa: Problems and solutions.* Lagos: Zomex Press.

Farag, S. M. (2009). The accounting profession in Egypt: Its origin and development. *The International Journal of Accounting, 44*, 403–414.

Faye, J. B. (2020). Indigenous farming transitions, sociocultural hybridity and sustainability in rural Senegal. *NJAS: Wageningen Journal of Life Sciences, 92*(1), 1–8.

Gorjestani, N. (2004). Indigenous knowledge for development. In S. Twarog & P. Kapoor (Eds.), *Protecting and promoting traditional knowledge: Systems, national experiences and international dimensions* (pp. 265–271). Geneva: United Nations.

Gregersen, B., & Johnson, B. (2009). Institutions and policy learning supporting economic development. In *Paper Presented at Globelics 2009: Inclusive Growth, Innovation and Technological Change: Education, Social Capital and Sustainable Development*, Dakar, Senegal. Retrieved from http://globelics2009dakar.merit. unu.edu/

Hanson, P. W. (2008). In R. Eversole, J.-A. McNeish, & A. D. Cimadamore (Eds.), *Indigenous peoples and poverty: An international perspective* (p. 320). London: Zed Books, 2005. ISBN 1-84277-679-7. Journal of International Development, *20*(2), 251–252.

Hoppers, C. A. O. (Ed.). (2002). *Indigenous knowledge and the integration of knowledge systems: Towards a philosophy of articulation.* Cape Town: New Africa Books.

Jackson, T., Amaeshi, K., & Yavuz, S. (2008). Untangling African indigenous management: Multiple influences on the success of SMEs in Kenya. *Journal of World Business, 43*(4), 400–416.

Igwe, P. A. (2022). Cross-cultural tribes, community and Indigenous entrepreneurship. In *The International Dimension of Entrepreneurial Decision-Making: Cultures, Contexts, and Behaviours* (pp. 163–179). Springer Nature. Retrieved from https://link.springer.com/book/10.1007/978-3-030-85950-3#bibliographic-information

Igwe, K. N. (2010). Resource sharing in the ICT era: The case of Nigerian university libraries. *Journal of Interlibrary Loan, Document Delivery & Electronic Reserve, 20*(3), 173–187.

Iwara, I. O., & Netshandama, V. O. (2021). Small-enterprise capital mobilization and marketing in rural areas: A review synthesis of Stokvel model. *Academy of Entrepreneurship Journal, 27*(2), 1–11.

Kinoti, A. M., & Otike, F. (2022). *Community knowledge and the role of libraries and librarians in the current digital age.* Library Hi Tech News, Vol. ahead-of-print No. ahead-of-print. doi:10.1108/LHTN-09-2022-0106

Mangaliso, M. P. (2001). Building competitive advantage from Ubuntu: Management lessons from South Africa. *Academy of Management Executive, 15*(3), 23–33.

Masango, C. A. (2010). Indigenous traditional knowledge protection: Prospects in South Africa's intellectual property framework? *South African Journal of Libraries and Information Science, 76*(1), 74–80.

Mkabela, Q. (2005). Using the Afrocentric method in researching Indigenous African culture. *The Qualitative Report, 10*(1), 178–189.

Monau, P., Raphaka, K., Zvinorova-Chimboza, P., & Gondwe, T. (2020). Sustainable utilization of indigenous goats in Southern Africa. *Diversity, 12*(1), 20.

Moyo, B. H. Z. (2009). Indigenous knowledge-based farming practices: A setting for the contestation of modernity, development and progress. *Scottish Geographical Journal, 125*(3–4), 353–360.

Moyo, B. H. Z., & Moyo, D. Z. (2017). Indigenous knowledge perceptions and development practice in northern Malawi: Lessons from small-scale farmers' agricultural practices. In *Handbook of research on social, cultural, and educational considerations of indigenous knowledge in developing countries* (pp. 280–302). Hershey, PA: IGI Global.

Mpofu, E. (Ed.). (2011). *Counseling people of African ancestry.* New York, NY: Cambridge University Press.

Mutenheri, E. (2003). *The determinants of corporate financial policy in Zimbabwe: Empirical evidence from company panel data.* PhD Manuscript, Loughborough University.

Ntumngia, R. N. (2009). Uncovering farmers' ethnobotanical knowledge: A methodology for assessing farmers' perceptions of cassava varieties. In *9th African Crop Science, Conference Proceedings*, Cape Town, South Africa, September 28–October 2, 2009 (pp. 467–473). African Crop Science Society.

Oghojafor, B. E. A., Alaneme, G. A., & Kuye, O. L. (2013). Indigenous management thoughts, concepts and practices: The case of the Igbos of Nigeria. *Australian Journal of Business and Management Research, 3*(1), 815.

Ojera, P. (2018). Indigenous financial management practices in Africa: A guide for educators and practitioners. In *Indigenous management practices in Africa*. Bingley: Emerald Publishing Limited.

Olaide, I. A., & Omolere, O. W. (2013). Management of Indigenous knowledge as a catalyst towards improved information accessibility to local communities: A literature review. *Chinese Librarianship: An International Electronic Journal, 35*, 87–98.

Olutayo, A. O., Akanle, O., & Fadina, O. A. (2017). The socio-economic developments of Aso-Oke of South-Western Nigeria. *Asian & African Studies, 26*(1), 41–68.

Oluwabamide, A. J. (2015). An appraisal of African traditional economy as an heritage. *International Journal of Research, 2*(12), 107–111.

Ovadje, F. (2016). The internationalization of African firms: Effects of cultural differences on the management of subsidiaries. *Africa Journal of Management, 2*(2), 117–137.

Oyewunmi, A. E., Esho, E., & Ukenna, S. I. (2021). Navigating the realities of intercultural research in sub-Saharan Africa: Insights from Nigeria. In *Field guide to intercultural research* (pp. 256–269). Cheltenham: Edward Elgar Publishing.

Pence, A., & Nsamenang, B. (2008). A case for early childhood development in Sub-Saharan Africa. In *Working Papers in Early Childhood Development*, No. 51. PO Box 82334, 2508 EH, The Hague: Bernard van Leer Foundation.

Stiansen, E., & Guyer, J. I. (1999). *Credit, currencies, and culture: African financial institutions in historical perspective*. Uppsala: Nordiska Afrikainstitutet.

Tanyanyiwa, V. I., & Chikwanha, M. (2011). The role of Indigenous knowledge systems in the management of forest resources in Mugabe area, Masvingo, Zimbabwe. *Journal of Sustainable Development in Africa, 13*(3), 132–149.

Tharakan, J. (2015). Indigenous knowledge systems-a rich appropriate technology resource. *African Journal of Science, Technology, Innovation and Development, 7*(1), 52–57.

Turyahikayo-Rugyema, B. (1976). Markets in precolonial East Africa: The case of the Bakiga. *Current Anthropology, 17*(2), 286–290.

Tsui, A. S. (2004). Contributing to global management knowledge: A case for high quality Indigenous research. *Asia Pacific Journal of Management, 21*, 491–513.

Uyar, A., & Kuzey, C. (2014). Determinants of corporate cash holdings: Evidence from the emerging market of Turkey. *Applied Economics, 46*(9), 1035–1048.

Wane, N. N. (2002). African women and spirituality: Connections between thought and education. In E. V. O'Sullivan, A. Morrell, & M. O'Connor (Eds.), *Expanding the boundaries of transformative learning: Essays on theory and praxis* (pp. 135–150). New York, NY: Palgrave.

West, A. (2014). Ubuntu and business ethics: Problems, perspectives and prospects. *Journal of Business Ethics, 121*(1), 47–61.

Yülek, M. A., & Yeda, V. (2018). Broadening financial intermediation in Sub-Saharan Africa. *Financing Sustainable Development in Africa*, 93–119.

Zafar, A. (2011). Mauritius: An economic success story. In P. Chuhan-Pole & M. Angwafo (Eds.), *Yes Africa can: Success stories from a dynamic continent* (pp. 91–106). Washington, D.C.: The World Bank.

Part 1
Indigenous Trade Practices and Production

Chapter 2

Challenges of Indigenous Black Soap (*Ọṣẹ Dúdú*) Entrepreneurs in Southwest Nigeria

Olayinka Akanle and Adedeji Adewusi

Abstract

Ọṣẹ dúdú production and sale constitute a major indigenous business among the Yoruba people. Scholars have noted that the business is capable of boosting the socio-economic status of black soap entrepreneurs and of countries. However, *ọṣẹ dúdú* enterprise has some significant threats and problems that are yet to be researched. This chapter examined the challenges of *ọṣẹ dúdú* entrepreneurs in Southwest Nigeria. Twenty-six interviews were conducted among indigenous black soap producers and sellers in Ogun, Oyo and Lagos States. Data were analysed in themes. Weather, financial, spiritual, copyright and succession challenges, as well as issues such as a large number of sellers, debt, lack of support, pricing and brand competition, were found to be problems faced by black soap entrepreneurs. This chapter concluded that certain controllable and uncontrollable factors were not only capable of limiting the development of *ọṣẹ dúdú* business but also have adverse implications for the achievement of the sustainable development goals through the indigenous resource. This chapter suggests that *ọṣẹ dúdú* business actors such as mechanical engineers, local fabricators, financial institutions, and governmental and non-governmental agencies collaborate with black soap entrepreneurs to ameliorate the challenges of the latter. It is only through this alliance that black soap entrepreneurs can contribute to indigenous business development and the achievement of sustainable development goals in Africa.

Keywords: Black soap (*ọṣẹ dúdú*) entrepreneur; challenge; indigenous knowledge; Nigeria; Yoruba; indigenous technology

Casebook of Indigenous Business Practices in Africa, 17–40
Copyright © 2023 Olayinka Akanle and Adedeji Adewusi
Published under exclusive licence by Emerald Publishing Limited
doi:10.1108/978-1-80455-762-420231005

Introduction

In less-developed nations, western knowledge systems have been receiving increasing criticisms for their inability to address the socio-economic and socio-technological problems affecting basic human needs in African countries (Olutayo, Akanle, & Fadina, 2017; Tharakan, 2015). This is because the solutions offered by foreign development projects do not fit well into the local knowledge systems; they lack autonomy and are inappropriately incorporated into African development plans (Akanle, Adesina, & Fakolujo, 2017). Hence, a development framework that works for a particular country may not work for another due to the difference in the content (i.e. the people and their belief system) and context (i.e. the social structures and their prevailing historical and social foundations) of the adopting country (Olutayo, 2012). This preceding argument may be linked to the reason several authors and experts have stressed that societal growth and development will be achieved if and only if the development plans and policies of less developed nations acknowledge the indigenous knowledge system prevailing in these African countries (Hoppers, 2017; Rist et al., 2011; Tharakan, 2015).

One of the problems of successful industrialisation in Nigeria is undoubtedly the utilisation of foreign means and/or resources to create social and economic values that are incongruent with the nation's social context. Perhaps, with the contact with '*mônîyâw*' (i.e. imported development initiatives), the beliefs and knowledge perpetuated about indigenous people have been cross-culturally mis-communicated and have propagated an unending misunderstanding. This has extended into appropriation through interpretations and representations domi-nated by non-indigenous people. Closely related to the above assertion is the submission of Olatokun and Ayanbode (2008), who concluded that the Third World countries had made mistakes in efforts to bring about development in Africa. They have depended on the developed world for aid and assistance for too long. This has made it challenging to achieve viable approaches to development in most African nations. The foregoing is a clear indication that the western knowledge system is not suitable for the propagation of development in Africa (Lwoga, Ngulube, & Stilwell, 2010; Olatokun & Ayanbode, 2008; Olutayo & Akanle, 2009; Sillitoe, 2006), especially for a sustainable one (Olutayo, Akanle, & Fadina, 2017; Rist et al., 2011).

Despite the importance of indigenous knowledge to the growth and develop-ment of African countries, Nigeria inclusive, these knowledge systems are fast eroding due to colonialism, globalisation, lack of proper commodification, codification and westernisation of African institutions (Jegede, 2016). Further-more, Nigeria is enormously blessed with both natural and human resources (Kalejaiye, Sokefun, & Adewusi, 2015). In terms of natural resources, Waziri (2017) pointed out that Nigeria could as well be the biblical Promised Land: a land endowed with large deposits of 44 different minerals spread across the country with a favourable topographical terrain. In a country of approximately 180 million persons (NPC, 2015), Nigeria is still faced with developmental chal-lenges despite these enormous human and material endowments (Kalejaiye et al., 2015). Some of these endowments, especially the forest resources, have been confirmed to have a close association with rural economic and health activities (Oluyole et al., 2005). Hence, they can only realise their full potential when their development is integrated into that of agriculture, large forest industries, natural resources development, rural manufacturing and health-based enterprises (Oluyole & Adeogun, 2005). For instance, researchers have identified some non-timber forest products (NTFPs) such as firewood and sawdust ash alongside agro-processing wastes generated from agro-processing enterprises being utilised by small-scale industries to produce consumer products such as black soap (Adewusi & Akanle, 2020; Oluyole & Adeogun, 2005; Yusuf & Okoruwa, 2006).

The primary aim of this chapter is to explore the challenges faced by *ọṣẹ dúdú* (indigenous black soap) producers and sellers in selected states in southwest Nigeria. This is mainly predicated on the fact that *ọṣẹ dúdú* occupies a critical place within the web of the indigenous knowledge system of the Yoruba people. Hence, black soap is an essential tool for the social and economic development of Nigeria. Indigenous knowledge to an appreciable degree, 'local content' can constitute the only sustainable engine of development. This is because indigenous knowledge is often acquired across generations with a deep understanding of the affected socio-cultural, economic and ecological environments (Aluko, 2018; Olutayo et al., 2017; Rist et al., 2011). Moreover, the use of 'local content' in development efforts pay attention to and understands local dynamics that determine the whole performance of the society in the short and long run. They also provide communities with experience and expertise as they pertain to societal survival and flourishing in the local environmental and resource context (Aluko, 2018; Tharakan, 2015).

Soaps produced from wood ash, such as *ọṣẹ dúdú*, which is largely produced by women (Alo, Achem, Mohammed, & Abdulquadir, 2012; Oluwalana et al., 2016), are well recognised in the traditional setting and served different cultures of the world due to its efficient bactericidal and dermatological properties. Of utmost importance here are the studies of Adewusi (2018) and Yusuf and Okoruwa (2006), which reported that *ọṣẹ dúdú* is being manufactured locally and capable of increasing the profitability of black soap entrepreneurs, generating employment and revenue opportunities for African countries, Nigeria inclusive. However, soap processing enterprises have some basic characteristics, problems and economic growth potentials that have to be researched. For instance, some authors confirmed that many entrepreneurs who found and managed SMEs lack the appropriate management skills (Olayide et al., 2021; Lawal, Kio, Sulaimon, & Adebayo, 2000). Additionally, due to the lack of adequate capital has been found to adversely affect black soap entrepreneurs (Alo et al., 2012; Oluwalana, Adekunle, & Okojie, 2012). Besides, sheer ignorance of technological advances, such that entrepreneurs purchase obsolete and inefficient equipment, thereby setting the stage ab initio, were also found to be responsible for a lower level of productivity, poor product output and market acceptability of black soap (Lawal et al., 2000). The outcome, of course, is the closure of some enterprises while many others drastically reduced their scale of operations. As a result of the foregoing, it is most important to document the peculiar problems of *ọṣẹ dúdú* entrepreneurs in order to safeguard the developmental prospects of the business concern.

This chapter was justified on the basis that previous studies on *ọṣẹ dúdú* in Nigeria have largely examined the microbiological constituents of the resource (Adebiyi & Adeniyi, 2004; Aliyu et al., 2012; Aliyu, Ladan, Ahmed, & Abdullahi, 2007; Beetseh & Anza, 2013; Egho & Emosairue, 2010; Ikotun, Awosika, & Oladipo, 2015; Ikpoh et al., 2012; Lucet et al., 2002; Oyekanmi, Adebayo, & Farombi, 2014; Oyeniran, 2015; Oyeniran & Oguniran, 2015; Oyeniran & Ogunleye, 2015; Oyeniran, Oladunmoye, & Aladeselu, 2015; Zauro et al., 2016), while the social science analysis of the resource is still lacking (Borokini & Lawal, 2014; George, Ogunbiyi, & Daramola, 2006; Lin, Nabatian, & Halverstam, 2017; Oluwalana et al., 2016). Moreover, previous studies have largely focused on the medicinal benefits of this soap (Ahmed et al., 2005; Ajaiyeoba, 2003; Ajose, 2007; Anyakoha, 2011; Ekwenye & Ijeomah, 2005; Getradeghana, 2000; Mike, 2008; Taiwo & Osinowo, 2001; Ugbogu, 2006). However, none of the aforementioned studies has examined the challenges faced by *ọṣẹ dúdú* entrepreneurs.

This chapter is further divided into six sections. The next section briefly examined the historical connection between the Yoruba ethnic group and the indigenous black soap, while the third section succinctly discussed the methodology adopted by the chapter. The fourth section unearthed the findings of the chapter, while the fifth section discussed the findings of the chapter vis-à-vis what was obtainable in previous studies on the subject matter. The chapter's summary and conclusion as well as policy recommendations were discussed in the sixth and seventh sections, respectively.

The Yoruba Ethnic Group and Indigenous Black Soap: A Brief Historical Overview

Nigeria is a multicultural nation with not less than 400 ethnic groups (Olutayo, 2012), with each having its respective indigenous ways of practically solving societal problems. The Yoruba people, popularly found in the southwestern part of Nigeria, are one of the major ethnic groups in Nigeria.

The southwestern part of Nigeria is commonly referred to as the Yoruba nation; 99.9% of residents in Lagos, Oyo, Osun, Ondo and Ogun states are affiliated with the Yoruba ethnic group. Scholars have estimated the population of the Yoruba people to stand at approximately 30 million, accounting for 21% of the entire Nigerian population (Ogundele, 2007). This is not to say that Yoruba people are only found in Nigeria. To Abimbola (2006), Yoruba communities are found in the modern Republics of Benin and Togo in West Africa and also in Cuba and some Caribbean countries. Some of the major settlements in Yorubabaland are Ibadan, Lagos, Abeokuta, Ijebu-Ode, Ilesha, Ado-Ekiti, Osogbo, Ogbomoso, Ilorin and Ile-Ife. Ile-Ife is the popularly accepted religious and cultural centre for all the Yoruba people (Borokini & Lawal, 2014). The Yoruba nation has several sub-groups like the Ekiti, Ijesa, Oyo, Egba, Ijebu, Yewa and Igbomina (Olagunju, 2012), in addition to Ondo, Akoko and even the Edos. Yorubaland is characterised by forest vegetation as well as patches of derived savanna types arising basically from human activities like bush burning for agricultural and hunting purposes. The main traditional occupations of the people include farming, fishing, blacksmithing, pottery and indigenous medical practices (Lucas, 1978).

Black soap, herbal or African black soap, originated amongst the Yoruba tribe in Nigeria and the Yoruba communities in Benin and Togo (Adewusi & Akanle, 2020; Aguh et al., 2017; Yusuf & Okoruwa, 2006). Black soap has, for centuries, been produced and marketed. The traditional methods of processing African black soap were mainly from wood ashes, until recently when the soap was produced from the ashes of natural waste materials such as cocoa pod husks, palm kernel branches, plantain peels and cassava peels (Yusuf & Okoruwa, 2006). Soaps produced from wood ash are well recognised in the traditional setting and serve cultures worldwide with their efficient bactericidal and dermatological properties.

Black soap is widely used by different tribes in Nigeria. It has different names, such as *ọṣẹ dúdú* or *abuwe* in Yoruba and *eko zhiko* in Nupe (Getradeghana, 2000). In the Western part of Africa, black soap is known as *anago simena* or *alata simena* in Ghana. In Hausa, it is known as *sabulun salo*. *Samina* means soap in the Twi dialect of the Akan language. *Alata samina* is used to refer to the resource throughout Ghana. As the name implies, *Alata* in the Yoruba language means 'pepper seller'. It is believed that Yoruba traders, specifically women traders, who sold tomatoes and peppers, introduced black soap to Ghana. These women were called *alata*s (i.e., pepper traders) and *alata Simena* was a term coined by the Ghanaians that meant 'the pepper traders' soap' (Adewusi, 2018).

In West Africa, especially Ghana, black soap is often made by women and fair-traded. The women use secret agro-family or agro-community recipes that have been handed down for generations for the production of black soap. First, they sun-dry the plant matter, such as plantain skins, palm tree leaves, cocoa pods and Shea tree bark, and burn it to ash. Next, they add water and various oils and fats, such as coconut oil, palm oil and Shea butter, cook the mixture until it solidifies, and hand-stir it for at least 24 hours. Finally, they scoop out the soap and let it solidify (Nelson, 2015; Strausfogel, 2015).

Chapter Methodology

This study was conducted in Lagos, Ogun and Oyo States of Nigeria. The justification for selecting the aforementioned states is that the history and origin of the Yoruba people, which constitute a focal point in this chapter, revolves around the southwestern part of Nigeria (Olutayo, 2012). The chapter was descriptive in nature. Qualitative method was used to gather data. The adoption of a qualitative approach was predicated on the fact that little has been known about the subject matter. Hence, the adoption of this method was germane due to the basic assumption that qualitative methods allow research participants to express themselves without restriction. Unrestricted discussion with participants helps to gain deep and rich insights into the subject matter (Adewusi, 2018).

The chapter adopted a multistage sampling technique (see Shodipe & Ohanu, 2020) to select two producers and 24 sellers of the black soap for the purpose of data collection. The two categories of participants were considered in order to gather a wide range of facts on the subject matter. First, Nigeria was clustered into the six major geopolitical zones, which were south-south, southeast, southwest, northwest, northeast and north central. The southwest was purposively selected because the chapter was interested in ọsẹ dúdú, which is largely produced by the Yoruba people. More so, the Yoruba people are known to dominate the southwestern part of the country (Olutayo, 2012). The southwestern part of Nigeria was further clustered into manageable units (i.e. states), out of which Oyo, Ogun and Lagos States were purposively selected (see Adewusi, 2018).

Three of the six states were purposefully selected to represent southwestern part of Nigeria since they all constituted the Yoruba nation. Major production sites and markets for the Yoruba indigenous black soap were considered through the adoption of purposive and snowball sampling techniques. Purposive sampling was used because the researchers knew few black soap production sites and markets. However, the production sites and markets identified by the researchers were insufficient for the study. Hence, the snowball technique was used to identify other production sites and markets. After much persuasion, only two of the producers of the 12 that were contacted from Ogun, Oyo and Lagos were willing to participate in the chapter. A major reason for the non-participation of these producers was to safeguard the knowledge of the black soap business from knowledge scavengers.

The instrument for data collection was an in-depth interview guide. To ensure validity, the guide was reviewed by three experts within the fields of Sociology and Anthropology, Entrepreneurship and Gender Studies. Suggestions were made by these experts, and they were carefully incorporated into the instrument (see Adewusi, 2018). Also, a pilot study was conducted to identify and correct ambiguities and plaque items in the instrument. The interviews with the producers and sellers of indigenous black soap were conducted in the Yoruba language. This is because the ọsẹ dúdú entrepreneurs in the study area had no formal education; thus, they were largely comfortable discussing with the researchers in their local language. Interview sessions were tape-recorded and transcribed by experts proficient in the Yoruba language.

Using a grounded theory approach (Strauss & Corbin, 1998), data were selected, simplified, classified and connected. A key element of this stage is the concept of coding, i.e. the making sense of the data. Thereafter, the coded data were displayed, which included reflecting the meaning and identifying the structure of the data for familiarity purposes (Adewusi, 2018; Adewusi & Akanle, 2020; Mason, 2002). In the existing data, recurring themes and ideas with regard to the challenges of ọsẹ dúdú entrepreneurs were searched for and identified. This coding process was done using Atlas ti software. Ethical considerations such as anonymity, privacy, voluntariness and non-maleficence were adhered to by the authors.

Findings

Both participants that were considered at the production phase of this chapter were women. This was because women were predominantly found in the *ọṣẹ dúdú* production business. This was similar to the finding of Alo et al. (2012) and Oluwalana et al. (2012), who discovered that the majority of black soap producers in southwestern Nigeria were females.

Socio-Demographics of Producers

Sl N	Variables	Responses	
		First Participant	**Second Participant**
1	Sex	Female	Female
2	Age	41 years old	85 years old
3	Highest educational qualification	Primary education	No formal education
4	Duration in business	32 years	47 years
5	Net worth of business	₦25,000 ($69.4[a])	₦17,000 ($47.2)
6	Frequency of production per month	6	3
7	Average income made per production	₦2,200 ($6.1)	₦2,000 ($5.6)

[a]Exchange rate was $1 to ₦360 as at the time of the study.

The domination of women in the soap production was because the occupation is historically perceived as feminine (Ogunbor, 2016), hence, became an occupation meant only for women in the context of traditional Yoruba belief (Osunwole, 2018). The table also revealed that *ọṣẹ dúdú* producers were poorly educated. The average age of *ọṣẹ dúdú* producers was 63 years, indicating that black soap is predominantly produced by the elderly. These were indications that the production of the soap was largely explored by older women with little or no education who are economically disadvantaged in Yorubaland. Meanwhile, the average worth of participants' businesses was of ₦21,000 ($58.3). This can be linked to the submission of Ogunbor (2016), who suggested that the production of black soap can be done with ease because it requires little capital. In addition, *ọṣẹ dúdú* producers stated that they make an average of ₦2,100 ($5.8) per production, totalling an average of ₦9,600 ($26.7) per month, which is 53.3% of the country's statutory minimum wage. This confirms that the profit from *ọṣẹ dúdú* business is largely dependent on its frequency of production. Therefore, the higher production frequency attracts higher profit and vice versa.

Socio-Demographics of Sellers

S/N	Variables and Categories	Frequencies	Percentages
1	*Sex*		
	Male	1	4.2
	Female	23	95.8
2	*Age (Mean Age = 65)*		
	Less than 50 years	3	12.5
	50 years or More	21	87.5
3	*Highest Educational Qualification*		
	No formal education	18	75.0
	Primary education	1	4.2
	Secondary education	5	20.8
	Tertiary education	0	0.0
4	*Religious Affiliation*		
	Christianity	5	20.8
	Islam	11	45.8
	ATR	8	33.4
5	*Marital Status*		
	Single	1	4.2
	Married	4	16.7
	Separated/Divorced	2	8.3
	Widow/Widower	17	70.8
6	*Ethnic Affiliation*		
	Yoruba	24	100.0
	Igbo	0	0.0
	Hausa	0	0.0
7	*Position Held*		
	Business Owner	22	91.7
	Apprentice/Employee	2	8.3
8	*Age of SME*		
	Less than 10 years	1	4.2
	10–20 years	2	8.3
	More than 20 years	21	87.5
Total		**24**	**100.0**

Approximately 96% of the participants were females, while only one of the participants was a male. Just like production, this portrays that majority of those involved in the black soap selling business were women. However, this is not to say that the males were not found engaging in the business but were a small fraction of the population. In probing this finding, the only male participant was engaged in an interview session to identify the motivation to venture into a business presumed to be gendered in nature. He stated that the business was initially conducted by his late mother, but he decided to venture into the business due to the already-created customer base. He specifically said that:

> ... reason being that my mum sells these kinds of stuff at a point in time, and I usually assist her at the market whenever I return from school during my childhood days. It was after her demise I decided to venture into the business since she still had some of those that patronise her coming around... I've been doing it ever since then.
> 54 years/Seller/Male/Lagos State

Also, the age category of participants depicted that the majority, constituting approximately 88% of the total participant, were expected to have stopped their menstrual activities as they were already aged 50 years or more. Hence, the majority of *ose dúdú* sellers in selected chapter locations are elderly women who are expected to have gotten to the menopause stage (Olaolorun & Lawoyin, 2009). Out of curiosity, the researchers inquired about the reasons behind the domination of elderly women in *ose dúdú* selling business. The domination of the elderly in *ose dúdú* sale was linked to the use of the soap by indigenous medical cum spiritual experts, such as the Babalawos and Oniseguns, Alfas, and Pastors who prefer to purchase *ose dúdú* from the elderly traders[1,2]:

> When any Babalawo want to buy *ose dúdú*, they prefer to buy it from an elderly woman because they would not want to patronise a woman that still observes their menstrual cycle. This is because buying the soap from the latter will adversely affect the functionality of what the Babalawo intends to use it for.
> 75 years/Seller/Female/Lagos state

It is, therefore, a truism that the purchase of *ose dúdú* by Alfas, Babalawos and Oniseguns among others, may have necessitated an increase of elderly women in *ose dúdú* selling business. Further, there is a belief that black soap sold by women who still menstruate are less functional for spiritual use. However, it is worthy to note that, just like the producers, the majority of the black soap sellers, constituting about 75.0%, were without formal education. Meanwhile, the majority (45.8%) of those into *ose dúdú* selling business were religiously affiliated with Islam while 33.4% were traditional worshippers and 20.8% were Christians. This is an indication that more Muslims were found in the black soap sale business than Christians.

Furthermore, the majority (70.8%) of those into *ose dúdú* selling business were widows. This indicated that *ose dúdú* sale constitutes an economic opportunity exploited by widows in southwest, Nigeria. It is, however, worthy to note that *ose dúdú* selling a business is exclusively dominated by the Yoruba. This may be linked to the fact that the study was conducted in a geographical space that is frequently tagged as the Yoruba nation (Olutayo, 2012). For the purpose of this chapter, the business owners were largely considered (91.7%) as against the idea of engaging their apprentices or employees. This was because employees/ apprentices of those selling the soap were relatively young, hence, perceived to lack sufficient knowledge of the subject matter. Lastly, the table shows that majority of the participants have been into the black soap business for more than two decades. This buttresses the point that *ọsẹ dúdú* business is a form of indigenous entrepreneurship that is passed from one generation to the other (Ogunbor, 2016).

Summarily, *ọsẹ dúdú* production and sale are largely conducted by older widowed women with low education. Therefore, *ọsẹ dúdú* business constitutes an occupation dominated by economically disadvantaged women in Yorubaland. While these economic activities serve as a means of livelihood it is also a truism that the engagement of these persons is needed to safeguard the functionality of the soap in traditional healing praxis. Therefore, the non-engagement of these persons in the production and sale of *ọsẹ dúdú* is endemic to the indigenous healing process in Yorubaland, where the soap constitutes one of the major components of traditional healing practices among the Yoruba.

Production Challenges of Ọsẹ Dúdú

A number of production challenges were faced by black soap entrepreneurs. Some of these challenges are controllable and thus man-made, while others are uncontrollable.

Weather Challenge

One of the uncontrollable factors that affect the production of *ọsẹ dúdú* is the downpour of rain. A black soap producer stated that during the production, there might be a sudden downpour of rain. This constitutes a challenge because when rainwater comes in contact with any of the ingredients of the soap; it poses a daunting challenge to the quality of the soap, especially its durability:

> When one is engaged in the production of black soap and rain suddenly starts, it poses a challenge to the quality of the soap. This is due to the fact that rainwater will affect the durability of the soap.
>
> 85 years/Producer/Female/Oyo State

In addition to the above response, another participant also reiterates the rain challenge but from a different dimension. She particularly stated that during the rainy seasons, she usually faces the challenge of preparing the ingredients that will be used for the production of *ọsẹ dúdú*, especially the ash. It is a fact that ash constitutes one of the major ingredients in *eyin aro* (i.e. mordant water) and the substantive production of the soap. When it rains, the burning of corn cobs and locust bean pods will almost be impossible. As a result, sales and income are affected, and this makes her divest for the main time:

> We make use of ash in the production of black soap. Burning/ roasting of *lasagba* (i.e., locus bean pod) or *kurukuru agbado* (i.e., corn cob) to form the needed ash is very difficult during rainy seasons. This makes me divest into other businesses for a period of time.
>
> 85 years/Producer/Female/Oyo State

One of the producers also commented on the implication of using wet firewood during the production process of *ọṣẹ dúdú*. As observed, firewood sellers practice the culture of exposing their firewood during both dry and rainy seasons. While the dry season enhances the quality of the firewood, rainy seasons deplete it. The quality depletion has several effects on the consumers and residents that were close to the production site. For example, a participant stated that when she uses wet firewood, aside from the fact that it consumes more kerosene and other supporting elements such as plastics to support the cooking, it produces excessive smoke that is not only inimical to the sight of those that are on the production site, but also to those residing around the production site:

> During rainy seasons, a large number of the firewood that will be found in the community will be the wet ones. When I use the wet ones; it consumes a lot of kerosene and plastics. It also results in the irritation of the eyes due to the smoke it produces. Even those residing within my production site complain a lot during rainy seasons, especially when I embark on the journey of the soap production before I know it, they (i.e., the residents) will start to hiss.
>
> 41 years/Producer/Female/Oyo State

Finance Challenge

Ọṣẹ dúdú producers are also faced with the problem of finance. A participant stated that her major source of finance is her personal savings, instead of getting a sizeable loan from financial institutions such as the Lift Above Poverty Organization (LAPO) microfinance bank. The participant explained that there was a time she needed to add more finance to her business only to be told by her Pastor not to apply for the loan to avoid embarrassment:

> The capital I invested in this business is mine. I didn't borrow money from anyone. Though there was a time I wanted to borrow money from LAPO microfinance, my Pastor told me not to request for the loan because he saw a vision that I won't be able

to repay it. Due to the fact that, truly, I didn't want to embarrass myself, I decided not to apply for the loan.

41 years/Producer/Female/Oyo State

Spiritual and Antagonist Challenges

Part of the challenges faced by *osẹ dúdú* entrepreneurs were spiritual difficulties and other ungodly acts perpetuated by people that will be referred to as antagonists who reside within the production site of the soap. The participant particularly stressed the need for one to safeguard oneself spiritually due to the fact that the business of *osẹ dúdú* production constitutes one of the so-called *ise aiye* (i.e. a type of profession that makes one vulnerable to spiritual attacks whose source may be from competitors among others). In addition to this, the participant also stressed that there were some persons who may decide to execute certain ungodly acts that will sabotage the quality of *osẹ dúdú*. The challenging aspect of this is that one may not be aware until the soap comes out bad:

> Owners of businesses of this type are vulnerable to spiritual attacks, especially when you engage in *ise aiye* such as this. So you have to take good care of yourself spiritually. The *olokiti* (one of the apparatuses used in the production of *osẹ dúdú*, which is made from mud) may suddenly get broken. Besides, when one is making the soap, it is expected that you won't leave the production site as your absence, even for a few seconds, may allow the 'enemies of progress' to poison the whole process either by dropping some pinch of salt in the *olokiti* or *osẹ dúdú* being prepared. In fact, some can do it to the extent of adding kerosene to *osẹ dúdú* you are preparing, and when this happens, there is a possibility that it will result in a fire outbreak.

41 years/Producer/Female/Oyo State

Copyright Challenge

Participants also lamented the attempted efforts of non-Africans in 'stealing' the knowledge of *osẹ dúdú* production from them. This was because of the belief that the 'whites' never reveal their own livelihood secret to them, hence, arguing that the knowledge of *osẹ dúdú* production is classified information:

> The whites have come to our production site on several occasions with the mindset of learning how black soap is being made, but we didn't teach them. Even those that proved adamant, we taught them halfway and didn't reveal the other processes to them. This is because they never taught us how they make their things, therefore we can't teach them ours too. In fact, if we teach them, they won't

be able to practice them on their own because of the process they have to go through... we cannot afford to lose our knowledge of soap production to them.

>   85 years/Producer/Female/Oyo State

Succession Challenge

A participant also stated that Oyo State, which is a renowned geographical space where the producers of the *ọsẹ dúdú* originated from, may lose her jurisdiction over the said resource, not only to towns like *Ikirun* and *Ada* of Osun state, Nigeria, but mainly to neighbouring countries like the Benin Republic. This is because the younger generations, which are meant to succeed these producers from the indigenous states of Yorubaland, were showing little or no interest in the profession. The participant buttressed this by stating that the children of those who were meant to help and learn from the older generations of soap entrepreneurs have increasingly been sent to tertiary institutions for the acquisition of formal education. This development has been paving the way for the engagement of foreigners, such as those from the Benin Republic, who now serve as maids for the black soap entrepreneurs, entrepreneurs that only want their children to acquire formal education. The challenge here is that, after the acquisition of education, the children of the soap entrepreneurs tend to lose interest in the business:

> Oyo is one of the pioneers of *ọsẹ dúdú*. However, towns like *Ikirun* and *Ada* have begun to take over. Civilisation had affected the people of Oyo producing *ọsẹ dúdú* because when Oyo dominated *ọsẹ dúdú* market, their children were the major apprentice they had. But most of them now send their children to higher institutions. Instead of using their children, they now pay for girls from the Benin Republic to serve the same function. Therefore, the knowledge of soap production is gradually moving to the Benin Republic because the children of the people of Oyo are not interested in the business again.
>
>   85 years/Producer/Female/Oyo State

Sale Challenges

Large Number of Sellers

One of the prominent challenges faced by *ọsẹ dúdú* sellers is the large number of dealers within a market. A participant stated that the number of those that deal with selling *ọsẹ dúdú* was large, hence, making it challenging to earn income, especially when sales were generally poor. However, the participants have been coping with this challenge via the pre-orders made by their respective customers:

> The challenge as regards sales is that I may not record any patronage for days due to the fact that everyone around me sells the same thing. However, each seller has his/her own customer who makes pre-orders.
>
> 61 years/Seller/Female/Oyo State

Another participant at *ita osu* market in Ogun State buttressed the large dealer size raised by the aforementioned participant. She mentioned that due to a large number of *ọṣẹ dúdú* dealers in the market, they usually compete for customers. However, the participant stated that this scenario has never resulted in a face-off among them; although none of the dealers will be able to relate easily when his/her potential customer(s) is poached by another person occupying the same selling space/lane. She later mentioned ways they cope with competition:

> ... the only issue is that, when there are low sales, we compete for buyers, and the 'winner' will be happy while the 'loser' will be angry. However, we consider ourselves as brothers and sisters here. We do not fight each other, we only compete for buyers, and this is common in all markets. Sometimes, when a buyer comes to my side, and I don't have what s/he requested for, I might call all other sellers to bring the request in other to sell to the buyer.
>
> 75 years/Seller/Female/Ogun State

Debt Issues

Furthermore, participants were also faced with debt issues. It is not out of place to have supplied a wholesaler or retailer without payment. However, participants stated that it is usually challenging to get the person supplied with the goods to pay, even when the latter might have sold all or a significant part of the soap. However, the issue of 'supply-in-advance' was not a problem to the black soap entrepreneurs when they were young and agile. This is because they could walk-in to wholesalers' or retailers' shops to demand the payment of *ọṣẹ dúdú* supplied to them. However, weak agility on the part of the seller has prevented the prompt request for payment. Lack of prompt payment could results in bad debt that could take the entrepreneur out of business:

> Some may buy and not pay. When we were still young, we'll demand our money from our debtors persistently by going to their shops. But now that we are old, if they pay, fine, if they don't 'uhm uhm'. So that's the challenge.
>
> 75 years/Seller/Female/Lagos State

Another participant reemphasised the unrecoverable debts recorded by *ọṣẹ dúdú* sellers.

The challenge we face is that some people buy and don't pay.

50 years/Seller/Female/Lagos State

Lack of Support

It was also discovered that *osẹ dúdú* entrepreneurs are also faced with a lack of support. This arises from the lack of financial, political and moral support from the government. Instead of providing support to the elderly women, the participant claimed that they were rather considered old people and less relevant to societal growth:

> We lack support from the government. There was a time we heard that the government stated that they don't have any business with us and that we are too old. We agree that we are old, but it is the responsibility of the government to provide for us as elderly beings rather than stigmatise us. It means they don't consider us as important to the growth of our society.
>
> 81 years/Seller/Female/Oyo State

Financial Challenge

Just like the soap producers are constrained by finance, sellers are also faced with the same challenge, however, in a different dimension. One of the eldest participants stated that she uses stipends from her children to trade the black soap. This constitutes a limiting factor as she could not invest big in the business. She, however, stated that the government could provide needed financial support for black soap sellers, as this will make them compete with other brands of black soap within Nigeria and beyond:

> Most of us use stipends given to us by our children to trade *osẹ dúdú*. If the government can support us financially, then we will be able to sell in large quantities and compete with other modern soaps in the country and beyond.
>
> 81 years/Seller/Female/Oyo State

The only male black soap seller sampled mentioned that he is also constrained by finance. This is because, as a father, he must perform his role by feeding his family and providing quality education for his children. These financial demands are usually fulfilled from the income from *osẹ dúdú* business. When this happens, he may end up expending the largest chunk of his business capital on his family's financial demands:

> It is basically a financial issue. You know everybody wants the best
> including for the children-education and all ... for e.g. he needs
> ₦100,000 naira for school, you remove it from it.
>
> 50 years/Seller/Male/Lagos State

Pricing Issue

Pricing issues were also faced by participants. A participant illustrated that some
consumers prefer to buy directly from the producers. This is due to the significant
price difference between wholesalers or retailers and producers selling to the final
consumers. This is particularly true as the price of the producers were usually
cheaper than that of the wholesalers and retailers. Hence, this constitutes a pricing
issue for sellers, making them less relevant in the value chain:

> Price issues we face generally is that when the wholesalers and
> retailers fix prices of different sizes of black soap, which is different
> from that of the producer. Buyers usually choose to buy from the
> one whose price is cheaper (i.e., the producer).
>
> 61 years/Seller/Female/Oyo State

Competition From Other Soap Brands

Competition with modern/packaged soaps also constitutes a challenge to *oṣẹ dúdú*
sellers. Although black soap was used for all washing purposes in the household.
However, the emergence of modern/packaged soap has reduced the relevance of
oṣẹ dúdú as it is presently considered old-fashioned:

> We have been recording poor sales since the inception of modern
> soap. Thirty years ago, when I started this business, I usually make
> sales because this soap is virtually used for everything such as the
> washing of hair, body, cloth, plates, car etc. However, we all know
> that there are now modern soaps that can cater to the
> aforementioned functions. Therefore, black soap is presently
> relevant among few people that consider it relevant for bathing.
>
> 81 years/Seller/Female/Oyo State

Discussion of Findings

The aim of this chapter was to examine the challenges associated with the production and sale of *oṣẹ dúdú*. First, the chapter identified five major challenges
faced by *oṣẹ dúdú* producers. These are weather, financial, spiritual, copyright,
and business succession challenges. The weather challenge stemmed from the fact
that, during rainy seasons, the use of wet firewood has several negative

implications, not only for the soap entrepreneur but also for residents within the production site of *ọṣẹ dúdú*. Specifically, the use of wet firewood produces excess smoke that could result in the irritation of the eyes. These implications also included an increase in the cost of kerosene and plastic used to support the cooking process. Additionally, this could also result in delays or outright sabotage of the production of ash used in the substantive production of the *ọṣẹ dúdú*, and it has an adverse effect on the durability of the soap. Furthermore, it was also discovered that *ọṣẹ dúdú* entrepreneurs were also faced with financial issues. This finding corroborates the findings of Alo et al. (2012), Oluwalana et al. (2012), and Oluwalana et al. (2016) which noted that black soap entrepreneurs lack access to formal financial assistance. Although these entrepreneurs had intentions to apply for loans from financing institutions such as LAPO, but some of them had certain constraints; like one of the seller had.

In addition, the chapter found that copyright issues were faced by *ọṣẹ dúdú* entrepreneurs. This was because the non-Africans have been keen on learning the soap knowledge possessed by these soap producers. However, these entrepreneurs were unwilling to reveal their livelihood secret to them because of the belief that the 'whites' never reveal their own, hence, they argued that the knowledge of *ọṣẹ dúdú* production is classified information. Furthermore, it was found that soap producers also face certain spiritual challenges due to the fact that their profession has been categorised as *ise aiye*. The chapter also discovered that soap entre-preneurs have to deal with certain ungodly acts perpetrated by community members. These ungodly acts either sabotage the quality of *ọṣẹ dúdú* or destroy some of the indigenous technologies (such as the *olokiti*). Lastly, *ọṣẹ dúdú* pro-ducers also faced succession challenges. This was because Oyo State, where the production of *ọṣẹ dúdú* originates, may lose its jurisdiction over the said resource, not only to towns like *Ikirun* and *Ada* of Osun State, but also to neighbouring countries like the Benin Republic. This is because the young ones who were meant to succeed these producers from the indigenous states in Yoruba land are showing little or no interest in the profession, due to their acquisition of formal education.

Furthermore, the chapter found that challenges such as large numbers of *ọṣẹ dúdú* sellers that necessarily led to competition for potential customers, lack of support from the government, and unavailability of financial support were faced by black soap sellers. Instead of providing support to the soap entrepreneurs, *ọṣẹ dúdú* sellers are perceived by the government as 'old', hence given less recognition in the socio-political and economic space. Besides, the manner and method used in the enforcement of loan repayment among erring borrowers also constituted some of the reasons sellers of *ọṣẹ dúdú* were unwilling to apply for a loan to boost their businesses. Pricing problems, such that customers patronise a certain set of people within the value chain (i.e., the producers) due to the lack of generally acceptable prices, have thwarted the relevance of value chain actors, especially the wholesaler and retailers, within the selling space. This constituted a major chal-lenge to *ọṣẹ dúdú* sellers.

Summary, Conclusion and Policy Recommendations

Ọṣẹ dúdú is being manufactured locally and capable of generating employment opportunities, increasing the profitability of black soap entrepreneurs and revenue of countries. However, ọṣẹ dúdú enterprise has certain threats and problems that were yet to be researched. It is against this backdrop that this chapter documented the challenges faced by ọṣẹ dúdú entrepreneurs in southwest, Nigeria. A total of 26 interviews were conducted among indigenous black soap producers and sellers in Ogun, Oyo and Lagos States. This chapter concluded that certain controllable and uncontrollable factors were not only capable of limiting the production and sale of ọṣẹ dúdú but also have adverse implications for the contribution of the soap to Nigeria's socio-economic development and the achievement of the Sustainable Development Goals, especially goal 1 (No Poverty), goal 3 (Good Health), goal 8 (Good Jobs and Economic Growth), goal 9 (Industry, Innovation and Infrastructure) and goal 10 (Reduced Inequalities). Policy recommendations are suggested in the next section.

Policy Recommendations

The chapter suggests some recommendations to *oṣẹ dúdú* business actors such as soap entrepreneurs, mechanical engineers, local fabricators, financial institutions, and governmental and non-governmental agencies. These recommendations are discussed in the next few paragraphs.

In light of the weather challenge identified in this chapter, there is a need for more efficient technologies to aid the production and processing of *eyin/omi Aro* and *oṣẹ dúdú*, respectively. However, local development of technologies is also paramount in advancing this initiative. The promotion of local ideas, experiments and discovery by indigenous stakeholders in areas of technology, system creation and implementation is very important in building sustainable production technology that will improve the level of acceptance and make it a vibrant industry in the economy. Also, in achieving this, there is a need for mechanical engineers, fabricators, welders and black soap entrepreneurs to collaborate in order to design, implement and evaluate the most appropriate 'modern' technology that could be used for the production of *oṣẹ dúdú*.

Closely related to the above, it was also found that the activities of black soap producers may only affect their health but also the health of nearby residents. Hence, there should be strict provision and implementation of policies regulating the activities of black soap producers as regards their health behaviours. For instance, it should be ensured that producers have and use the necessary protective gear such as nose masks, hand gloves and transparent goggles during the production of the soap. In addition, the provision should also restrict black soap users from using technologies that would affect nearby residents or, better still, *oṣẹ dúdú* production site may be (re)located to nonresidential sites.

It was also revealed that copyright issues were faced by *oṣẹ dúdú* entrepreneurs. To avoid potential copyright issues, this chapter hereby implores indigenous social organisations, trademarking establishments, indigenous legal experts and the Nigerian government to safeguard the knowledge of this resource from cultural appropriation and cultural property theft as efforts are presently being deployed by the West to harness this intellectual property. This is important so as to prevent Africa's indigenous knowledge from theft.

To alleviate the financial challenge of black soap entrepreneurs, stakeholders such as the government, microfinance and investment banks, non-governmental organisations, and private investors should design a system through which funds can be collated and then loaned to new and existing *oṣẹ dúdú* entrepreneurs. The suggested loan infrastructure should attract low-interest rates and flexible loan conditions such as collateral and repayment plans. Closely related to this suggestion is that more friendly ways be established by financiers as loan repayment strategies to prevent discouragements among *oṣẹ dúdú* entrepreneurs in assessing finance to boost their businesses.

The chapter found the prevalence of pricing issues among *oṣẹ dúdú* entrepreneurs, such that customers patronise certain set of vendors within the value chain (i.e. the producers) due to the lack of generally acceptable prices. This has thwarted the relevance of value chain actors, especially the wholesaler and the retailers, within the selling space, hence constituting a major challenge to *ọṣẹ dúdú* sellers. Therefore, this chapter suggests that *ọṣẹ dúdú* association be constituted to check these shortcomings.

Case Questions

(1) How is Indigenous knowledge important to the development of Africa?
(2) What is the history of the African black soap?
(3) What are the benefits of black Soap?
(4) What are the challenges of black soap entrepreneurs and possible suggestions to address these challenges in order to scale up the practice?

Acknowledgement

The authors would like to acknowledge the Chairman of the Lift Above Poverty Organisation (LAPO), Dr Godwin Ehigiamuso, and the entire governing and management staff at LAPO for the small grant awarded for the purpose of this study.

Notes

1. These are commonly used to describe traditional clerics in Yoruba land.
2. This means an Islamic cleric.

References

Abimbola, K. (2006). *Yoruba culture: A philosophical account*. Birmingham: Iroko Academic Publishers.

Adebiyi, O., & Adeniyi, B. (2004). Do Aloe vera and Ageratum conyzoides enhance the anti-microbial activity of traditional medicinal soft soaps (Osedudu). *Journal of Ethnopharmacology*, *92*, 57–60.

Adewusi, O. A. (2018). *Ọṣẹ Dúdú (Indigenous black soap) value chain in Southwest, Nigeria*. An Unpublished M.Sc. Thesis Submitted at the Department of Sociology. University of Ibadan, Ibadan.

Adewusi, A. O., & Akanle, O. (2020). Ọṣẹ Dúdú: Exploring the benefits of Yoruba indigenous black soap in Southwest, Nigeria. *The International Indigenous Policy Journal*, *11*(1), 1–20.

Aguh, C., Jhaveri, M., He, A., Okoye, G. A., Cohen, B. E., & Elbuluk, N. (2017). Ethnic hair considerations for people of African, South Asian, Muslim, and Sikh origins. In C. Aguh & G. Okoye (Eds.), *Fundamentals of ethnic hair* (pp. 137–149). Cham: Springer.

Ahmed, A., Odunukwe, N., Akinwale, P., Raheem, Y., Efienemokwu, E., Ogedengbe, O., & Salako, L. A. (2005). Knowledge and practices of traditional birth attendants in prenatal services in Lagos State, Nigeria. *African Journal of Medicine & Medical Sciences*, *34*(1), 55–58.

Ajaiyeoba, E. (2003). Phytochemical and antibacterial properties of Parkia biglobosa and Parkia bicolor. *African Journal of Biomedical Research, 5,* 125–129.

Ajose, F. (2007). Some Nigerian plants of dermatologic importance. *International Journal of Dermatology, 1,* 48–55.

Akanle, O., Adesina, J., & Fakolujo, O. (2017). Jedijedi: Indigenous versus Western knowledge of Rectal Haemorrhoids in Ibadan, Southwestern Nigeria. *African Studies, 76*(4), 530–545.

Aliyu, M., Ladan, T., Ahmed, B., & Abdullahi, J. (2007). Studies on the efficacy of black soap and kerosene mixture on the control of Pod sucking bugs on Cowpea. *Emirates Journal of Food & Agriculture, 19*(2), 8–14.

Aliyu, S., Tijjani, M., Doko, M., Garba, I., Ibrahim, M., Abdulkadir, S., … Zango, U. (2012). Antimicrobial activity of Sabulun Salo a local traditional medicated soap. *Nigerian Journal of Basic and Applied Science, 20*(1), 35–38.

Alo, R., Achem, B., Mohammed, B., & Abdulquadir, A. (2012). Profitability analysis of black soap production in Ekiti State, Nigeria. *Continental Journal of Agricultural Economics, 6*(3), 8–14.

Aluko, Y. (2018). Women's use of indigenous knowledge for environmental security and sustainable development in Southwest Nigeria. *The International Indigenous Policy Journal, 9*(3), 1–23.

Anyakoha, U. (2011). *Home economics for junior secondary schools.* Onitsha: Africana First Publisher.

Beetseh, I., & Anza, K. (2013). Chemical characterization of local black soap (chahul mtse) made by using cassava peels ashes (alkali base) and palm oil in North Central Zone of Nigeria. *Civil and Environmental Research, 3*(4), 82–91.

Borokini, T. I., & Lawal, I. O. (2014). Traditional medicine practices among the Yoruba people of Nigeria: A historical perspective. *Journal of Medicinal Plants Studies, 2*(6), 20–33.

Egho, E., & Emosairue, S. (2010). Evaluation of native soap (local black soap) for the control of major insect, pests and yield of cowpea, Southern Nigeria. *Agriculture and Biology Journal of North America, 1,* 938–945.

Ekwenye, U., & Ijeomah, C. (2005). Antimicrobial effect of palm kernel oil. *KMTL Science Journal, 6,* 22–26.

George, A., Ogunbiyi, A., & Daramola, O. (2006). Cutaneous adornment in the Yoruba of south- western Nigeria - past and present. *International Journal of Dermatology, 45,* 23–27.

Getradeghana, B. (2000). Evaluation of African traditional soap. *Global Journal of Pure and Applied Sciences, 6,* 174–179.

Hopper, C. A. O. (2017). Indigenous knowledge and the integration of knowledge systems. In C. A. O. Hoppers (Ed.), *Indigenous knowledge and the integration of knowledge systems: Towards a philosophy of articulation* (pp. 2–22). Cape Town: New Africa Books.

Ikotun, A., Awosika, A., & Oladipo, M. (2015). The African black soap from Elaeis guineensis (Palm kernel oil) and Theobroma cacao (Cocoa) and its transition metal complexes. *African Journal of Biotechnology, 16*(18), 1042–1047.

Ikpoh, I., Lennox, J., Agbo, B., Udoekong, S., Ekpo, A., & Iyam, S. (2012). Comparative studies on the effect of locally made black soap and conventional medicated soaps on isolated human skin microflora. *Journal of Microbiology and Biotechnology Research, 2*(4), 533–537.

Jegede, O. (2016). The indigenous medical knowledge systems, perceptions and treatment of mental illness among the Yoruba of Nigeria. *Studies in Sociology of Science*, *7*(5), 12–20.

Kalejaiye, P., Sokefun, E., & Adewusi, A. (2015). Leadership and human resource development in Nigeria: Factors for national development. *The Nigerian Journal of Sociology and Anthropology*, *13*(1), 127–144.

Lawal, A., Kio, S., Sulaimon, A., & Adebayo, O. (2000). *Entrepreneurship development in small scale business*. Lagos: Labson Resource Nigeria Ltd.

Lin, A., Nabatian, A., & Halverstam, P. C. (2017). Discovering black soap: A survey on the attitudes and practices of black soap users. *The Journal of Clinical and Aesthetic Dermatology*, *10*(7), 18–22.

Lucas, O. J. (1978). *The religion of the Yoruba*. Lagos: CMS Press.

Lucet, C., Rigaud, P., Mentre, F., Kassis, N., Deblangy, C., Andremont, A., & Bouvet, E. (2002). Hand contamination before and after different hygiene techniques: A randomized clinical trial. *Journal of Hospital Infection*, *50*, 276–280.

Lwoga, E., Ngulube, P., & Stilwell, C. (2010). Managing indigenous knowledge for sustainable agricultural development in developing countries: Knowledge management approaches in the social context. *The International Information & Library Review*, *42*, 174–185.

Mason, J. (2002). *Qualitative researching* (2nd ed.). London: Sage.

Mike, L. (2008). Phenolic constituents of shea (Vitellaria paradoxa) kernels. *Journal of Agricultural and Food Chemistry*, *51*, 6268–6273.

National Bureau of Statistics. (2015). *Annual abstract of statistics*. Federal Republic of Nigeria.

Nelson, J. (2015). *What is African black soap?* Retrieved from https://www.treehugger.com/what-is-african-black-soap-4864029

Ogunbor, E. (2016). What are the beauty benefits of "black soap"? Retrieved from https://www.bellanaija.com/2016/03/lola-oj-has-answers-to-your-black-soap-questions-watch/

Ogundele, S. O. (2007). Aspects of indigenous medicine in South Western Nigeria. *Studies on Ethno-Medicine*, *1*(2), 127–133.

Olagunju, O. S. (2012). The traditional healing systems among the Yoruba. *Archaeological Science Journal*, *1*(2), 6–14.

Olaolorun, F. M., & Lawoyin, T. O. (2009). Experience of menopausal symptoms by women in an urban community in Ibadan, Nigeria. *Menopause*, *16*(4), 822–830.

Olatokun, W., & Ayanbode, F. (2008). Use of indigenous knowledge by women in a Nigerian rural community. *Indian Journal of Traditional Knowledge*, *8*(2), 287–295.

Olayide, O. E., Obisesan, D., Nitturkar, H., Adesida, A., Alegieunu, B., & Obisesan, O. (2021). Cassava seedpreneurship, determinants of varietal adoption, profitability, and women empowerment in Nigeria. *Resources, Environment and Sustainability*, *6*, 1–5.

Olutayo, A. (2012). "Verstehen", everyday sociology and development: Incorporating African indigenous knowledge. *Critical Sociology*, *40*(2), 229–238.

Olutayo, A., & Akanle, O. (2009). Aso-oke (Yoruba's hand-woven textiles) usage among the youths in Lagos, Southwestern Nigeria. *International Journal of Sociology and Anthropology*, *1*(3), 62–69.

Olutayo, O., Akanle, O., & Fadina, A. (2017). The socio-economic developments of Aso-Oke of South-Western Nigeria. *Asian & African Studies*, *26*(1), 41–68.

Oluwalana, O., Adekunle, M., Aduradola, A., Okojie, L., Ashaolu, O., & Sanusi, A. (2016). Determinants of herbal soap small enterprises and market-led development in South West, Nigeria. *Journal of Humanities, Social Sciences and Creative Arts*, *11*(1&2), 76–87.

Oluwalana, E., Adekunle, M., & Okojie, L. (2012). Economic efficiency of forest-based small scale herbal soap enterprise utilizing agricultural-wastes in Southwest Nigeria. In *Proceedings of the 3rd Biennial National Conference of the Forests and Forest Products Society, held at University of Ibadan*, Ibadan, 3rd–6th April (pp. 428–432).

Oluyole, K. A., & Adeogun, S. O. (2005). Determining the profitability level of black soap production from cocoa pod husk in Lagelu Local Government Area of Oyo State. *Journal of Agriculture, Forestry and the Social Sciences*, *3*(1), 69–80.

Osunwole, A. (2018). *Ọṣẹ Dúdú: Traditional African soap in Youbaland*. Ibadan: Clemeve Media Konsult.

Oyekanmi, A., Adebayo, O., & Farombi, A. (2014). Physiochemical properties of African black soap, and it's comparison with industrial black soap. *American Journal of Chemistry*, *4*(1), 35–37.

Oyeniran, K. (2015). Antagonistic activities of microorganisms associated with indigenous black soap on some selected skin pathogens. *British Journal of Pharmaceutical Research*, *8*(2), 1–7.

Oyeniran, K., & Ogunleye, A. (2015). Synergistic potentials, comparative antibacterial activities of Ficus exasperata (Vahl) leave extract and indigenous black soap. *Journal of Microbiology and Antimicrobial Agents*, *2*(1), 4–8.

Oyeniran, A., Oladunmoye, K., & Aladeselu, O. (2015). Comparative studies in the release of sodium and potassium ions by indigenous black soaps from some selected skin pathogens. *Research Journal of Microbiology*, *10*(12), 592–599.

Rist, S., Boillat, S., Gerritsen, P., Schneider, F., Mathez-Stiefel, S., & Tapia, N. (2011). Endogenous knowledge: Implications for sustainable development. In U. Wiesmann & H. Hurni (Eds.), *Research for sustainable development: Foundations, experiences, and perspectives. Perspectives of the Swiss National Centre of Competence in Research (NCCR) North–South* (pp. 119–146). Bern: University of Bern.

Shodipe, T. O., & Ohanu, I. B. (2020). Antecedents of entrepreneurial intentions of electrical installation and maintenance work students' in technical colleges. *Asia Pacific Journal of Innovation and Entrepreneurship*, *14*(2), 127–137.

Sillitoe, P. (2006). Introduction: Indigenous knowledge in development. *Anthropology in Action*, *13*(3), 1–12.

Strausfogel, S. (2015). *African black soap*. Retrieved from https://web.archive.org/web/20160911203826/https://www.highbeam.com/doc/1P3-3711852681.html

Strauss, A., & Corbin, J. (1998). *Basics of qualitative research techniques*. London: SAGE.

Taiwo, O., & Osinowo, F. (2001). Evaluation of various agro-wastes for traditional black soap production. *Bioresource Technology*, *79*, 95–97.

Tharakan, J. (2015). Indigenous knowledge systems – A rich appropriate technology resource. *African Journal of Science, Technology, Innovation and Development*, *7*(10), 52–57.

Ugbogu, O. (2006). Lauric acid content and inhibitory effect of palm kernel oil on two bacterial isolates and Candida albicans. *African Journal of Biotechnology*, *5*(11), 1045–1047.

Waziri, A. (2017, October 8). Extractive sector transparency, value maximisation and Nigeria's economic recovery. *This Day*. Retrieved from https://www.thisdaylive.com/index.php/2017/10/08/extractive-sector-transparency-value-maximisation-and-nigerias-economic-recovery-2/

Yusuf, S. A., & Okoruwa, V. O. (2006). Transforming wastes into money: The case of black soap making using cocoa pod husks. In: *Cocoa revolution in Nigeria. Proceedings of a national seminar on revolutionizing Nigeria's cocoa industry* (pp. 101–112). Ibadan: University of Ibadan.

Zauro, S., Abdullahi, M., Aliyu, A., Muhammad, I., Abubakar, I., & Sani, Y. (2016). Production and analysis of soap using locally available raw-materials. *Elixir Applied Chemistry*, *96*, 41479–41483.

Chapter 3

Preparation for Business Negotiation at the Livestock Auction Market in Tanzania: The Case of Maasai Livestock Traders

Felix Adamu Nandonde

Abstract

This chapter focuses on how Maasai traders prepare for business negotiations at the livestock auction market. The Maasai community live in the forest, rearing their animals; they are characterised by less education and appear to be bound by their traditional practices. The current study utilised a qualitative method; interviews and focus group discussions were employed for data collection from the livestock auction market with a focus on the techniques that Maasai livestock traders use in preparation for business negotiations. Content qualitative analytical technique was used for data analysis. Four issues emerged as important for pre-negotiation, namely goal setting, advice from others, seeking assistance and apprenticeship. In general, the study shows that livestock keepers prepare young learners to master the art of negotiations through an apprenticeship approach. Additionally, the study has implications for business development services (BDS) and institutions that offer negotiation training to include the practices of the Indigenous societies in their courses, either as short courses or long-term programmes.

Keywords: Business negotiation; Maasai; exchange theory; Tanzania; livestock auction market; livestock keepers

Introduction

The study aims to explore the pre-negotiation preparation of livestock keepers at primary livestock auction markets in Tanzania. Livestock business is estimated to be worth Tshs 1.5 trillion in 2021 (URT, 2022). Different livestock such as goats, sheep and cattle are sold at the primary, secondary, border and international

Casebook of Indigenous Business Practices in Africa, 41–51
Copyright © 2023 Felix Adamu Nandonde
Published under exclusive licence by Emerald Publishing Limited
doi:10.1108/978-1-80455-762-420231007

livestock markets in the country. Based on the country's guidelines for conducting livestock business at the primary livestock auction market, livestock keepers must take their animals to a primary livestock auction for selling. In practice, business negotiations are characterised by unethical practices such as cheating, threatening tactics and overpricing. Jackson, Amaeshi, and Yavuz (2008) show that there is a relationship between firm's success and the blending of the management style to meet local content in Africa. In this regard, it is very important to understand how livestock keepers who participate in the primary livestock auction market prepare for negotiations.

Previous studies on negotiation with producers, farmers or livestock keepers focused on the dyadic interactions with distributors and paid attention to strategies that actors employ to build their relationships. For example, the study by Prado and Martinelli (2018) found that producers and distributors of farm inputs employ integrative strategies in their negotiations to build relationships. Nandonde and Liana (2013) conducted a study on women's business negotiation skills for traders and farmers in the open market and skills that farmers lack in the market. Furthermore, studies on negotiations focused on farmers' bargaining power during negotiations with buyers such as retailers (Cohen, 2020; Velazquez, Buffaria, & Commission, 2017). Despite the previous efforts on producers' negotiation practices, some of the stages of negotiations seem to be marginalised by researchers in the previous studies, such as pre-negotiation stage. Previous studies concentrated more on the negotiation stage and strategies farmers can use to increase their power. We understand these efforts, but we argue that understanding how livestock keepers undertake pre-negotiation is very important in increasing their persuasion at the market.

One of the studies conducted in South Africa identified that an increase in negotiation cost might limit livestock keepers' ability to sell their animals at the livestock auction market compared to selling to speculators (Ndoro, Mudhara, & Chimonyo, 2015). This suggests that empowering farmers to have business negotiations skills is very important. In Tanzania's business environment, if livestock keepers view that their negotiation skills are low or negotiations costs are high, it is likely that farmers can decide to sell at their farm gate price. This may lead to high administration costs of levy collection and cess (taxes administrated by local authorities). In some cases, some traders or buyers may not pay levies or cess to the government. Therefore, empowering livestock keepers with negotiation skills is very important so that they can negotiate fair deals in the market, and this will influence them to participate in the formal livestock market. However, we cannot train livestock keepers if we do not understand their practices and the challenges they are currently faced with. The current study intends to unearth pre-negotiation practices of Maasai livestock keepers in Tanzania with the case of Kololo primary livestock auction market and Melela ward in Mvomero district in the Morogoro region.

In general, business negotiation literature is dominated by corporate research practices such as Shell, Enron and Unilever in foreign and domestic markets. Further, these previous studies focused more on two stages of the negotiation process, which are during and after negotiation stages (see Lindholst, Bulow, &

Fells, 2020; Geiger, 2017). Little attention has been given to the preparation stage of business negotiation stages, and livestock keepers were not considered by business negotiations scholars. The current study seeks to fill that knowledge gap with a focus on Maasai community in Tanzania. Specifically, the current study aimed to understand how livestock keepers prepare themselves for business negotiations that occur at livestock primary auction markets. To achieve this objective, the current study seeks to answer the research question; what activities are livestock keepers conducting at the pre-negotiation stage?

Literature Review

Literature on business negotiation is dominated by corporate firms' techniques and implemented strategies (Geiger, 2017; Lindholst et al., 2020). Furthermore, these studies focused on during and after negotiations, with few studies on the preparation stage. We argue that understanding what happens at pre-negotiation stage is also important for negotiators as well. In that regard, the current study aimed to understand what activities take place during pre-negotiation stage with a focus on livestock keepers at livestock auction markets in Tanzania. General dynamics which occur in livestock business in developing economies, including Tanzania, show that there is need for more research on business negotiations among actors. Business of animals (cattle, ships and goats) at the livestock market in Tanzania is estimated to be worth Tshs 1.5 trillion (URT, 2022). This suggests that it is very important to study how actors develop their skills, tactics and strategies to engage with buyers in the market. The current study centres on the pre-negotiation stage among the Maasai community in the country.

Different theories have been used to understand how partners interact in business negotiation, including exchange theory (ET) by Homas (1958). Homas (1958) posits that, for any exchange, social interaction has to occur. The author argued that social interaction is an exchange of goods, material goods and non-material ones, such as symbols of approval or prestige. The ET has different paradigms, such as sociology, psychology and economics, and the current study adopts the economic approach. The economic approach assumes that an individual tends to approach a potential exchange with the aim of maximising their benefits and minimising loss (Tarver & Haring, 1988).

In a spot market that is featured with a win–lose relationship where no one is looking for a long-term relationship, it is likely that unfair practices are very common. In practice, the livestock auction market is characterised by a short-form relationship. Success of a firm in this business environment depends much on local knowledge that developed from long-term experience of working in a similar market situation (Kusumastuti, Silalahi, Asmara, Hardiyati, & Juwono, 2022). This makes actors in that market have a low level of loyalty, trust and mutual commitment, which are key components of ET. This means actors prefer a short-term relationship instead of developing a long-term relationship through their negotiation practices.

The ET sees social units as 'exchange processes' (Tarver & Herring, 1988). That means actors will develop some understanding based on what they have experienced before, and this will help develop some of the practices to safeguard their interests in the future. For the Maasai community with low literacy levels, it is important to understand how they develop negotiation practices based on the nature of relationship that exists at the livestock auction market. The assumption is that actors will develop that reciprocal relationship based on the market practices. Therefore, the current study paid attention to pre-negotiation stage for Maasai as sellers of livestock and the spot market characterised by short-term relationships.

Pre-negotiation is one of the three important stages of negotiations, the other stages being during and after negotiations. Studies show that actors conduct a number of activities before negotiations, such as collecting intelligence information on counter teams and goal setting (Lindholst et al., 2020). Previous studies vary on the number of activities that constitute this stage; for example, Peterson and Shepherd (2010) mentioned 32 activities, while Lindhost (2015) named 58 activities. In spite of the contradictions, pre-negotiation is considered one of the very important stages. In general, the pre-negotiation stage is important to individuals selling food crops or live animals at the market or corporate representatives sitting in a certain room representing their companies.

Goal setting is one of the important activities for negotiators to take into consideration. We understand that for any negotiations occurring for the live animal, buyers and sellers at the livestock auction market are considered to set a goal before negotiations. For example, negotiators can set goals on the lowest price that they can accept and the number of animals they intend to sell. Despite its importance, literature shows that in some cases, negotiators are going to the negotiation table without a goal that has been set (Peterson & Lucas, 2001).

Collecting market intelligence on the counterparts is another activity performed by the parties before negotiations. This information will enable actors to understand their strengths and weaknesses. Furthermore, this information can be collected to understand the previous history of the counterparts in fulfilling their promises to other players in the market. By understanding the fact that the agribusiness value chain is characterised by unethical behaviour makes collecting the marketing intelligence to be one of the important pre-negotiations stage activities by market actors. However, the nature of small livestock market players in developing economies like Tanzania is characterised by financial budget constraints which limit their involvement in these activities. Building on that, it is likely that they will not invest in collecting market intelligence to understand their counterparts' previous activities at the livestock markets. Furthermore, the nature of the livestock auction market, which operates on the principle of free entry and exit, is also likely that the collection of marketing intelligence information before negotiations becomes challenging for actors. This does not mean that the market is characterised by actors who will not act in good faith towards counterparts. Literature that is dominated by corporate negotiations practices failed to indicate how livestock keepers will protect their interests and prepare themselves before business negotiations. The current study intends to fill that gap with the practices of Maasai livestock keepers in Tanzania.

Methodology

The study employed a qualitative method to examine activities performed by Maasai livestock keepers during the pre-negotiation stage to increase their participation in the market. Social constructivism epistemology has been used to understand how Maasai livestock traders develop knowledge and skills at the pre-negotiation stage. In general, social constructivism assumes that knowledge is constructed rather than discovered (Berger & Luckmann, 1991). That means individuals tend to develop their own understanding of a certain phenomenon that they are going through, and through that, they attach meaning based on their experience. In that regard, for that knowledge to be shared among individuals, interactions are very important. The current study assumes that Maasai livestock traders do not have enough resources to invest in intelligence information collection on their potential counterparts as the stage of pre-negotiation proposed. Further, these traders do not have formal education as many of their counterparts do. This suggests that the likely means through which the required skills and knowledge are developed is through life experiences. Social constructivism paradigm seems to be appropriate as the lens that can be used to understand how to generate that knowledge from the field.

A researcher introduced himself to the Kololo Ward Executive Officer by delivering his introduction letter, and was allowed to collect data at the Kololo primary livestock auction market. Two focus group discussions (FGD) with six people each were organised, and seven face-to-face interview sessions with livestock keepers at the primary livestock auction market were conducted. Table 1 shows that 100% of the participants are male, and this is because in the Maasai community, men are involved in the business of selling animals, and women are involved in selling milk. FGD took 30 minutes, and face-to-face interview sessions took 20 minutes. As Creswell (2013) and Plummer (1983) suggest, for qualitative research, it is very important to have participants who are marginal, great or ordinary. Participants were selected after a proper introduction had been done.

Table 1. Participants' Profile.

Item	Parameter	Frequency	Percentage
Age	18–35	19	100%
Gender	Male	19	100%
Education	Not attended formal education	13	68
	Attended primary school	6	32

Some other persons who were not initially involved were invited to participate in the study to obtain more information.

In general, issues of whether or not to participate in negotiations at the livestock market in the Maasai community occur more at the family level. Someone who is elderly has more chance to represent the family in market negotiation than younger ones. For this study, those without experience selling animals at the market were excluded. In that respect, this study took the initiative to find other participants who had experience selling animals; they were asked some questions like: Do you have experience selling animals at the livestock market? How many animals have you sold in this livestock auction market in the past five months?

The aim was to find experienced livestock keepers and not traders who are buying and selling at the same primary livestock market. Patton (1988) argues that the key factor for selecting and making decisions about the appropriate unit of analysis is to decide which unit to be discussed. Therefore, it becomes important to understand and identify contextual factors surrounding the unit of analysis. Thus, the goal of the study is to explore pre-negotiation practices used by livestock keepers in Tanzania with a focus on the Maasai community in Kololo ward in Kilosa, District, Morogoro region. In this regard, the study employed relationship as a unit of analysis.

This study used a semi-structured interview for the selected participants. The interview guidelines were used to guide the interviewer. Interview questions were developed from the previous literature on negotiation with a focus on pre-negotiation stage (Peterson & Lucas, 2001). A voice recorder was used in the data collection process. The researcher sought the permission of the participants before the voice recorder could be used. The researcher informed the participants of the purpose of the voice recording and explained the importance of the exercise to the study and, more specifically, the importance of recording at the data analysis stage. Some of the participants accepted, and some others declined. In addition, a field notebook was used to record conversations for all interviews.

The focus of the interviews included activities they engage in before coming to the livestock auction market; planned actions to be taken when price does not relate to their expectation and the type of training they take to help them participate at the auction market. Interviews were conducted in Kiswahili and transcribed in Kiswahili first and then translated from Kiswahili into English. Transcripts were filed for manual analysis.

Findings

Four issues emerged to be prevalent among livestock keepers for pre-negotiation: goal setting, seeking advice from others, seeking assistance from others and apprenticeship. In general, the study shows that livestock keepers prepare younger ones to master the art of negotiations through an apprenticeship approach.

Negotiation Goals Setting

One of the activities that take place before negotiations is goal setting. This allows actors to ask themselves why they have to engage with counterparts and what they would like to achieve from the coming negotiation (Swaab, Lount, Chung, & Brett, 2021; Tasa, Celani, & Bell, 2013). The study shows that there are a number of issues that occur at the family level. For instance, before selling an animal, people can decide how much they want and how many animals will be sold to meet their goal. Some of the important things such as food, clothes and medical-related issues can help family set goals for negotiations. These issues will determine how much is required and which animal must be sold to collect the respective amount. One of the participants in FGD said:

> Issues that need to be solved in the family can be determined by the price and amount of animals to be sold. This will help a family to set a goal for talk [FGD 7].

Seeking Advice From Others

In pre-negotiation, livestock keepers seek advice from their fellow keepers within their village. This is done so that they can make the right decisions on the purchasing or selling price. In general, livestock keepers' community literacy level is low due to their pastoral lifestyles in the forest and continuous grazing activities. This limits them from conducting a thorough market intelligence to understand the market and even their counterparts. However, what they do is interact with one another to share the experience of price setting during purchasing or selling. This helps them to prepare before the negotiation by obtaining knowledge from others on pricing. One of the participants said:

> Some five years ago, when I was new at the livestock auction market, I sold cattle for Tshs 350,000. After that, my friends asked me why I had sold that animal at a throw-away price. If you had asked us, we could have advised you to sell at Tsh 500,000/=. Since that mistake, I don't come to the market without seeking advice from my fellow livestock keeper [Interview participant 3].

Seeking Assistance From Relatives

Interviews show that before negotiation, some of the market participants with limited negotiation skills seek support from their relatives to assist them during negotiations. Family can make a decision on who to accompany them at the market and help them during the process of selling and negotiations. This decision is influenced by the fact that some of the family members do not have market experience and expertise. This assistance has to be decided before the market day.

Furthermore, this assistance is also intended for overcoming language barriers because a good number of livestock keepers stay in the wild forest raising their animals, and they can only speak their mother tongue. This makes them uncomfortable with Kiswahili which is a common language at the livestock market. With this in view, they have to ask for assistance from their relatives during negotiations at the market. One of the participants stated:

> You know at the livestock auction market, there are people coming with different backgrounds and some of the sellers are shy and have bad tempers. Family can decide before the market day, that tomorrow we want you to assist us in selling our animals during the time of talking with buyers at the market. You know we know each other [Interview participant 5].

> I came here today with my elder brother to assist him to sell his goats, because he cannot speak Kiswahili fluently. He had to stay with me during negotiations I talk to him about the offer from the buyer using Maasai language until we get a fair deal for our animals. We manage to sell all of our goats today [Interview participant 6].

Apprenticeship Practices

When they were asked how they developed those skills, participants mentioned that one has to be old enough to participate in negotiations at the livestock market. However to reach that process, an individual has to engage in that apprenticeship by frequently going to the market with elders staying nearby them and learning the negotiation practices at the market.

> Today I am here at the market accompanied by my friends who are selling five goats and two cows and together with us there is one boy here. He is here so that he can learn the negotiation practices, next time we can send him alone to sell our animals [Interview participant 1].

Conclusion

The results of this study show that pre-negotiation preparation is one of the very important stages among livestock keepers, as performed by the Maasai community in Tanzania. The stage is different from corporate practices, and four important issues emerged: goal setting, seeking advice from fellow livestock keepers, seeking assistance from fellow livestock keepers and apprenticeship practices. Livestock keeper's pre-negotiation stage is guided by setting clear goals of selling animals. Also, apprenticeship for the younger generation is one of the important activities conducted by livestock keepers to prepare members of the family to develop skills in business negotiation.

Goal setting emerged to be one of the activities that livestock keepers conduct in the pre-negotiation stage because it helps livestock keepers to identify accepted price for their animals. In practice, farmers in Tanzania depend on their animals to help them solve their personal financial challenges at their family level, such as buying food and clothes for children, such as school uniforms. This indicates that goal setting is one of the important factors in meeting the family needs, and this helps them to engage in business negotiation and, in particular, for the livestock keepers to identify if they can achieve their goals through the market price offered. The use of apprenticeship is aimed at preparing the next generation of negotiators and is performed at the livestock market by allowing young people to come with elders to the market and observe the process of negotiation. Through this process, they can learn some of the important skills required to be good negotiators at the livestock market.

The pattern of the results supports the ET that governs the stage of negotiation literature. The pre-negotiation stage emphasises the interest in setting goals among actors. The study shows that livestock keepers engage in setting goals. The study did not indicate that the Maasai community engaged in collecting marketing intelligence at the pre-negotiation stage. This is because the market is characterised by short-term relationships, suggests that there is freedom of entry and exit for actors. This makes the process of engaging in collecting market intelligence difficult for livestock keepers who are selling at primary livestock markets because you do not know who your next counterpart in the next animal auction market will be.

Despite its contribution, the current study has some limitations, such as negotiation, which is a dyadic process. This suggests that the study will add value if buyers are interviewed to understand how they prepare for business negotiations, and we can compare the findings from two livestock actors. Furthermore, the current study is exploratory in nature that utilised the qualitative method; therefore, future studies can use a quantitative method survey in more than one auction market at different levels, such as secondary and border livestock markets. These elements will have different perspectives on how traders and farmers participate in various levels of the market and how they prepare. The current study found that one of the activities that are currently conducted by Maasai negotiators in the pre-negotiation stage is goal setting; therefore, it is important in the future to conduct research to understand the effect of goal setting on the behaviour of negotiation and how do they set their goal and factors influence them.

Practical Implication

The findings from this study have practical implications for policymakers and traders. It is well known that acquiring negotiation skills is important for improved performance of livestock keepers at livestock markets. Further, the study has indicated that the pre-negotiation stage is very important for Maasai livestock keepers in Tanzania and has four components which are practiced. Policymakers need to pay attention to how they can build up the capacity of Indigenous community with training on soft skills and negotiation skills. Currently, negotiation training in a number of African countries, including Tanzania, is more focused on supporting corporate and government officers. The current findings suggest that more has to be done to support natives with the aim of improving their business practices. By understanding the fact that livestock keepers, especially Maasai, move around with their animals in the search for pasture and water for the livestock. This type of training can be offered through cooperatives or farmers' groups at the livestock auction markets during the auction day or a day before the auction.

Additionally, the study shows that Maasai livestock keepers do not invest in searching for intelligence information on their counterparts as the corporate pre-negotiation stage suggests. This is due to the costs associated with this process and the nature of doing business at the primary livestock market. However, this can be fulfilled by government officers, especially at the district level, such as district business officers who can conduct business intelligence information on the traders and the market situation and share them with livestock keepers. This can be in the form of weekly reports that can be delivered at the livestock auction market by the market manager to livestock keepers through their elders.

Case Questions

(1) If you were a district marketing officer, what course content would you design to train livestock keepers in business negotiation skills at the livestock market?
(2) Maasai livestock keepers move around with their animals to search for water and pasture; what will you do to ensure you reach them for training?
(3) If you were the marketing officer at the Mvomero district, what would you do to assist Maasai livestock keepers in having access to market intelligence information?
(4) What are some valuable negotiation lessons for agribusiness actors operating in Africa?

References

Berger, P., & Luckmann, T. (1991). *The social contracution of reality*. London: Penguin Book.
Cohen, A. J. (2020). Negotiating the value chain: A study of surplus and distribution in Indian markets for food. *Law and Social Inquiry*, *45*(2), 460–492.
Creswell, J. W. (2013). *Qualitative inquiry and research design* (3rd ed.). London: Sage.
do Prado, L. S., & Martinelli, D. P. (2018). Analysis of negotiation strategies between buyers and sellers: An applied study on crop protection products distribution. *RAUSP Management Journal*, *53*(2), 225–240.

Geiger, I. (2017). A model of negotiation issue-based tactics in business-to-business sales negotiations. *Industrial Marketing Management, 64*, 91–106.

Homas, G. C. (1958). Social behavior as exchange. *American Journal of Sociology, 63*, 597–606.

Jackson, T., Amaeshi, K., & Yavuz, S. (2008). Untangling African indigenous management: Multiple influences on the success of SMEs in Kenya. *Journal of World Business, 43*, 400–416.

Kusumastuti, R., Silalahi, M., Asmara, A. Y., Hardiyati, R., & Juwono, V. (2022). Findings the context indigenous innovation in village enterprise knowledge structure a topic modeling. *Journal of Innovation Entrepreneurship, 11*(1), 1–15.

Lindholst, M., Bulow, M., & Fells, R. (2020). The practices of preparation for complex negotiations. *Journal of Strategic Contracting and Negotiation, 4*(1–2), 1–22.

Lindhost, M. (2015). *Complex business negotiation: Understanding preparation and planning.* Unpublished PhD Thesis submitted at Copen Hagen Business School, Denmark.

Nandonde, F. A., & Liana, P. J. (2013). Analysis of women small scale entrepreneurs practices during business negotiations in Tanzania agribusiness. *Journal of Language, Technology and Entrepreneurship in Africa, 4*(2), 28–45.

Ndoro, J. T., Mudhara, M., & Chimonyo, M. (2015). Farmer's choice of cattle marketing channels under transaction costs in rural South Africa: Multinomial logit model. *African Journal of Range and Forage Science, 32*(4), 243–252.

Patton, M. Q. (1988). *How to use qualitative method.* Thousand Oak, CA: Sage.

Peterson, R. M., & Lucas, G. H. (2001). Expanding antecedent component of traditional business negotiation model: Pre-negotiation literature review and planning-preparation proposition. *Journal of Marketing Theory and Practice, 9*(4), 37–49.

Peterson, R. M., & Shepherd, C. D. (2010). Preparing to negotiate: An exploratory analysis of activities comprising the pre-negotiation process in a buyer-seller interaction. *Marketing Management Journal, 20*(1), 66–75.

Plummer, K. (1983). *Documents of life: An introduction to the problems and literature of humanistic method.* London: Unwin Hyman.

Swaab, R. I., Lount, R. B., Chung, S., & Brett, J. M. (2021). Setting the stage for negotiation: How superordinate goal dialogue promote trust and joint gain in negotiations between team. *Organization Behaviour and Human Decision Processes, 167*, 157–169.

Tarver, J. L., & Haring, R. C. (1988). Improving professional selling: A social exchange approach. *Marketing Intelligence and Planning, 6*(2), 15–20.

Tasa, K., Celani, A., & Bell, C. M. (2013). Goals in negotiation revisited: The impact of goal setting and implicit negotiation beliefs. *Negotiation and Conflict Management Research, 6*(2), 114–132.

URT. (2022). Ministry of livestock and fisheries. Budget Speech, 2022/2023, Dodoma.

Velazquez, B., Buffaria, B., & Commission, E. (2017). About farmers' bargaining power within the new CAP. *Agricultural and Food Economics, 5*(16), 1–13.

Chapter 4

Sustainability of Indigenous Butchery Business in Ghana

Mohammed Majeed, Prince Gyimah and Adiza Sadik

Abstract

The study explores the sustainability practices among Indigenous butchery businesses in a developing country, and in this context, Ghana. Qualitative interview data are employed to understand the start-up procedures, sustainable factors, benefits, opportunities, challenges and strategies that advance the sustainability of butchery businesses. The results show that starting a butchery business depends on a person's tradition or cultural heritage, apprenticeship, training and skills or past experiences. Other factors include support from family and suppliers, dedication and diligence to work, managerial experiences and good luck that may be relatively linked to religious prayers. This study is one of the few studies that extensively explore the possibility and sustainability of Indigenous butchery businesses in Ghana. The approach used does not only provide practicable findings limited to research purposes but also suggestions that are applicable to daily practices and policy formulation.

Keywords: Small and medium-scale enterprises (SMEs); sustainability; Indigenous butchers; Sustainable Development Goals (SDGs); Ghana; butchery business

Introduction

Poverty and unemployment continue to be one of the very pressing challenges confronting most developing countries (Gyimah & Lussier, 2021). The contributions of small and medium-scale enterprises (SMEs) have been a panacea to these problems, and this has spurred the government and other stakeholders to focus on the creation, growth and sustainability of small businesses in order to alleviate poverty (Adeola, Gyimah, Appiah, & Lussier, 2021). In terms of demographic distribution, 40% of the population in the northern region of

Casebook of Indigenous Business Practices in Africa, 53–69

Copyright © 2023 Mohammed Majeed, Prince Gyimah and Adiza Sadik

Published under exclusive licence by Emerald Publishing Limited

doi:10.1108/978-1-80455-762-420231008

Ghana, which has about 1.3% populace, is considered poor (Abdulai, Bawole, & Kojo Sakyi, 2018). Asuming-Bediako, Aikins-Wilson, Affedzie-Obresi, and Adu (2018) thus argue that advancing the butchery businesses can help alleviate poverty and create more jobs in developing countries. For instance, the butchery industries predominantly reduce poverty and sustain growth in the North, a region with the most considerable rate of poverty (Abdulai et al., 2018; Okpala, Nwobi, & Korzeniowska, 2021). In Ghana, native Butchers from Wulensi, Bimbilla and Yendi from the Northern region of Ghana buy livestock (cow, goat and ram), make specialty meat, process and package the meats for wholesale and retail sales. The butchery businesses contribute to employment, economic development, and basically, public health and well-being by ensuring that healthy meat are provided for human consumption (Asuming-Bediako et al., 2018; Okpala et al., 2021).

Thus, the sustainability of the butchery businesses is crucial to the attainment of United Nations (UN) Sustainable Development Goals (SDGs). Some of the goals the butchery industry is targeted at achieving are poverty alleviation (SDG 1), zero hunger (SDG 2), good health and well-being (SDG 3), and work and economic growth (SDG 8). In spite of the well-articulated SDGs agenda, the butchery businesses are positioned to achieve; it is not uncommon to see that thousand of butchery businesses fail within the first five years of establishment (Klimas, Czakon, Kraus, Kailer, & Maalaoui, 2021). Surprisingly, extant literature predicting business sustainability is limited; in recent times, scholarship calls for more research studies to explore businesses' challenges and sustainability factors (Adeola et al., 2021; Gyimah & Adeola, 2021). In addition, findings from existing studies on the sustainability of businesses are fragmentary, and presently, to the best of our knowledge, no valid theories are advancing a firm's sustainability (Gyimah et al., 2020). The crux of this research is to fill this gap by investigating successful entrepreneurs' start-up processes, challenges, opportunities and sustainability factors among Indigenous butchery businesses in the Northern region of Ghana, coupled with a high business failure rate in the region.

Our scholarly contributions are fourfold. First, the study would assist butcher entrepreneurs in adjusting their business practices and implementing new tactics to enhance their ability to grow, multiply, and replicate and also contribute to sustainable employment. Second, this research can assist government and regulatory agencies such as the National Board for Small Scale Industries (NBSSI) and the stakeholders of the butchery industry to utilise existing scarce resources for the sustainability of the business. In addition, the findings would reveal the best possible strategies to deploy to help businesses remain in operations for unforeseeable years. Thirdly, nascent and existing butchery entrepreneurs can use the findings to make investment decisions, and finally, we contribute to business and management literature on firm's sustainability focusing on Indigenous butchery businesses from a developing country's perspective.

The rest of the study is structured as follows: section 'Butchery Business in Ghana' presents the context and brief history of butchery businesses; section 'Methodology' provides the methods used to conduct the study; section 'Results and Discussions' discusses the results; section 'Conclusion and Implications' provides concluding remarks, including policy implications; and section 'Limitations and Further Research' gives the limitations and suggestions for further studies.

Butchery Business in Ghana

A butcher is a person whose line of work is cutting up and selling meat in a shop (Reynolds, 2022). Put differently, a butcher is a person who slaughters and cuts up animals for food (Reynolds, 2022). The butchery business is one mediaeval trade where livestock was domesticated (Okpala et al., 2021). Butchery businesses can be primary and secondary (Asuming-Bediako et al., 2018). Primary butchery is the dismemberment of a carcass, whereas secondary butchery is the boning and trimming by separating an animal's carcass and preparing it for sales (Asuming-Bediako et al., 2018). Asuming-Bediako et al. (2018) add that butchery businesses do not only contribute significantly to job creation and profitability of entrepreneurs but also have a positive influence on public health by ensuring meat safety for consumption. Butchers ensure that livestock or meats are made available for every individual irrespective of their budget, and meat demand is expected to increase at a higher rate, especially in developing countries (Okpala et al., 2021). Thus, this research unveils the sustainability factors of Indigenous butchery businesses that will serve as benchmarks for research and practice. We contribute to literature, investigating the sustainability tactics that butcher businesses employ to sustain their operations in Ghana.

In Ghana, butchers were incorporated into Dagomba Society by Naa Dimani. Naa Dimani is the first butcher. He is the grandfather of all the butcher families (Dolsi-naa Abubakari Lunna, May 21, 1993) who happened to be a traveller from Hausa land, which now is in Nigeria, visited Dagbɔŋ. In ancient times, when travellers visited any town within the Dagomba Kingdom without having any relatives therein, it was customary for them to go to the chief's house. This man told the chief that he was a butcher, and he was allowed to settle in the community. He started working in Yendi at a place called the 'butchers' tree' (the place they sit and kill the animals). Several boys followed him whenever this man went to work, including one of the young princes [the young Naa Dimani]. The Hausa man used to cut the meat and put it on a plate (called Pong, in Dagbani) for the boys to go around and sell. At first, people did not know the name to call this man. No one knew the Hausa man's name, so they called him 'Baaba'. Baaba means father. The young prince and his friends started to know how to do the work. The Hausa man grew old in Dagbɔŋ. When the old man was close to the grave, he gathered all the trade tools, the knives and other things, and presented them to the prince, and told him, 'When I die, continue my work. Do not leave it' (AfroRoman, 2010). Since then, the butchery business continues to dominate among the young and active workforce in the Northern area of Ghana, especially amongst Nanumbas and Dagombas.

Literature suggests that men are predominantly in the butchery industry in Northern Ghana (Asuming-Bediako et al., 2018). It is no surprise that Muslims dominate the butchering industry (Adzitey, Teye, & Dinko, 2011). Most Christians and other religions do not care who killed an animal for its flesh, but Muslim slaughterers have an essential duty to ensure that the meat is acceptable to Muslims worldwide (Asuming-Bediako et al., 2018). Butchery in Ghana appeared to be a family industry, passed down through the generations, and the butchers were all related to one other. According to Teye and Bortir (2012), butchery in the North is a family industry passed down from generation to generation. Although it is a modern practice, butchery in Ghana has its root in the past. Meat sold from their establishments could not be ruled out because the working benches were composed of porcelain tiles or wood wrapped in cardboard, not stainless steel. The industry lacks professionalism if equipment like axes, cutlasses and simple weighing scales are still used in butchery activities. So the butchery business in Ghana is eagerly awaiting the implementation of cutting-edge technology to modernise its operations (Asuming-Bediako et al., 2018).

Although Ghana's butchery industry has several obstacles, the increasing demand for animal products suggests more prospects for companies along the value chain. There are excellent opportunities for investment in local animal production because of the low output level, and entrepreneurs can jump-start their company plans by setting up a meat delivery service. Another business opportunity is the supply of cold storage facilities for the storage of unsold meat. A butchery module in a post-secondary institution or research centre could help modernise the industry in Ghana in addition to its commercial appeal (Asuming-Bediako et al., 2018).

Methodology

Design and Context

We employ a qualitative case study to examine the abilities needed by butcher entrepreneurs to remain in and sustain their businesses. The qualitative research method allows one to have a better understanding of how butchery businesses have maintained their operations and delve into an in-depth investigation of their sustainability tactics and practices. Patton (2015) argues that a qualitative case study such as face-to-face interviews provides a deeper understanding of situations that are not well known and are ideal for eliciting information about people's thoughts, feelings and motivations. For the sake of the research, we conducted a 30-minute face-to-face interview each to gather primary data to achieve the study's objectives. The purposive sampling technique was used to select four small butchery entrepreneurs to achieve the study's objectives. Semi-structured interviews conducted are on the small butchery retail entrepreneurs (respondents) from three traditional cities in the North: Bimbilla, Wulensi and Yendi. Bimbilla and Wulensi are the two largest communities in Nanung.

Yendi is the traditional seat of Dagbɔnŋ and the second largest city in the Dagbɔnŋ kingdom, whilst Bimbilla is the traditional city of Nanung kingdom. History reveals that the butchery businesses originated from these traditional cities and merit the study's size, tradition and location standards.

The butchery business of Wulensi is conducted based on the chiefs and the hierarchy. The chief of butchers (Nakɔhnima) (called *Nakɔh-Naa*) conducts business on Thursdays, Fridays and Saturdays. The second in command of the chieftaincy hierarchy of Butchers in Wulensi is *Barba*, who conducts business on Sundays and Mondays. The third in the hierarchy is *Taribabu*, who conducts business on Tuesdays and Wednesdays. The animals slaughtered are mostly cattle (cows and bulls). Similarly, the butchery business of Bimbilla is the same as in Wulensi and is conducted based on the chiefs and the hierarchy. The chief of butchers (Nakɔhnima) (called *Nakɔh-Naa*) conducts business Fridays, Saturdays and Sundays. The second in command of the chieftaincy hierarchy of Butchers in Bimbilla is *Barba*, who conducts business on Mondays and Tuesdays. The third in the hierarchy is *Taribabu*, who conducts business on Wednesdays and Thursdays. The animals slaughtered are mostly cattle (cows and bulls). The case of the Yendi butchery hierarchy is different from the whole of Dagbɔnŋ and Nanung. At Yendi, *Yidann Barba* is the head, followed by *Zɔhi Nakɔh-Naa, Balɔgu Nakɔh-Naa* and *Taribabu*. The weekly schedule of business is as follows: *Yidann Barba* (Head of Nakɔh Family in Yendi) conducts his business on three days (Monday, Tuesday and Wednesday) and two days for *Zɔhi Nakɔh-Naa* (Thursday and Friday). Finally, one day each (Saturday and Sunday) for *Balɔgu Nakɔh-Naa* and *Taribabu*, respectively.

Selection Criteria and Interview Guide

The selection criteria for respondents included the following: (1) The participants own butcher businesses; (2) the butcher has been in business and making a profit for at least five years; (3) the owners of butcher businesses are residents in Ghana and (4) the butcher is not a minor (age of participants should be more than 18 years). We sought approval from each respondent through a phone call to participate in the research. We reach saturation after the fourth person. Data saturation happens when no new information or themes can be discovered from more interviews or cases (Fusch & Ness, 2015). Qualitative researchers discontinue data gathering and analysis when they reach saturation (Tran, Porcher, Tran, & Ravaud, 2017).

The language of the selected respondents for the face-to-face interview is Dagbani. Hence, the interview was conducted and recorded in Dagbani. A linguistic lecturer from Tamale Technical University did the transcription. The interview guide includes the following research questions (*RQs*):

RQ1: How did you start the butchery business?

RQ2: What strategies have you used to sustain your butchery business beyond 5 years?

RQ3: What benefits and opportunities do you derive from the butchery business?

RQ4: What challenges or barriers, if any, did you encounter in implementing your strategies for business?

RQ5: How did you address the barriers you encountered in implementing your strategies for sustainability?

Results and Discussions

Demographic Statistics

The first respondent is the son of Mba Mahamud Divela in Wulensi, who is 40 years old with over 20 years of butchery business experience. He retails beef in Accra in the Madina butcher house. He learnt the business from his parents in Wulensi, but later moved to Accra to start meat retailing. We interviewed him at his butcher house, and he underlined the necessity of using technology (refrigerator) to assist everyone in the industry during the interview.

The second respondent is the son of Gbantohgu Nakɔh-Naa, who is 42 years of age. He is a Nanumba man from Wulensi. He was interviewed in his new residence in Wulensi. He deals in meat retailing and selling live animals. He buys from Wulensi, Bimbilla, and other villages and Bawku in the upper East region of Ghana. He sells mainly in Accra. He joined the business because it is ancestral and inherited from the father.

The third respondent is a 40-year-old Dagomba man who had a table retailing meat at the Yendi Butcher house. His highest qualification of education was senior high school. From his shop, he took part in the interview. He has been in the industry for 12 years. Throughout the discussion, he underlined the butchery industry's economic and cultural values and importance.

The final respondent is a 49-year-old Nanumba man who worked for Bimbilla Nakɔh-Naa. He has a senior high school certificate as his highest degree of education. He *underlined* the importance of goal setting and traditional Dagomba butchery values.

Interview Results and Discussions

We present the results of the face-to-face interviews of the selected four respondents. The following paragraphs provide the responses and discussion relating to the research questions on how the entrepreneurs started their butchery businesses, the sustainability tactics and strategies, benefits or opportunities they have derived from them, challenges encountered and solutions proffered.

Start-Up

Regarding how entrepreneurs start the butchery business, Respondents 1 and 3 said they understudied or followed their parents or brothers to gather experiences before starting the butchery business. Thus, the participants anticipate that starting a butchery business is based on an apprenticeship or internship (training) to gather the requisite experiences or skills to be a successful butchery entrepreneur. These are their responses:

> I understudied my parents in the Wulensi butcher house. I started selling the meat at the butcher house. But I moved to Accra 20 years ago.
>
> 40 years/Retailer/Male/Wulensi

> I followed my brothers for ten clear years later they asked me to start slaughtering. Now I use our father's slaughtering space or tools.
>
> 40 years/Retailer/Male/Yendi

However, Respondents 2 and 4 argue that they started the butchery business due to heritage, inheritance or tradition. Like the native butchers of Wulensi, Bimbilla and Yendi, it is an automatic and organic business for the children of the butcher chiefs in those communities.

> ….it is our heritage when I started going to the butcher house and was able to cater for my small things like table and chair in school. I joined it fully after senior high school. I started with GH₵60, generated by myself. I now sell on the table and buy animals to Accra to retail to butchers/individuals.
>
> 42 years/Retailer/Male/Wulensi

> Is a tradition, and inherited the business from my dad. I was learning while in the butcher house. So, I will say is a family business.
>
> 49 years/Retailer/Male/Bimbilla

Sustainability

Regarding business sustainability, Respondents 1 and 3 link this to access to external support or capital from family and suppliers or trade payables, respectively. For instance, the respondents said:

> I give my best to the job because it is my source of livelihood since I dropped out after senior high school. I used to borrow to support

the animal selling business, but now I am ok. I give my customers what they want.

> 40 years/Retailer/Male/Wulensi

My sisters have supported me all this while. But today, I am doing good and have started supporting them. I am also serious when it comes to business and debt collection.

> 40 years/Retailer/Male/Yendi

Other Respondents (2 and 4) stated that the butchery business sustainability is due to hard work, managerial experiences, good luck due to religious prayers and providing quality animals and meats. They provided these responses during the interview:

I work hard, I have boys, and I am patient with the boys. Now the boys understood the business was continuous. We slaughter healthy animals all the time, and we sell good-looking animals too.

> 42 years/Retailer/Male/Wulensi

I will say it is by luck because my business grows every day though I pray every day for Allah's support. We also work hard and follow food sellers for our money (debt collection), and I give customers low prices and make a small profit.

> 49 years/Retailer/Male/Bimbilla

Access to external capital or credit, managerial experiences and religion are contributing factors that have impacted the longevity of small businesses in Ghana (Gyimah et al., 2020; Meyer, 1998). As stated by Amankwah-Amoah, Boso, and Antwi-Agyei (2018), Gyimah and Adeola (2021), and Gyimah and Lussier (2021), the high failure rate of SMEs is because they have restricted access to external capital. Gyimah and Boachie (2018), Ibrahim and Shariff (2016), and Wang (2016) agreed that a lack of financial resources was one of the most significant hurdles to SMEs' long-term viability.

Benefits and Opportunities

In terms of the benefits they derived from the butchery businesses, they have tangible assets, complete a university or college, marry and are very responsible, and contribute to the nation's development by paying taxes. Here are the responses:

I have a number of properties from the butchery business. I take care of my four kids and their schooling and my wife too.

> 40 years/Retailer/Male/Wulensi

The job is a blessing; we pay taxes; make money to take care of my needs, build a house and look after my parents. I now have a herd of cattle, and I have a lot of assets.

42 years/Retailer/Male/Wulensi

It helped me to complete my first degree last two years. All my income comes from it. I used it to marry, feed my home and change my motor every year.

40 years/Retailer/Male/Yendi

Though I am now in charge, I still provide for my wife and children and take care of my parents. I have started building a house through that.

49 years/Retailer/Male/Bimbilla

These findings suggest that butchery businesses help alleviate poverty and contribute to the country's socio-economic development (Okpala et al., 2021). However, the business sector among Dagombas/Nanumbas is a mix of self-employment outlets and dynamic enterprises primarily concentrated in rural areas (Moyo & Mandizwidza-Moyo, 2017). Due to their low international competitiveness, butchers mainly focus on retailing to the domestic market.

For the opportunities, the ability to affect positive social change starts with the owners of SME crafting, modelling, harmonising and directing sustainability activities and efforts for emerging opportunities. The 40-year-old butcher retailer at Wulensi said the demand for local beef/meat is expected to stay or increase in the future.

Challenges

Three respondents outline that lack of credit support from the government or family, payment of taxes, refrigerator costs for leftover meats and cost of animal transportation are the challenges facing the butchery business. Here are their responses:

The government does not help butchers despite the fact that we pay tax. Some of the animals die during transportation; as a Muslim, you have to throw the carcass away. Cost of animal transportation.

42 years/Retailer/Male/Wulensi

...paying for refrigerator cost for leftover meats. This time you have to go to the bush to get the animal you want. There are credit facilities and sometimes your customer will switch to other butchers.

42 years/Retailer/Male/Wilensi

I am from poor family background, no one supports me apart from my sisters, who used to support me and I am now helping them back. This time cattle are expensive, and paying for refrigerator costs for leftover meats. There are no credit facilities in Bimbilla.

49 years/Retailer/Male/Bimbilla

Another respondent outlines that import of frozen meats, unstable demand during festive seasons, cost of handling the animals and spirituality are the challenges facing the butchery business. He said:

Demand is not stable, especially during the Christmas season. Sometimes you do not have plenty of money to buy. Paying for refrigerator costs for leftover meats, the cost of treating and feeding animals, the spiritual aspect from the butcher house by colleagues (especially Yendi), and the importation of frozen meats are some of the challenges.

40 years/Retailer/Male/Yendi

The large importation of frozen meat – ranging from frozen chicken to frozen beef – that comes from Western European and Latin American countries is another challenge curtailing the butchery business. The imported meat is cheaper than the local beef, so most chop bar operators (food sellers) prefer to buy imported meat instead of from local butchers. Water shortages result in unclean meat in the urban areas of Ghana. The tax government takes from butchers; they see it as a problem. According to Zvarivadza (2018), governments' tax and regulatory frameworks significantly impact SMEs' smooth operation, growth and development. Large corporations, lack of water and raw materials, and a lack of financial aid are only some of the problems small and medium-sized businesses face. As indicated in the study, the lack of credit for butchers is also exemplified in literature since the SMEs' development rate was slow in Ghana because of a lack of access to credit (Gyimah & Lussier, 2021; Nkuah, Tanyeh, & Gaeten, 2013). The pitiable commercial practices and uncomplimentary strategies contributed to the inability to access credit (Avortri, Bunyaminu, & Wereko, 2013). Financial limitations are often an interruption to the thriving of SMEs.

Solutions

Despite these numerous challenges facing the butchery business, the respondents stated that prayers and borrowing funds contribute to sustainability. Respondent

2 (42-year-old retailer at Wulensi) and Respondent 3 (40-year-old retailer at Yendi) stated that continuous prayers contribute to the probability of their sustainability. However, Respondent 1 (40-year-old retailer at Wulensi) states that the availability of credit facilities and the flexibility of payment contribute to the sustainability of the butchery business.

Conclusion and Implications

The contributions of small butchery businesses are seen as the panacea for alleviating poverty and creating jobs among Indigenous individuals in developing countries. This study explores the sustainability practices among Indigenous butchery businesses in a developing country context, Ghana. Qualitative interview data from respondents from Ghana is used to understand how butchers start their business, the business sustainability factors, benefits and opportunities, barriers or challenges, and solutions or strategies implemented to advance their sustainability. The interview results reveal that starting a butchery business depends on a person's tradition or heritage, apprenticeship or making money for livelihood. Provision of quality meats and access to external capital are the main drivers of the sustainability of butchery businesses. The benefits of butchery businesses include having properties or assets, payment of tax for infrastructural development, assistance to complete a university and taking care of family. The challenges of the butchery businesses include demand fluctuations, large imports of frozen meat, inadequate financial aid or credit, colossal payment of taxes, refrigerator or electricity costs and transportation and handling of the animal's costs. However, the increasing demand for local meat shows that the butchery industries have prospects and opportunities.

Our findings indicate that butchery businesses need prior training or some level of apprenticeship and adequate capital to increase their sustainability before starting the business. Financial institutions and government agencies should provide external finance with low-interest rates to help butchery businesses grow and achieve the SDGs, such as end poverty alleviation (SDG 1), zero hunger (SDG 2), good health and well-being (SDG 3), and work and economic growth (SDG 8). Again, the government should use some tax from the butchery businesses to stimulate and advance butchery entrepreneurship by halting the importation of foreign frozen meats into the country. Food and Drug Authority requires communal butchery vendors to be hygienically approved and regulated, and national medical outreach programmes should be expanded to guarantee that operators in Ghana's butchery business remain compliant. Fortunately, the future beef demand is expected to be high, and thus, both butchers and the government must improve cow production levels by reducing bottlenecks in animal husbandry. Advocacy, technology modelling, capacity building and practitioner training can all benefit from establishing a strong Butchers' Association.

Limitations and Further Research

This study has three main limitations, and we provide suggestions to improve them in future research. First, we interviewed butchers in Ghana, excluding other developing and advanced economies. There should be a replication studies from other countries to generalise the respondents' opinions. Second, we adopted a subjective qualitative interview guide to achieve the study's objectives. Future studies can use a quantitative objective approach to examine the sustainability factors, opportunities or challenges of butchery industries in developing and advanced countries. Finally, the study excludes questions on entrepreneur characteristics, culture and micro- and macro-economic indicators of butchery businesses in developing countries. Future studies should include these factors in their interview guide to understand the butchery activities, sustainability, and performance.

Notwithstanding the limitations, our study provides an in-depth understanding of how butchers start businesses, the challenges, benefits and opportunities of butchery firms, and the sustainability factors of butchery firms in developing countries. Our findings add to theory to utilising scarce resources for the sustainability and performance of butchery businesses.

Acknowledgement

The following people provided oral literature for the paper: Ms. Iddrisu Rukaya, Mr. Fusheini Zakari, Ridwan Yussif and Ms. Mohammed Safia.

References

Abdulai, A. G., Bawole, J. N., & Kojo Sakyi, E. (2018). Rethinking persistent poverty in Northern Ghana: The primacy of policy and politics over geography. *Politics & Policy, 46*(2), 233–262.

Adeola, O., Gyimah, P., Appiah, K. O., & Lussier, R. N. (2021). Can critical success factors of small businesses in emerging markets advance UN Sustainable Development Goals? *World Journal of Entrepreneurship, Management and Sustainable Development, 17*(1), 85–105.

Adzitey, F., Teye, G. A., & Dinko, M. M. (2011). Pre and post-slaughter animal handling by butchers in the Bawku Municipality of the Upper East Region of Ghana. *Livestock Research for Rural Development, 23*(2), 1–8.

AfroRoman. (2010). The story of Nakohi-waa, dance-drumming for butchers. DDD AfroRoman 2010 Nakohi-waa History Story DL1. Retrieved from https://dl.tufts.edu

Amankwah-Amoah, J., Boso, N., & Antwi-Agyei, I. (2018). The effects of business failure experience on successive entrepreneurial engagements: An evolutionary phase model. *Group and Organization Management, 43*, 648–682.

Asuming-Bediako, N., Aikins-Wilson, S., Affedzie-Obresi, S., & Adu, E. K. (2018). Challenges in the Butchery industry: Potential opportunities for business in Ghana. *Ghana Journal of Agricultural Science, 52*, 121–129.

Avortri, C., Bunyaminu, A., & Wereko, T. B. (2013). Factors that hinder access to credit by small and medium scale enterprises despite the financial sector liberalization in Ghana. *International Journal of Management Sciences, 1*(10), 386–390.

Fusch, P. I., & Ness, L. R. (2015). Are we there yet? Data saturation in qualitative research. *The Qualitative Report, 20*, 1408–1416.

Gyimah, P., & Adeola, O. (2021). MSMEs sustainable prediction model: A three-sector comparative study. *Journal of the International Council for Small Business, 2*(2), 90–100.

Gyimah, P., Appiah, K. O., & Lussier, R. N. (2020). Success versus failure prediction model for small businesses in Ghana. *Journal of African Business, 21*(2), 215–234.

Gyimah, P., & Boachie, W. K. (2018). Effect of microfinance products on small business growth: Emerging economy perspective. *Journal of Entrepreneurship and Business Innovation, 5*(1), 59–71.

Gyimah, P., & Lussier, R. N. (2021). Rural entrepreneurship success factors: An empirical investigation in an emerging market. *Journal of Small Business Strategy, 31*(4), 5–19.

Ibrahim, M. A., & Shariff, M. N. M. (2016). Mediating role of access to finance on the relationship between strategic orientation attributes and SMEs performance in Nigeria. *International Journal of Business and Society, 17*(3), 473–496.

Klimas, P., Czakon, W., Kraus, S., Kailer, N., & Maalaoui, A. (2021). Entrepreneurial failure: A synthesis and conceptual framework of its effects. *European Management Review, 18*(1), 167–182.

Meyer, B. (1998). Commodities and the power of prayer: Pentecostalist attitudes towards consumption in contemporary Ghana. *Development and Change, 29*(4), 751–776.

Moyo, B., & Mandizwidza-Moyo, E. (2017). SMEs management practices in a hostile business environment in Zimbabwe. *Journal of Entrepreneurship and Business Innovation, 4*(1), 13–24.

Nkuah, J. K., Tanyeh, J. P., & Gaeten, K. (2013). Financing small and medium enterprises (SMEs) in Ghana: Challenges and determinants in accessing bank credit. *International Journal of Research in Social Sciences, 2*(3), 12–25.

Okpala, C. O. R., Nwobi, O. C., & Korzeniowska, M. (2021). Assessing Nigerian butchers' knowledge and perception of good hygiene and storage practices: A cattle slaughterhouse case analysis. *Foods, 10*(6), 1165.

Patton, M. Q. (2015). *Qualitative research & evaluation methods: Integrating theory and practice* (4th ed.). Thousand Oaks, London: Sage Publications, Inc.

Reynolds, T. (2022). Are butcher shops a thing of the past? *Quora*. Retrieved from https://www.quora.com/Are-butcher-shops-a-thing-of-the-past

Teye, G. A., & Bortir, C. E. (2012). Butchering and meat handling standards in the SawlaTuna Kalba and West Gonja Districts in the st Northern Region. In *Proceedings of the 31 Ghana Animal Science Association Conference*, Accra, 23–24 August 2012. CSIRAnimal Research Institute.

Tran, V. T., Porcher, R., Tran, V. C., & Ravaud, P. (2017). Predicting data saturation in qualitative surveys with mathematical models from ecological research. *Journal of Clinical Epidemiology, 82*, 71–78.

Wang, Y. (2016). What are the biggest obstacles to the growth of SMEs in developing countries? An empirical evidence from an enterprise survey. *Borsa Istanbul Review, 16*, 167–176.

Zvarivadza, T. (2018). Sustainability in the mining industry: An evaluation of the National Planning Commission's diagnostic overview. *Resources Policy, 56*, 70–77.

Appendix

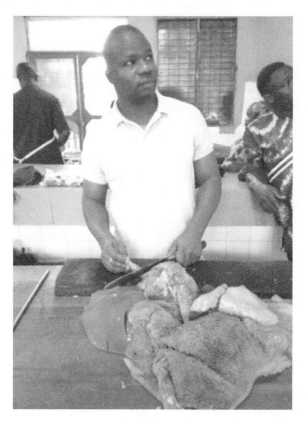

Fig. 1.   Abdulai Mahamud in a Butcher House Cutting Meat for
Customers.

Fig. 2.   Haruna Iddris in a Butcher House Cutting Meat for
Customers.

Fig. 3.   Ridwan Retailing Sheep From Wulensi, Bimbilla, in Accra.

Fig. 4.   Carcass for Retailing by Alidu Mohammed.

Chapter 5

What Is Peculiar in the Sustainability Practices of Indigenous Female Business Owners in Uganda?

Patricia Isabirye

Abstract

Businesses have increasingly been urged to shift their emphasis away from a purely profit-driven economic perspective to a more sustainable approach to growth that holistically captures people, the planet and profits. Indigenous businesses are well suited to creatively integrate sustainability principles within their internal culture. This enables them to cope with the dominance created by non-indigenous enterprises while also promoting long-term business success. The Triple Bottom Line (TBL) concept has been applied to explore how indigenous businesses in Uganda manifest their best practices by incorporating sustainability principles for lasting economic performance. A multiple case study approach was adopted, and three well-established female-owned indigenous businesses were investigated using in-depth interviews. Integrating sustainability in the business is a fulfiling process if done holistically by embracing a range of interdependent variables that include environmental, social and economic dimensions. The author contributes an innovative culturally sensitive sustainability scope that reflects practical insights on how internal sustainability efforts can be streamlined for long-term economic prosperity without compromising the wider social and physical environment.

Keywords: Indigenous business; business sustainability; female-owned businesses; Uganda; female business owners; female entrepreneurship

Introduction

This chapter introduces and unpacks the two concepts of indigenous entrepreneurship and business sustainability within the Ugandan context. It also explores

Casebook of Indigenous Business Practices in Africa, 71–103
Copyright © 2023 Patricia Isabirye
Published under exclusive licence by Emerald Publishing Limited
doi:10.1108/978-1-80455-762-420231009

how indigenous entrepreneurship and business sustainability translate into long-term economic performance, especially for female-owned indigenous businesses, which are often ignored during sustainability discussions (Loucks, Martens, & Cho, 2010). The ultimate focus is to equip more female-owned indigenous businesses with the necessary sustainability tools from a Ugandan perspective and to stimulate further discussions on the importance of incorporating sustainability lens within the internal company culture, especially for female-owned indigenous businesses said to be ideal for integrating sustainability principles (De Bruin, Brush, & Welter, 2007).

Indigenous Entrepreneurship

Indigenous peoples according to The World Bank (2010) are populations that possess strong historical links with societies that existed before colonial settlement. They associate with and use ancestral lands and natural resources; have a distinct language, culture, customary, economic, social and political institutions; and are resolute about their distinctiveness. Colonisation led to numerous injustices for indigenous communities in Africa (Conway, 2011; Dana, 2015; Imhonopi, Urim, & Iruonagbe, 2013; Tabuti & Van Damme, 2012). This impacted their sustainability and economic development negatively and produced an uncertain future for their communities (Conway, 2011; Tabuti & Van Damme, 2012) by diverting resources meant for indigenous people to settler communities. Also, the focus shifted to state interest at the expense of the interest of the indigenes and the right to exercise self-determination and control of their assets and resources were not accorded full recognition. Indigenous peoples are now reviving their traditional culture and values to restore their identity and ensure survival through indigenous-focused economic development and sustainability (Conway, 2011). Entrepreneurship has been a critical driver for the economic and social development of indigenous communities, and it also creates an avenue to promote economic gains which embrace community values and attitudes (Hindle & Moroz, 2007; Mika, Fahey, & Bensemann, 2019; Vazquez-Maguirre, 2020a).

Conway (2011) defines indigenous entrepreneurship as activities that focus on new venture creation and economic opportunity to reduce indigenous disadvantages through the creation of culturally viable and community acceptable wealth. Indigenous entrepreneurs create new ventures by and for the benefit of indigenous people which further generate economic returns for social and economic advantage (Dana, 2015; Hindle & Lansdowne, 2002; Mika, 2020; Tabuti & Van Damme, 2012; Vazquez-Maguirre, 2020a; Vazquez-Maguirre, 2020b). It is a means of generating sustainable revenue streams by employing indigenous people in businesses and embracing indigenous cultural and social norms. This puts them in touch with contextual issues, which are usually non-existent in mainstream entrepreneurship. The emphasis of indigenous entrepreneurship is on innovative economic ventures to overcome disadvantages while participating actively and competitively in the global economy (Hindle & Moroz, 2007; Tabuti & Van Damme, 2012; Vazquez-Maguirre, 2020a).

Indigenous enterprises are often environmentally sustainable and, to the barest minimum, avoid wasting resources (Dana, 2015). Findings from a study by Ring, Peredo, and Chrisman (2010) on rural communities in the United States suggest that culturally sensitive business practices which are crucial to sustainability are central to indigenous businesses. Vazquez-Maguirre (2020a) points out that indigenous enterprises in Latin America tend to embrace humanistic principles, which at times contradict mainstream entrepreneurial assumptions to generate a positive impact on the communities in which they reside. Shinde (2010), for example, reveals how indigenous religious entrepreneurs drive religious tourism in India by innovating and developing new products and expanding the cultural economy of rituals and performances to suit the demands of their flourishing tourism.

Tapsell and Woods (2010) analysed entrepreneurial activities in Maori communities, specifically their innovations in the form of social organisation that occur through interactions between the young Potiki communities and the Rangatira who are the elders/states representative within the community. These interactions demonstrate how culture and heritage can creatively contribute to innovation while bridging the gap between chaos and stability. In their case study analysis of Australian Aborigines, native Hawaiians and Maori entrepreneurs, Foley and O'Connor (2013) investigated networking activities by these groups of indigenous entrepreneurs. Their findings depicted that networking, characterised by fundamental social dimensions unique to their context, contributes significantly to their business ambitions.

Indigenous business culture and internal structure are socially and communally oriented (Maguirre, Ruelas, & De La Torre, 2016; Mika et al., 2019; Vazquez-Maguirre, 2020a, 2020b) and less formal, which makes them flexible in establishing sustainable business practices. Their internal financial resource mechanisms are less complex, which means easy adaptability to sustainability initiatives. Therefore, more user-friendly sustainability practices tailored for indigenous businesses are necessary to produce good results (Loucks et al., 2010). This calls for more innovative models of value creation, which can be unearthed during indigenous entrepreneurship research and which provide hope of addressing some of the challenges faced by indigenous communities. The diverse insights generated in this regard will also expand the horizons and relevance of the entrepreneurship scholarship (Hindle & Moroz, 2007). Therefore, additional research is needed on the practical aspects of sustainability (Bergquist, 2017; Petrini & Pozzebon, 2010), especially for indigenous businesses not sufficiently covered within sustainability discussions (Loucks et al., 2010).

Business Sustainability

Sustainable development was initially coined by the United Nations (1987) and is defined as 'meeting the needs of present stakeholders without compromising how future generations meet their needs'. Although considered vague (Lee, 2020), naïve and lacking focus (Loucks et al., 2010), this definition captures practical aspects that include human, economic and environmental dimensions (Lee, 2020;

Lesnikova & Schmidtova, 2020; Sukawati, Riana, Rajiani, & Abbas, 2020) with regard to equity in the distribution and utilisation of resources (Greco & De Jong, 2017). Sustainable development embraces the Triple Bottom Line (TBL) concept, also known as the three Ps (People, Profits and Planet) determined by Elkington (1997) with the aim of holistically achieving social, economic and environmental benefits. Business sustainability is an emerging concept (Bergquist, 2017; Lesnikova & Schmidtova, 2020) that has increasingly become critical in promoting corporate competitiveness (Epstein & Yuthas, 2012), long-term entrepreneurial success (Lee, 2020; Lesnikova & Schmidtova, 2020; Sukawati et al., 2020) and features as an aspect of growth and survival of business enterprises (Akhtar, Ismail, Ndaliman, Hussain, & Haider, 2015).

There has been an increased tendency for organisations to integrate society's expectations into their business strategies in response to rising pressure from consumers, employees and other stakeholders while exploring opportunities for competitive advantage (Jha & Rangarajan, 2020; Lesnikova & Schmidtova, 2020; Sukawati et al., 2020). Businesses have been urged to shift their emphasis away from a purely profit-driven economic perspective to a more holistic focus (Bateh, Heaton, Arbogast, & Broadbent, 2013) through a comprehensive system of stakeholder engagement (Newell & Moore, 2010). Sustainability-driven entrepreneurship focuses on pursuing social, environmental and economic objectives in an equal, altruistic, holistic and integral manner (Muñoz, 2013; Lee, 2020; Lesnikova & Schmidtova, 2020). This includes sustainable measures for making and delivering products and services and maintaining global standards and certification schemes such as the Global Reporting Initiative (GRI), which presents global best practices for reporting publicly on economic, environmental and social impacts; the SA 8000 standards for social responsibility, ISO 14001 for environmental priorities and ISO 9001 for economic sustainability (Lesnikova & Schmidtova, 2020).

Business sustainability connects stakeholders with the natural environment, aligns social progress with planetary issues and ultimately generates reasonable economic returns (Ahlström, Williams, & Vildåsen, 2020; Prasad, Mishra, & Bapat, 2019). It is grounded in creating a balance between the principles of integrity through environmental consideration and equity by focusing on society and prosperity for economic gains (Jha & Rangarajan, 2020). This includes deliberate actions that harmonise strategies for profitability, social responsibility and environmental protection to meet present needs without compromising how future generations meet their needs (Lee, 2020; Lesnikova & Schmidtova, 2020; Muñoz, 2013; Sukawati et al., 2020).

The Uganda indigenous entrepreneurship context, including female entrepreneurship, is explored in the next section. This builds into the case for indigenous female business sustainability.

The Uganda Indigenous Entrepreneurship Context

SMEs in Uganda play a major role in the Ugandan economy through employment and wealth creation, which leads to poverty eradication (Khayesi,

Sserwanga, & Kiconco, 2017; Nuwagaba & Nzewi, 2013; Sebikari, 2014). The Ugandan government acknowledges the important role SMEs play in the economy (Khayesi et al., 2017; UBOS, 2012), which calls for urgent public and private investment in developing successful indigenous businesses (Mwangi et al., 2013). Indigenous entrepreneurs were the most marginalised immediately after Uganda's independence because state officials and non-citizens with large businesses mostly acquired business licences (Verhoef, 2017). The colonial and post-colonial influx of different cultures and ethnic groups created obstacles to the emergence and growth of indigenous businesses in Uganda and hampered their ability and right to manage their own economic and social affairs (Briggs, 2009; Tabuti & Van Damme, 2012). Uganda has seen a remarkable increase in foreign investment with multinational businesses that have continued to thrive, but indigenous enterprises still face high attrition rates, low investment and capital formation levels (Mwangi et al., 2013).

Indigenous entrepreneurs in Uganda own and manage indigenous cultural heritage and resources and are better positioned to positively influence and determine entrepreneurial activities in their domain (Mapunda, 2007; Tabuti & Van Damme, 2012). Mwangi et al. (2013) reveal that indigenous businesses in East Africa (Uganda inclusive) hardly last beyond three years and focus on survival with less than five employees and an annual income below USD 60,000. However, they experience challenges related to increased multi-cultural competitive markets (Mwangi et al., 2013; Tabuti & Van Damme, 2012). This and their lack of legitimacy have resigned indigenous business owners to peripheral status, with foreign entrepreneurs primarily occupying the formal sector. Briggs (2009) attributes this divide to gaps in access to knowledge and financial resources and constraints in internal leadership capacity of indigenous businesses.

Uganda ranked 125th out of 137 countries in the 2019 annual Global Entrepreneurship Index (Ács, Szerb, Lafuente, & Márkus, 2019) and is ranked highly in female entrepreneurship in Africa (Mastercard, 2017), which reflects some improvement in the development of female-owned businesses since the early 2000s (Muagbi, 2014). However, their survival beyond three and half years is quite low compared to businesses owned by men (Kelley, Brush, Greene, & Litovsky, 2012). Female entrepreneurs in Uganda experience challenges during the start-up, growth and management of their businesses more than men. They lack the necessary skills, resources and capacities and face legal barriers, negative cultural norms and overwhelming domestic responsibilities. Therefore, efforts are needed to enable female business owners to own and manage sustainable enterprises (Mugabi, 2014).

Case for Indigenous Female Businesses Sustainability

Loucks et al. (2010) assert that one of the consistent conclusions found in indigenous business sustainability literature is the lack of knowledge about sustainability practices and tools. The issue of sustainability is also reportedly mainly prevalent among large corporations (Bergquist, 2017), probably because small businesses especially indigenous enterprises operating in the informal sector, lack the necessary expertise, resources or commitment found in larger companies (Newell et al., 2010). Sustainability reporting is a crucial component of corporate reporting (Lesnikova & Schmidtova, 2020), but it is mainly practised within large companies, which have the required resources to measure and report on such intangibles. Therefore, the question remains about why indigenous SMEs remain hesitant about including sustainability in their overall corporate reporting (Newell et al., 2010). Sustainable capacity development and empowerment strategies are therefore necessary for indigenous entrepreneurs to clearly understand their circumstances. Exploring their best practices in the sustainability sense through rigorous research will benefit indigenous and mainstream entrepreneurship considerably (Hindle & Moroz, 2007), especially since there are still gaps in the existing data on indigenous entrepreneurial activities (Mika et al., 2019).

Indigenous communities embrace sustainability naturally, which contributes to their survival. They are practically and spiritually in sync with their environment and have a wealth of highly relevant traditional ecological knowledge (Dana, 2007, 2015; Mika, 2020; Mika et al., 2019; Tabuti & Van Damme, 2012). Indigenous entrepreneurs apply unique approaches to innovation and wealth creation, useful in tackling social dynamics and climate change, which distinguishes them from mainstream entrepreneurial actors (Dana, 2015; Hindle & Moroz, 2007; Mika, 2020; Shinde, 2010; Tapsell & Woods, 2010; Vazquez-Maguirre, 2020a, 2020b). They use their extensive traditional knowledge and skills to design quality tools and products adaptable to their environment to facilitate trade, livelihood and survival (Conway, 2011; Mika et al., 2019; Tabuti & Van Damme, 2012). Indigenous entrepreneurs embrace relationships, coexistence, mutual benefit, respect and harmony, which are relevant for business success (Dana, 2007, 2015). They focus on capacity building for economic independence and operate for the social benefit of the indigenous collective, which contributes significantly to their business ambitions (Conway, 2011; Foley & O'Connor, 2013; Hindle & Moroz, 2007; McDonald, 2019; Mika, 2020; Vazquez-Maguirre, 2020a; Vazquez-Maguirre, 2020b). These moral obligations are critical aspects of the contemporary sustainability agenda (Jha & Rangarajan, 2020).

Indigenous female entrepreneurship is fostered by social dimensions such as relationships and community and has continued to attract academic interest (Meléndez & Lorenzo, 2014). Female entrepreneurs contribute meaningfully to the stability and wellbeing of communities and the global economy while focussing on minorities and disadvantaged groups (Ascher, 2012; Maguirre et al., 2016). They embrace context as a relevant factor, with emphasis on relationships between individuals and their environment (De Bruin et al., 2007), which are critical indigenous business (Hindle & Moroz, 2007) and sustainability features (Jha & Rangarajan, 2020; Petrini & Pozzebon, 2010). Therefore, it is imperative to explore the extent to which well-established female-owned indigenous businesses in Uganda have manifested their best practices to promote business sustainability using the TBL approach.

An analysis of the three case studies, which includes their case profiles and the criteria for their selection is presented in the next section.

A Description of Three Case Studies

The indigenous businesses targeted by the author are owner-operated and are responsible to a single or at most a few shareholders, with the owners' values driving the organisation. Some of them focus on natural resources and agriculture, which are pre-dominant economic activities practised by indigenous populations (McDonald, 2019). Loucks et al. (2010) suggest that if individual small business owners prioritise sustainability, their business is likely to prioritise sustainable development. They further assert that the small size means shorter lines of communication between the top managers, shareholders and employees, which make them more agile meaning they are able to implement changes quickly. Hence, the empirical component of this chapter is embedded in a multiple case study approach using a sample of three varied but extensive cases to reveal and describe similar but different recurring experiences and contextual features (Bhattacherjee, 2012; Creswell, 2013). These female-owned indigenous businesses were allocated case identifiers OUGA, KWBA and MGFM, derived from the names of their businesses for anonymity.

Case Selection

The case studies were selected using the judgemental sampling technique based on their availability, a set of selection criteria and the author's personal judgement (Howitt, 2019). The author incorporated some of the characteristics of indigeneity and business sustainability to determine the criteria for selecting the three cases in line with global sustainability standards with the aim of targeting participants with extensive knowledge and experience that can be replicated in other African settings. The criteria included female-owned indigenous businesses that (1) have been operating for more than 5 years; (2) embrace indigeneity, an indigenous world-view that connects people, the planet and mutual responsibility for each other (Mika, 2020), employ and contract indigenous members of the population, use locally produced/sourced raw materials, appreciate their cultural heritage; (3) have strong internal sustainability priorities in line with global corporate sustainability guidelines (GRI, ISO14001, SA8000, ISO9001) and (4) with a proven commitment to the same (incorporate quality/value-addition, uplift vulnerable/marginalised persons, implement ecologically conscious actions). Based on these criteria, three female-owned indigenous businesses were selected. The author sought to recount these experiences and construct an account of how they managed to establish a niche for themselves in a challenging business environment while ensuring that the needs of the wider social and environmental context are adequately met.

Case Profiles

Table 1 presents the organisational profiles of the three case studies.

Table 1. Organisational Profiles of the Three Female-Owned Indigenous Businesses.

Sample: Three (3) Female-Owned Indigenous Businesses

OUGA – Based in Kampala District, Central Uganda; 6 years of operations; Textile & Communications industry
Textile brand created to improve Uganda's image; use the power of words to showcase experiences made in Uganda; produce and sell gift items and sanitary packs for girls.
Indigeneity: Employs local staff; out-sources local partners + raw materials; cultural heritage: Promotes the Kabaka (King) of Buganda's image (a prominent cultural figure), focuses on patriotism (local language, national colours, Ugandan-ness)

KWBA – Based in Kitgum District, Northern Uganda, with over 16 years of operations, Bee-keeping industry
Work with women in bee-keeping: harvesting and processing honey, products from beehives (wax, ointment, soap, candles); produce shea oil/butter; sim-sim and groundnut paste for sale.
Indigeneity: Has worked with over 300 indigenous bee-keepers from in and around Kitgum; cultural heritage: practices bee-keeping (cultural practice in Northern Uganda), understands medicinal aspects of honey and local tree species that produce good quality honey; locally produced honey, shea products, sim-sim and groundnuts; locally sourced raw materials; conducts women trainings locally.

MGFM – Based in Fort Portal District, Western Uganda, 7 years in operation, Agriculture industry
Commercially grow and process coffee, matooke (staple Ugandan banana food), a forest of trees on over 200 acres of land; practice bee-keeping (350 beehives: produces and sell honey, beeswax and honeycombs); employs about 30 permanent workers and approximately 120 community workers.
Indigeneity: Employs local staff, source farmers/workers from surrounding communities; grows/produces coffee, matooke and honey (cultural products); preserves the national heritage (surrounding flora, fauna, game reserve); upholds cultural practices

---

Source: Author's Own work.

The case discussion questions and research methods applied are described in the next section.

Case Data Gathering

The three case studies were investigated intensively, during which large amounts of descriptive data were collected. Significant aspects of their businesses were gathered using in-depth interviews as the typical primary data collection technique (Bhattacherjee, 2012; Creswell, 2013; Howitt, 2019; Ponelis, 2015; Yin, 2014). The case participants revealed various perspectives on indigenous business sustainability. These were replicated in each of the selected cases using Yin (2008)'s reasoning of replication while taking note of their unique characteristics. A narrative literature review approach was applied to unpack intellectual content on indigenous and female entrepreneurship, business sustainability and related topics to produce various synopses relevant to this chapter (Snyder, 2019; Walliman, 2011).

In line with the standard case study research protocol, data from each case were triangulated by comparing responses from each participant (Bhattacherjee, 2012; Creswell, 2013; Ridder, 2017). Primary data were also triangulated with reviewed literature to substantiate empirical data while ensuring smooth correlation between all data gathering techniques (Howitt, 2019; Korstjens & Moser, 2018). Primary case data contained background information (age, size, industry, ownership and management), internal culture and innovativeness regarding business sustainability. This included variables such as ecologically conscious activities; unique social impact, sustainable efforts to generate profits and improve brand value, their business context and relevant cultural terrain, which provided a vivid picture of internal business sustainability decisions. The data also focused on their sustainability strategy or the lack thereof, as described by each business owner and the challenges encountered when running their businesses.

Case Data Analysis

Case data were manually analysed by the author with enough time devoted to the analysis process (Taylor, Bogdan, & DeVault, 2016). The female business owners were the unit of analysis (Bhattacherjee, 2012; Ponelis, 2015) based on their business experiences and sustainability practices. Primary data and reviewed literature were condensed into summarised formats (Creswell, 2013; Howitt, 2019). Braun and Clarke's (2013) guide on coding was used during thematic analysis to familiarise with the data; generate codes; search for and review themes and define the final themes generated. Colour coding mechanisms were used (O'Connor & Joffe, 2020) to distinguish between different participants' views in the transcribed case data, during which similar patterns and distinct ideas were categorised and consolidated under major themes depicted in the findings.

Ethical Considerations

Standard ethical practice was incorporated into the design and execution of this study (Brough, 2019). This entailed gaining the three participants' verbal and written informed consent voluntarily agreeing to participate in the study with no force, duress and coercion involved. Participants were availed of the necessary amount of information about all aspects of the research prior to their participation (Bhattacherjee, 2012; Creswell, 2013; Haslam & McGarty, 2014; Howitt, 2019). The appropriate time, clarity on the research purpose and privacy of the participants' identities and their participation were all ensured (Haslam & McGarty, 2014; Howitt, 2019; Sutton & Austin, 2015).

A discussion on how best practices by female-owned indigenous businesses in Uganda are manifested into business sustainability is presented in the next section.

Best Practices Adopted by Female-Owned Businesses to Promote Business Sustainability

Management researchers have continued to seek new ways of identifying essential aspects in facilitating the effective integration of sustainability into organisational practices (Petrini & Pozzebon, 2010). Nagel, Hiss, Woschnack, and Teufel (2017) denote that there is no single generally accepted best practice that measures sustainability. The multi-dimensional aspect of business sustainability requires more than one corporate action (Lesnikova & Schmidtova, 2020; Sukawati et al., 2020). Jansson, Nilsson, Modig, and Vall (2017) state that commitment to business sustainability is measured by exploring participants' views on sustainability in terms of their philosophy, strategic product decisions, competitiveness and strategic planning. Epstein et al. (2012), Lesnikova and Schmidtova (2020), and Sukawati et al. (2020) suggest deliberate ways of analysing decision outcomes, costs and benefits of programmes that have environmental or social impacts with the assumption that these programs are both operationally and sustainably beneficial. An effective sustainability strategy is therefore useful and requires numerous steps, processes and communication (Petrini & Pozzebon, 2010) to translate into social and environmental performance, improved internal efficiency and brand value (Arbogast & Thornton, 2010).

Epstein and Yuthas (2012)'s Enhanced Cost–Benefit Analysis

Epstein et al.'s (2012) enhanced Cost–Benefit Analysis model is a valuable tool in assessing the impact of sustainability initiatives that extend beyond traditional business partners such as customers or suppliers to sustainability performance and stakeholder reactions (Fig.1).

Programs/Activities: targeted internal actions by business enterprises to initiate and operate sustainability initiatives that impact favourably on stakeholders, the environment and profit generation.

Sustainability Performance: outcomes relating to social or environmental impacts as reported by business owners.

Operational performance: from sustainability programs such as reduced processing and shipping time due to simplified packaging and use of swift delivery methods as reported by the business owners.

Stakeholder reactions to sustainability performance outcomes including media (plus social media) reactions to environmentally focused actions, improved stakeholder engagement, which may in turn, increase brand awareness, attract new customers, a healthier workplace, more satisfied employees, attention by regulators, which all benefit the business.

Monetary Costs and Benefits: financial outcomes related to operational performance, arising directly from sustainability initiatives and indirectly as stakeholder reactions, which translate into monetary impacts.

Sustainability performance increases when community benefits increase; through employee goodwill towards the company = increased internal loyalty + subsequent monetary benefits due to employee retention/reduced cost of recruitment and training.

Fig. 1.   Expanded Cost–Benefit Analysis With Sustainability Outcomes. *Source:* Adapted from Epstein et al. (2012, p. 29).

A Proposed Sustainability Scope Based on Insights of Indigenous Female Business Owners

In responding to questions about their perceptions of business sustainability, the case participants denoted:

> *"I would say that when we talk about business sustainability, we are looking at what makes that business long-lasting, the business value of that business, the capital it injects and so on." KWBA*

> *"The aspects of business sustainability that I really understand is very biblical; it is spiritual, it is based on the fact that anyone who is connected to your business... you had better grow the business because if you don't, their livelihood depends on you... So, the more I innovate, the more I create work for them...their livelihood depends on the business...that keeps me grounded. Then the other spiritual aspect is that you have to multiply and subdue, it's in the bible. Multiplication and subduing is, your business has to grow to hire more people." OUGA*

> *"I would look at it in terms of people, what we do and what we have achieved at the farm. Our first principle is whether you want to go or*

not, you get paid for your work, maybe that has also helped us in terms of sustainability. No one will ever go out there and say, 'you know that farm, maybe they didn't pay me, maybe they never fed me.' We make sure we feed them, we accommodate them, and we pay their salaries." MGFM

They provided varied responses to questions regarding a sustainability strategy including:

"No, those are for these big corporate organisations...Why does it need to be on paper? What does being on paper mean?" OUGA

"No I haven't...I think I wouldn't really mind, I would really want to learn more about it. I would really embrace it." MGFM

"To be honest with you, what is really written that defines our work, it is there, but I would say it verbally but not on paper." KWBA

Although the three indigenous female-owned businesses seemingly lack a well-defined business sustainability framework, they focus on indigeneity and embrace distinct values which exhibit sustainability in unique and creative ways.

Epstein et al. (2012)'s cost–benefit analysis tool was used to assess the case participants' sustainability actions from which findings have been generated and categorised into thematic elements retrieved from the cost–benefit tool to develop the sustainability scope below (Table 2).

All three business owners demonstrate a common thread of being socially responsible and depict activities that are geared towards sustainability using a range of deliberate internal practices, outlined in their different organisational profiles (Table 1) and in the sustainability scope developed. These provide a culturally sensitive approach to embracing sustainability and a rich illustration of unique sustainability practices. The participants propose innovative solutions to social problems with the opportunity to create initiatives that can have a long-term positive impact, socially, environmentally and economically. The sustainability scope determines how creativity is applied by the three indigenous businesses from a community, moral and ethical perspective to promote growth and provides a useful sustainability reporting tool with information for decision-making and integration of sustainability into operational and capital decisions, which potentially results in economic benefits. The various programmes and activities reflect internal sustainability actions of the three female-owned indigenous businesses and their corresponding social, environmental and economic impact, while sustainability performance displays outcomes resulting from the social or environmental impacts reported by the business owners. Operational performance resulting from sustainability programs is also indicated, including stakeholder reactions towards sustainability performance outcomes and the monetary benefits resulting from operational performance.

Table 2. A Proposed Sustainability Scope Derived From Internal Practices of Female-Owned Indigenous Businesses.

Programme and Activities	Sustainability Performance	Stakeholder Reactions	Operational Performance	Monetary Benefits
OUGA *Social sustainability* **Strong social component:** Responsibility that goes beyond making profits – work with stakeholders who promote gender equity; positive dealings with the Buganda kingdom; support a range of local male and female suppliers (tailors, printers, boda boda (motor cycle) riders, bakers, packaging staff, gift suppliers) who rely on their business; engage female bakers on a monthly basis to bake cakes for the Kabaka of Buganda (proceeds go to developmental projects for women in Buganda); allocate 12% of their profits to charity and do not reveal this because 'giving spiritually is not something you shout about;' support female-owned businesses; train local entrepreneurs on branding fundamentals. **Cultural innovations:** Produce culturally defining locally translated	Assured growth of all stakeholders that work in the business Preserve the local culture Advance gender equity Contribute to environmental sustainability	Good reputation on the market Collaboration/good relationships with cultural institutions Collaborate with corporate entities to supply gift items for their employees Public goodwill: trademark issues are usually resolved by well-wishers; customers who travel wearing their brands attract goodwill in foreign cities, immigration points and on international flights	*Rythming* strategy translates into reduced time + improved efficiency in production/sales. Use familiar suppliers = speed and efficiency Use of motorcycles for deliveries = speed and efficiency	People aspire to buy their brands for local use, international travel and for gifting in the Diaspora = increased sales/ financial performance Good returns from profits made from all sales 30% of which is allocated to future investments = business growth

Table 2. (*Continued*)

Programme and Activities	Sustainability Performance	Stakeholder Reactions	Operational Performance	Monetary Benefits
printed apparel (for travellers, children, the Buganda Kingdom) with messages that convey positive Ugandan expressions.		Trust and loyalty from various circles because of their indigenous Ugandan brands		
		Goodwill among suppliers = quality assurance		
Environmental sustainability **Eco-friendly operational practices**: Use paper packaging; plan to adopt the use of sisal cloth for packaging; use digital payments; minimise printing; do online banking; limit electricity usage; conduct virtual meetings; use motorcycles instead of vehicles for deliveries.				
Economic sustainability **Income diversification:** Produce and sell a range of apparel products; innovative use of personal branding to create gift items; package and sell menstruation packs for girls.				

Value addition/quality assurance:

Produce shirts using appropriate colours for black skin, incorporate laundry habits of Ugandans/effect of ordinary soap on fabric (using products that withstand indigenous washing practices); work with suppliers whose fabrics have been tested with assurances of more than 10 washes; apply branding principles that improve on the quality of all brands; a unique operational mechanism ('rhythming') for quality and efficiency: 'Every product has a rhythm. The male shirt has a rhythm, the female shirt has a rhythm, and the rhythm means how long do 100 shirts go. So we know that every 10 days, we have to deliver 30 shirts to client X, that's a rhythm. Now what does delivering 30 shirts to client X mean? That means (1) they have to be tailored (2) branded (3) packed (4) the boda rider has to know that they are going to be delivered (5) when the order is made (6) when client puts the money on account'.

Table 2. (Continued)

Programme and Activities	Sustainability Performance	Stakeholder Reactions	Operational Performance	Monetary Benefits
Profitability ideology: Predominantly roll out products assured of generating 100% profits. *Strive to innovate, prove themselves and use challenges as learning opportunities in a market with limited open bidding for jobs; delays in payments; cut-throat competition, which limits sale of ideas; cultural/ societal expectations/ responsibilities of women and negative COVID-19 effects.*				
KWBA *Social sustainability* **Community support:** Have targeted over 300 vulnerable female bee-keepers (school dropouts, young mothers, child/women-headed households) who possess land but with no income source and provide them with a range of direct and indirect support (mentorship, training, marketing, financial) for sustainable business growth.	Financial independence = improved social and economic wellbeing and quality of life for an extensive community of women in Kitgum Environmental conservation	Government linkages = opportunities to access raw materials; credit facilities which improves efficiency Invitation to conduct bee-keeping training in other districts = increased visibility; personal motivation to continue supporting women	Training/mentoring (improved technical skills) for women bee-keepers; provision of capital; market and government linkages = increased efficiency in production and sale of products	Income generation and diversification for female bee-keepers in Kitgum

Preserve the cultural heritage: 'In my culture, honey is a source of food and medicine, when someone gets burnt, we use honey. You can even mix sim-sim and honey and eat it with our millet. So in our culture, if someone like your granny used to keep bees when they go to harvest, they don't leave the young ones. As I speak, it is women taking up bee-keeping and they are very smart, even their honey is very clean and quality...the widows, took up that initiative from where their husband left it and started keeping bees. They started paying for their children from the products, paying school fees using honey money. That is why on our logo, we say 'honey is money, get out of poverty'.

Environmental sustainability
Discourage harmful environmental practices like cutting trees, charcoal burning, brick making; encourage environmental conservation through planting of environmentally friendly tree species; educate women on

Cultural preservation Improved raw materials production (grow trees which attract bees for good quality honey/shea butter/oil + other medicinal products)

Invitation to participate in national agricultural events/trade shows, international events = improved visibility, productive business networks/ linkages, improved learning, market/sale of produce.
Certified by the Uganda Bureau of Statistics (UBOS)

Are a learning site due to their knowledge and practical experience in bee-keeping

Table 2. (*Continued*)

Programme and Activities	Sustainability Performance	Stakeholder Reactions	Operational Performance	Monetary Benefits
planting flowery and medicinal plants (sunflowers, shea trees) beneficial for honey production + conduct training on the benefit of specific tree species.				
Economic sustainability				
Income diversity: Production and sale of honey and beeswax (used for candles, soap, ointment); shea oil/ butter; sim-sim and groundnuts paste **Value addition:** Networking and partnership activities (with markets, government and other institutions and linkages for women bee-keepers); facilitate training/ mentorship for women bee-keepers on how to operate beehives and harvest quality/ medicinal honey; 'We train our people so that they do the best hives, we always tell our women that when you harvest honey, however little it is you are not supposed to put water in it and then we locally know how to measure				

honey when there is no water in it. You stand in the sunshine, get a small spoon of honey and put it in the sun, if it makes a round circle that means there is no water. When it has not been made, just know there is water. That goes back to our culture, we have been trained to know that this honey is watery or it is not watery. So, we train them to make the best honey…you cannot convince me who has been in the bee industry that honey from cassia is the best honey like the shea nut tree or an orange and mango tree. There are some tree species that are medicinal like the green honey, so we train them on quality honey production'.

Embrace challenges: such as local vulnerabilities, limited business and technical skills, minimal capital access, the aftermath of the COVID-19 pandemic, funding constraints, logistical hiccoughs, non-compliance for the environment and lack of sufficient processing equipment with a sense of resolve, resilience and positivity.

Table 2. (*Continued*)

Programme and Activities	Sustainability Performance	Stakeholder Reactions	Operational Performance	Monetary Benefits
MGFM				
Social sustainability				
Food security: Employ around 120 community farmers (men, women and youth) and allocate them land to grow food and keep a percentage of the produce; provide them with seeds to grow vegetables; farmers, in turn, till their land for coffee and matooke production some of which is provided to farmers as food.	Financial growth + improved quality of life for a wide community of farmers in the Fort Portal and surrounding Semilki Game reserve areas.	Collaboration with institutions like UCDA = improved quality and yields through support in form of certified nursery operators, seedlings, technical advice, local and international market opportunities + other assistance	Improved efficiency and increased coffee, matooke and honey yields due to close proximity of farmers/ other workers	Generate income from sale of coffee, honey/honey products + matooke Networking (referrals from friends, orders from overseas clients) = monetary gains
Opportunities for farming: Discourage surrounding communities from hunting/poaching wild animals within the nearby National Park by providing farming as an alternative means of generating income; women are the majority of community workers; discourage child labour and discrimination	Promote gender equality Environmental conservation			
Cultural sensitivity: produce coffee, honey and matooke (cultural produces); adopt the local language and embrace other cultural practices which ease community integration.	Cultural preservation	Agro-tourism = Farm attracts numerous visitors and is a learning site for different coffee experiences (how coffee is grown, processed and consumed)		

Goodwill among local community members; staff and recruiters = quality assurance

Environmental sustainability

Preserve national heritage and conserve wildlife: Grow herbal plants beneficial for bees and people; plant indigenous trees that attract birds, chimpanzees; produce matooke which also provides food for birds (retain the bird species), discourage poaching.

Environmental Conservation:

Replacing eucalyptus trees with good indigenous trees 'we are getting rid of the eucalyptus, we realised that the eucalyptus trees were not very environmentally friendly. They drain the land of all the nutrients, so we are trying to get rid of them and grow some good indigenous trees for birds, for animals.'

Economic sustainability

Income diversity: Operate 350 beehives that produce honey/honey products; over 200 acres of land for commercial coffee + matooke production.

Quality assurance: Follow national regulations (getting Fair Trade + UBOS certification, their coffee has

Table 2. (*Continued*)

Programme and Activities	Sustainability Performance	Stakeholder Reactions	Operational Performance	Monetary Benefits
been tested by the Uganda Coffee Development Authority (UCDA); coffee samples are accompanied by vital sanitary certification). **Value addition:** Produce value-added coffee (dry, roast, grind, package and brand their coffee) **Marketing:** Attend monthly farmers' markets and other coffee events to display products; provide and distribute free samples of brewed coffee and use feedback to improve on quality. **Long-term growth plans:** 5-to- plan to maximise expansion by investing in marketing while working towards producing the best quality coffee and honey. **Use challenges:** like exploitation by bigger coffee players; frequent staff				

turnover, disobedient employees, unfavourable local work culture, domestic burdens faced by female workers; unfavourable weather patterns, costly production process; financial liquidity challenges, effects of the COVID-19-induced lockdown as learning opportunities and apply business ethics for improved quality.

Source: Adopted from Epstein et al. (2012).

Discussion of Findings

The author explored how sustainability is integrated into the three indigenous businesses' internal practices from a Ugandan perspective using the TBL approach identified in existing literature as a useful mechanism for exploring how people, the planet and profits can be innovatively assimilated into internal business culture (Elkington, 1997). Epstein et al. (2012)'s cost–benefit analysis tool was adopted in assessing the case participants' sustainability actions and generate findings, which were categorised into themes.

Theme 1: Programme Activities

One of the major thematic elements was determined as programme activities under which the author categorised the three sub-themes of social, environmental and economic sustainability. These three sub-components have been merged together by the author to display their holistic importance in the growth and sustainability of the three indigenous businesses.

The social sustainability sub-theme captured responsibility that goes beyond making profits where the business owners work with stakeholders in various aspects. This includes promoting gender equity; positive dealings with cultural leaders; mutual support towards local male and female suppliers, promoting female bakers in various ways, allocating a percentage of their profits to charity, peer support to other female-owned businesses and training local entrepreneurs on branding fundamentals. Other social responsibility mechanisms entailed producing culturally defining apparel to promote a positive image about Uganda. Social sustainability is also depicted through community support during which over 300 vulnerable female bee-keepers are targeted and provided with a range of direct and indirect support for sustainable business growth. The social component also includes food security that sees one of the indigenous businesses employing over 100 community farmers and allocating land to them for food and providing them with seeds to grow vegetables, while they in turn, till their employer's land for coffee and matooke production. These are all standards for social responsibility as depicted by Lesnikova and Schmidtova (2020) and Sukawati et al. (2020) which focus on cultivating social change while addressing social needs.

Environmental sustainability is another sub-theme categorised under programme activities and includes what Dana (2015) depicts as favourable environmental behaviour adopted by indigenous businesses such as eco-friendly operational practices by one of the businesses including the use of paper packaging and potential adoption of sisal material for packaging; using digital payments; minimising on printing; online banking; limiting electricity usage; conducting virtual meetings; and using motorcycles instead of vehicles for delivery of products to customers. Other environmentally sustainable activities include discouraging harmful environmental practices like cutting of trees, charcoal burning, and brick making; encouraging environmental conservation through tree planting; and education on planting flowery and medicinal plants for honey production. Another participant preserves the national heritage and conserves wildlife by growing herbal plants that are beneficial for bees and people; planting indigenous trees that attract birds and animal species and discouraging poaching among their surrounding communities. Environmental conservation is also demonstrated by replacing eucalyptus trees with good indigenous trees that are environmentally friendly.

The economic sustainability sub-theme echoes the notions of Mika (2020), Tabuti and Van Damme (2012), and Vazquez-Maguirre (2020a, 2020b) about how indigenous businesses tend to create socially innovative business ventures that generate economic returns. This includes income diversification where one business is seen producing and selling a range of apparel products; innovatively using personal branding to create gift items for sale and packaging and selling menstruation packs for girls. Value addition and quality assurance is seen through the production of shirts using appropriate colours for black skin, incorporating indigenous washing practices and habits, working with suppliers whose fabrics have been tested with assurances of more than 10 washes, applying branding principles that improve on the quality of all brands, and applying a unique operational mechanism ('rhythming') for quality and efficiency. This participant predominantly rolls out products that are assured of generating 100% profits. Another indigenous business ensures income diversity by producing and selling a range of products (honey, beeswax, shea oil/butter, sim-sim and groundnuts paste) and ensures value addition through networking and partnership activities to market her produce. She has also established relationships with the government and other institutions to improve on learning while facilitating training and mentorship for women bee-keepers and embracing challenges with a sense of resolve, resilience and positivity. Income diversity is prioritised by the coffee producer by operating over 300 beehives that produce honey and honey products; and cultivating over 200 acres of land for commercial coffee and matooke production. They enhance quality assurance by following national regulations during production and value addition by producing value-added coffee and implementing marketing strategies that include displaying their different products at coffee marketing events and aim to produce the best quality coffee and honey while also making use of existing challenges to improve on the quality of their business.

Theme 2: Sustainability Performance

Sustainability performance was determined as a corresponding theme which according to Epstein et al. (2012), refers to outcomes of social and environmental impact and increases when the benefits directed to the community are substantial. This was demonstrated by the assured growth of all stakeholders that are part of the value chain for one of the indigenous businesses, their preservation of the local culture and how they have advanced gender equity. Sustainability performance is also displayed through financial growth and independence demonstrated by improved social and economic wellbeing and quality of life for an extensive community of women and men farmers, female bee-keepers, improved gender equality as well as environmental conservation, cultural preservation and improved raw materials production within the environs of these indigenous businesses. These are all necessary elements in an effective sustainability strategy (Arbogast & Thornton, 2010).

Theme 3: Stakeholder Reactions

Epstein et al. (2012) also demonstrated that stakeholder reactions are an important element in measuring sustainability performance. Therefore, this has been determined as the third thematic element in the findings. One of the indigenous businesses has built a good reputation in the market, their collaboration and relationships with cultural institutions and corporate entities have been strengthened, they have acquired public goodwill locally and internationally and attract trust and loyalty from various circles because of their indigenous Ugandan brands.

Another business has promoted good linkages with government representatives, which has provided them with opportunities to access raw materials, credit facilities and improved efficiency, invitation to conduct bee-keeping training in other districts all of which have improved their image and increased their visibility. Their personal motivation to continue supporting women bee-keepers, participation in national and international agricultural event have also improved their visibility and helped them build productive business networks, improved their learning, market and sale of their produce as well as earning certification by the Uganda Bureau of Statistics (UBOS). They are also a learning site due to their knowledge and practical experience in bee-keeping.

The coffee producer collaborates with institutions like the Uganda Coffee Development Authority in various aspects which has improved their quality and yields through the support they receive in form of certified nursery operators, seedlings, technical advice, local and international market opportunities and other assistance. Their focus on agro-tourism has earned them a farm that attracts numerous visitors and is a learning site for different coffee experiences during which visitors learn how coffee is grown, processed and consumed. They have also attracted a lot of goodwill among local community members; their staff and recruiters which has contributed to quality assurance. These all reaffirm the importance of integrating society's expectations and stakeholder engagement within internal culture to explore opportunities for competitive advantage (Jha & Rangarajan, 2020; Lesnikova & Schmidtova, 2020; Sukawati et al., 2020).

Theme 4: Operational Performance

Operational performance has been determined as the fourth principal theme and according to Epstein et al. (2012) refers to performance that results from sustainability programmes. Some of the sustainability programmes revealed included the rythmning strategy by one of the businesses which translates into reduced time and improved efficiency in production and sales. They also use familiar suppliers as well as motorcycles for the delivery of products to customers which promotes speed and efficiency. Another business conducts training and mentoring for women bee-keepers which leads to improved skills. Their market and government linkages have led to increased efficiency in production and sale of their products. While the major coffee producer has improved efficiency and increased coffee, matooke and honey yields due to close proximity of farmers and other workers. These all reflect how useful sustainability programmes can be in improving operational performance as Petrini and Pozzebon (2010) and Arbogast and Thornton (2010) suggest.

Theme 5: Monetary Benefits

Monetary benefits is the fifth and final theme generated from this study and refers to the financial outcomes resulting from sustainability actions (Epstein et al., 2012). Some of the monetary benefits for the apparel business owner include people's aspiration to buy their brands for local and international use which has seen increases in their sales and financial performance. They are assured of favourable returns from profits made from all sales 30% of which is allocated to future investments which leads to business growth. For the bee-keeping business owner, income generation and diversification for female bee-keepers in Kitgum is assured while the coffee producer generates income from the sale of coffee, honey and honey products and matooke. Their strong networks and linkages with stakeholders have earned them several referrals from friends and orders from overseas clients which translates into monetary gains. This therefore demonstrates the importance of sustainability practices in generating reasonable economic returns (Ahlström et al., 2020; Prasad et al., 2019).

Recommendations for Business Actors in Africa

The need to contextualise actions or solutions for sustainability on a case-by-case basis grounded in best practices as opposed to generalised solutions is critical. Focusing on the 'one size fits all' approach is not appropriate for meeting the needs of the wider community as depicted by the different initiatives by each indigenous business. The idea is to move towards more effective solutions, which should be achieved in line with specific stakeholders who constitute investors, employees, community, government representatives, suppliers and consumers, among others. This entails practising environmental compliance to contribute towards environmental sustainability; integrating the social aspect within company culture while maintaining the ultimate goal of generating profits in a unique and contextual manner which all contribute to goodwill, better brand perception and brand loyalty.

The author contributes an innovative sustainability scope that incorporates reporting on socially responsible actions which capture Afrocentric cultural values and gender-responsive business practices as a social dimension. This includes a comprehensive and holistic stakeholder engagement aligned with environmentally sustainable practices that are both fundamentals in enforcing sustainability. The author provides practical insights on how sustainability can be manifested within female-owned indigenous businesses from the Ugandan perspective based on reflections from a group of relatable business owners. The triple bottom line approach has been maximised by showcasing user-friendly business solutions that can be replicated by indigenous businesswomen within even the most localised settings.

In terms of practical implications, first, the perspectives presented on business sustainability and how this impacts indigenous entrepreneurship development will provide researchers, policymakers, institutional heads, academics and other practitioners across the African continent, with new and diverse insights into the heterogeneous nature of female business performance. Second, the insights gathered will expand on the horizons and relevance of the entrepreneurship scholarship and contribute to ongoing discussions on female entrepreneurship in general and its impact on economic development, specifically how business sustainability can innovatively be incorporated, implemented, measured and reported within informal female-owned indigenous enterprises for their long-term economic success. This is essential, especially at a time when female entrepreneurship is gathering momentum globally as part of the women's economic empowerment agenda.

Conclusion

Business sustainability entails a look at the bigger picture by taking into consideration long- and short-term outcomes using innovative means while recognising the economic prominence of nature and human capital beyond measuring success solely against financial performance. Integrating sustainability into female-owned indigenous businesses is a normative, complex and dynamic initiative that includes multiple interactions between actors and factors, which need to be implemented, measured and reported for long-term success. It focuses on saving the planet and entails social inclusion which means making sure that the have-nots have access to social and economic opportunities and ultimately be elevated out of poverty. Mechanisms should therefore be in place to account for externalities like the environment and communities as demonstrated by the three indigenous business owners who blend social, economic and environmental priorities with activities that respond to local community needs.

Business sustainability can essentially be a fulfilling process if done holistically and altruistically within female-owned indigenous businesses by embracing a range of interdependent variables that capture environmental, social and economic dimensions. Applying culturally sensitive social and environmental standards are outstanding sustainability features demonstrated by the female business owners who align short-term incentives for employees, beneficiaries, suppliers, consumers and producers with the long-term collective goals of their businesses while incentivising people to work towards their sustenance. This has led to lasting relationships, true loyalty and real trust as an outstanding social impact with a moral imperative that is reflected in responsive standards of quality and value addition in production and an internal culture that reflects characteristics critical in ensuring financial performance.

References

Ács, Z. L., Szerb, L., Lafuente, E., & Márkus, G. (2019). *The Global Entrepreneurship Index 2019.* Washington, DC: The Global Entrepreneurship and Development Institute (GEDI). Retrieved from https://thegedi.org/wp-content/uploads/2021/02/2019_GEI-2019_final_v2.pdf. Accessed on February 7, 2022.

Ahlström, H., Williams, A., & Vildåsen, S. S. (2020). Enhancing systems thinking in corporate sustainability through a transdisciplinary research process. *Journal of Cleaner Production, 256,* 1–10. doi:10.1016/j.jclepro.2020.120691

Akhtar, C. S., Ismail, K., Ndaliman, M. A., Hussain, J., & Haider, M. (2015). Can intellectual capital of SMEs help in their sustainability efforts? *Journal of Management Research, 7*(2), 82–97. doi:10.5296/jmr.v7i2.6930

Arbogast, G. W., & Thornton, B. A. (2010). A global corporate sustainability model. *Journal of Sustainability and Green Business,* 1–9. Retrieved from http://www.aabri.com/manuscripts/10732.pdf. Accessed on July 21, 2021.

Ascher, J. (2012). Female entrepreneurship – An appropriate response to gender discrimination, journal of entrepreneurship. *Management and Innovation, 8*(4), 97–114.

Bateh, J., Heaton, C., Arbogast, G. W., & Broadbent, A. (2013). Defining sustainability in the business setting. *American Journal of Business Education, 6*(3), 397–400.

Bergquist, A. (2017). *Business and sustainability: New business history perspectives.* Working Paper 18-034. Boston, MA: Harvard Business School. Retrieved from https://www.hbs.edu/ris/Publication%20Files/18-034_39d7d71d-9e84-4e8b-97c0-0e626f75293c.pdf. Accessed on July 27, 2021.

Bhattacherjee, A. (2012). *Social science research: Principles, methods and practices* (2nd ed.). Tampa, FL: University of South Florida.

Braun, V., & Clarke, V. (2013). *Successful qualitative research: A practical guide for beginners.* Thousand Oaks, CA: Sage.

Briggs, B. R. (2009). Issues affecting Ugandan indigenous entrepreneurship in trade. *African Journal of Business Management, 3*(12), 786–797.

Brough, P. (2019). *Advanced research methods for applied psychology design, analysis and reporting.* London: Routledge.

Conway, D. M. (2011). Promoting indigenous innovation, enterprise and entrepreneurship through the licensing of Article 31 indigenous assets and resources, indigenous innovation, enterprise and entrepreneurship. *SMU Law Review, 64*(3), 1095–1103.

Creswell, J. W. (2013). *Qualitative inquiry & research design, choosing among five approaches* (3rd ed.). Thousand Oaks, CA: Sage.

Dana, L. P. (2007). Toward a multidisciplinary definition of indigenous entrepreneurship. In L. P. Dana & R. B. Anderson (Eds.), *International handbook of research on indigenous entrepreneurship.* Cheltenham: Edward Elgar.

Dana, L. P. (2015). Indigenous entrepreneurship: An emerging field of research. *International Journal of Business and Globalisation, 14*(2), 158–169. doi:10.1504/ IJBG.2015.067433

De Bruin, A., Brush, C. G., & Welter, F. (2007). Advancing a framework for coherent research on women's entrepreneurship. *Entrepreneurship Theory and Practice, 31*, 323–339. doi:10.1111/j.1540-6520.2007.00176

Elkington, J. (1997). *Cannibals with Forks: The triple bottom line of twenty-first century business.* Oxford: Capstone.

Epstein, M. J., & Yuthas, K. (2012). Analysing sustainability impacts. *Strategic Finance*, 26–33. Retrieved from https://pdxscholar.library.pdx.edu/cgi/viewcontent. cgi?article=1011&context=busadmin_fac. Accessed on July 21, 2021.

Foley, D., & O'Connor, A. J. (2013). Social capital and the networking practices of indigenous entrepreneurs. *Journal of Small Business Management, 51*(2), 276–296. doi:10.1111/jsbm.12017

Greco, A., & De Jong, G. (2017). *Sustainable entrepreneurship: Definitions, themes, and research gaps, centre for sustainable entrepreneurship.* Working Paper Series 1706-CSE. University of Groningen, Leeuwarden. Retrieved from https://www. rug.nl/cf/pdfs/cse/wps6_angela.pdf. Accessed on July 20, 2021.

Haslam, S. A., & McGarty, C. (2014). *Research methods and statistics in psychology* (2nd ed.). London: Sage.

Hindle, K., & Lansdowne, M. (2002). Brave spirits on new paths: Towards a globally relevant paradigm of indigenous entrepreneurship research. In L. Dan & R. B. Anderson (Eds.), *International handbook of research on indigenous entrepreneurship* (pp. 8–19). Cheltenham: Edward Elgar.

Hindle, K., & Moroz, P. W. (2007). Indigenous entrepreneurship as a research field: Developing a definitional framework from the emerging canon. *International Entrepreneurship and Management Journal, 6*, 357–385. doi:10.1007/S11365-009-0111-X

Howitt, D. (2019). *Introduction to qualitative research methods in psychology: Putting theory into practice* (4th ed.). Harlow: Pearson Education Ltd.

Imhonopi, D., Urim, U. M., & Iruonagbe, T. C. (2013). Colonialism, social structure and class formation: Implication for development in Nigeria. In D. Imhonopi & U. M. Urim (Eds.), *A panoply of readings in social sciences: Lessons from Nigeria* (pp. 107–122). Ota: Covenant University.

Jansson, J., Nilsson, J., Modig, F., & Vall, G. H. (2017). Commitment to sustainability in small and medium- sized enterprises: The influence of strategic orientations and management values. *Business Strategy and the Environment, 26*(1), 69–83. doi:10.1002/bse.1901

Jha, M. K., & Rangarajan, K. (2020). Analysis of corporate sustainability performance and corporate financial performance causal linkage in the Indian context. *Asian Journal of Sustainability and Social Responsibility, 5*(10), 1–30. doi:10.1186/ s41180-020-00038-z

Kelley, D. J., Brush, C. G., Greene, P. G., & Litovsky, Y. (2012). *Global Entrepreneurship Monitor, 2012.* Women Report. Babson College, Babson Park, MA. Retrieved from https://www.babson.edu/media/babson/site-assets/content-assets/ about/academics/centres-and-institutes/centre-for-womenx27s-entrepreneurial-leadership/about/collaborations/GEM-2012-Womens-Report-(1).pdf. Accessed on August 25, 2021.

Khayesi, J. N. O., Sserwanga, A., & Kiconco, R. (2017). Culture as a facilitator and a barrier to entrepreneurship development in Uganda. *Entrepreneurship in Africa, 15,* 307–322. doi:10.1163/9789004351615_014

Korstjens, I., & Moser, A. (2018). Series: Practical guidance to qualitative research. Part 4: Trustworthiness and publishing. *European Journal of General Practice, 24*(1), 120–124. doi:10.1080/13814788.2017.1375092

Lee, S. H. (2020). Achieving corporate sustainability performance: The influence of corporate ethical value, and leader-member exchange on employee behaviours and organisational performance. *Fashion and Textiles.* doi:10.1186/s40691-020-00213-w

Lesnikova, P., & Schmidtova, J. (2020). Development of corporate sustainability in enterprises through the application of selected practices and tools. *Organizacija, 53*(2), 112–126. doi:10.2478/orga-2020-0008

Loucks, E. S., Martens, M. L., & Cho, C. H. (2010). Engaging small and medium-sized businesses in sustainability, sustainability accounting. *Management and Policy Journal, 1*(2), 178–200. doi:10.1108/20408021011089239

Maguirre, M. V., Ruelas, G. C., & De La Torre, C. G. (2016). Women empowerment through social innovation in indigenous social enterprises. *Mackenzie Management Review, 17*(6). Retrieved from http://doi.org/10.1590/1678-69712016/administracao.v17n6p164-190. Accessed on February 8, 2022.

Mapunda, G. (2007). Entrepreneurial leadership and indigenous enterprise development. *Journal of Asia Entrepreneurship and Sustainability, 3*(3), 1–28.

Mastercard. (2017). *Mastercard Index of Women Entrepreneurs 2017, Index of women entrepreneurs (MIWE).* Mastercard. Retrieved from https://newsroom.mastercard.com/mea/files/2017/03/Report-Mastercard-Index-of-Women-Entrepreneurs-2017-8-Mar2.pdf. Accessed on July 20, 2018.

McDonald, C. (2019). *Promoting indigenous community economic development, entrepreneurship and SMEs in a rural context.* OECD Regional Development Working Papers, 2019/03. OECD Publishing, Paris. doi:10.1787/20737009

Meléndez, A. P., & Lorenzo, A. M. C. (2014). Women entrepreneurs in indigenous communities. In *The Case of Tiquipaya (Bolivia), XXIV Congreso Nacional De Acede,* Septiembre 2014, Castellón.

Mika, J. P. (2020). Indigenous entrepreneurship: How indigenous knowing, being and doing shapes entrepreneurial practice. In D. Deakins & J. M. Scott (Eds.), *Entrepreneurship: A contemporary & global approach* (pp. 1–32). Thousand Oaks, CA: Sage.

Mika, J. P., Fahey, N., & Bensemann, J. (2019). What counts as indigenous enterprise? Evidence from Aotearoa New Zealand. *Journal of Enterprising Communities: People and Places in the Global Economy, 13*(3), 372–390. doi:10.1108/JEC-12-2018-0102

Mugabi, E. (2014). *Women's entrepreneurship development in Uganda: Insights and recommendations.* Geneva: International Labour Office. Retrieved from https://www.ilo.org/wcmsp5/groups/public/-ed_emp/-emp_ent/-ifp_seed/documents/publication/wcms_360427.pdf. Accessed on April 24, 2018.

Muñoz, P. (2013). Distinctive importance of sustainable entrepreneurship, current opinion in creativity. *Innovation and Entrepreneurship, 2*(1), 1–6. doi:10.11565/cuocient.v2i1.26

Mwangi, R. M., Sejjaaka, S., Canney, S., Maina, S., Kairo, D., Rotich, A., … Mindra, R. (2013). *Constructs of successful and sustainable SME leadership in East*

Africa. ICBE-RF Research Report No. 79/13. Investment Climate and Business Environment Research Fund, Dakar. doi:10.13140/RG.2.1.4966.8248

Nagel, S., Hiss, S., Woschnack, D., & Teufel, B. (2017). Between efficiency and resilience: The classification of companies according to their sustainability performance. *Historical Social Research, 42*(1), 189–210. doi:10.12759/hsr.42.2017.1. 189-210

Newell, C. J., & Moore, W. B. (2010). Creating small business sustainability awareness. *International Journal of Business and Management, 5*(9), 19–25. doi:10.5539/ijbm.v5n9p19

Nuwagaba, A., & Nzewi, H. (2013). Major environment constraints on growth of micro and small enterprises in Uganda: A survey of selected micro and small enterprises in Mbarara Municipality. *International Journal of Cooperative Studies, 2*(1), 26–33. doi:10.11634/216826311302298

O'Connor, C., & Joffe, H. (2020). Intercoder reliability in qualitative research: Debates and practical guidelines. *International Journal of Qualitative Methods, 19*, 1–13. doi:10.1177/1609406919899220

Petrini, M., & Pozzebon, M. (2010, October/December). Integrating sustainability into business practices: Learning from Brazilian firms. *Brazilian Administration Review, 7*(4), 362–378.

Ponelis, S. R. (2015). Using interpretive qualitative case studies for exploratory research in doctoral studies: A case of information systems research in small and medium enterprises. *International Journal of Doctoral Studies, 10*, 535–550. Retrieved from http://ijds.org/Volume10/IJDSv10p535-550Ponelis0624.pdf. Accessed on April 29, 2021.

Prasad, M., Mishra, T., & Bapat, V. (2019). Corporate social responsibility and environmental sustainability: Evidence from India using energy intensity as an indicator of environmental sustainability. *IIMB Management Review, 31*(4), 374–384. doi:10.1016/j.iimb.2019.07.014

Ridder, H. (2017). The theory contribution of case study research designs. *Business Research, 10*, 281–305. doi:10.1007/s40685-017-0045-z

Ring, J. K., Peredo, A. M., & Chrisman, J. J. (2010). Business networks and economic development in rural communities in the United States. *Entrepreneurship Theory and Practice, 34*(1), 171–195. doi:10.111/j.1540-6520.2009.00307.x

Sebikari, K. V. (2014). Entrepreneurial performance and small business enterprises in Uganda. *International Journal of Small Business and Entrepreneurship Research, 2*(4), 1–12.

Shinde, K. A. (2010). Entrepreneurship and indigenous entrepreneurs in religious tourism in India. *International Journal Tourism Research, 12*, 523–535. doi:10.1002/jtr.771

Snyder, H. (2019). Literature review as a research methodology: An overview and guidelines. *Journal of Business Research, 104*, 333–339. doi:10.1016/j.jbusres.2019. 07.039

Sukawati, T. G. R., Riana, I. G., Rajiani, I., & Abbas, E. W. (2020). Managing corporate sustainability by revitalising Balinese cultural identity. *Polish Journal of Management Studies, 21*(1), 382–393. doi:10.17512/pjms.2020.21.1.28

Sutton, J., & Austin, Z. (2015). Qualitative research: Data collection, analysis and management. *The Canadian Journal of Hospital Pharmacy, 68*(3), 226–231.

Tabuti, J. R. S., & Van Damme, P. (2012). Review of indigenous knowledge in Uganda: Implications for its promotion. *Afrika Focus, 25*(1), 29–38.

Tapsell, P., & Woods, C. (2010). Social entrepreneurship and innovation: Self-organisation in an indigenous context. *Entrepreneurship & Regional Development: An International Journal, 22*(6), 535–556. doi:10.1080/08985626.2010.48840

Taylor, S. J., Bogdan, R., & DeVault, M. (2016). *Introduction to qualitative research methods: A guidebook and resource* (4th ed.). Hoboken, NJ: John Wiley and Sons.

The World Bank. (2010). *Indigenous peoples: Still among the poorest of the poor.* Indigenous Peoples Policy Brief, Washington, DC. Retrieved from http://www.miqols.org/howb/wp-content/uploads/2016/06/World-Bank_Status-of-First-Indigenous-Peoples.pdf. Accessed on November 17, 2021.

Uganda Bureau of Statistics (UBOS). (2012). Statistical Abstract. Kampala.

United Nations. (1987). *Report of the World Commission on Environment and Development: Our common future.* Transmitted to the General Assembly as an Annex to document A/42/427, Nairobi. Retrieved from https://digitallibrary.un.org/record/139811. Accessed on November 17, 2021.

Vazquez-Maguirre, M. (2020a). Building sustainable rural communities through indigenous social enterprises: A humanistic approach. *Sustainability, 12.* doi:10.3390/su12229643. Accessed on February 8, 2022.

Vazquez-Maguirre, M. (2020b). Restoring, protecting and promoting human dignity through indigenous entrepreneurship. *International Journal of Entrepreneurship, 24*(3), 1–12.

Verhoef, G. (2017). *The history of business in Africa: Complex discontinuity to emerging markets.* Cham: Springer International Publishing.

Walliman, N. (2011). *Research methods, the basics.* London: Routledge.

Yin, R. K. (2008). *Case study research: Design and methods.* (4th ed.). London: Sage.

Yin, R. K. (2014). *Case study research. Design and methods.* (5th ed.). London: Sage.

Chapter 6

Informality, Control/Management Practices and Performance of Small Congolese Enterprises: A Focus on SMEs in the City of Bukavu

Marcellin Chirimwami Luvuga,
Deogratias Bugandwa Mungu Akonkwa and Didier Van Caillie

Abstract

In recent times, the operating landscape of Small and Medium Enterprises (SMEs) environment can be described as constantly changing. Their performance is more dependent on the managers' ability to implement effective control/management practices suitable for their context and operating environment. Through a multi-site case study, we examine the peculiarities of control/management practices in four SMEs in the city of Bukavu to ascertain whether and how those practices contribute to SMEs' performance. Our findings indicate the predominance of informal practices, which include coordination methods similar to the balanced scorecard, budgeting practices, cost imputation, cash monitoring and inventory management. Compared to the results from literature, these practices did not differ much from those observed in the SMEs of developed countries and are likely to contribute to performance achievement, which corroborates the proposition of the contingency theory.

Keywords: Management control practices; management practices; performance; SMEs/small organisations; Congolese; Bukavu

Introduction

Small enterprises' socio-economic importance and role in the development of nations have been extensively recognised in the literature (Benaziz & Koubaa,

Casebook of Indigenous Business Practices in Africa, 105–121
Copyright © 2023 Marcellin Chirimwami Luvuga, Deogratias Bugandwa Mungu Akonkwa and Didier Van Caillie
Published under exclusive licence by Emerald Publishing Limited
doi:10.1108/978-1-80455-762-420231011

2016; BIT, 2015; OECD, 2000, 2002; Torres, 2007). In an ever-turbulent environment, studies support that the growth and survival of these enterprises are increasingly dependent on the ability of their leaders to equip themselves with management tools capable of ensuring their performance (Chapellier, 1997). Management control could prove to be one of such important tools allowing firms' to achieve strategic objectives. From the premise of Simons' (1994, 1995) model, the adoption of management control is the heart of SMEs' governance and management and ensures the firm's performance. Notably, performance can have implications on stakeholders such as: customers, suppliers, employees and the society (Giraud, Saulpic, Naulleau, Delmond, & Bescos, 2004).

Indeed, the quest for performance through SMEs' responsible practices differs from one context to another due to the strong embeddedness that characterises these organisations (Elbousserghini, Berger-Douce, & Jamal, 2019). This embeddedness leads to broader governance, which would ensure management control practices that serves the interests of the owner and other stakeholders. The formal and informal practices of control/management must thus empower managers to act in an optimal way for the company, by aligning their interests with those of the stakeholders with a view to achieving a more sustainable performance.

For SMEs in Africa, specifically, SMEs in Congo, this implies questioning the management control practices put in place. In terms of management control systems that can be adapted to the context and profiles of the actors to facilitate the performance of SMEs (Barbelivien & Meyssonnier, 2018), the contingency theory seems appropriate. This theory recognises that all organisations are different and that there are no formal structures that are superior, although there are ideal structures for given contexts. In this sense, the achievement of a 'balanced' performance for SMEs depends on the ability of their leaders to match these elements (Magaji, Lawan, & Naziru, 2018), especially when the firm's environment is complex and uncertain (Meyssonnier, 2015).

The research underlines that mastering the motivations of the owner-manager of the SME assumes a thorough understanding of his profile (Raymond, Blili, & EL-Alami, 2004) and provides an indication of the types of strategies that are likely to be mobilised by the latter for its control system(s) (Amanze & Nitesh, 2012). Characteristics such as the level, type of training, culture and experience of the leader (Chapellier, 2003) and the leader's extent of capital contribution (Lavigne, 2002; Ngongang, 2007) greatly determine the system of control in place in the company. The observation of Congolese SMEs suggests that the family culture of the leader could be very decisive in the implementation of control/management practices and that these could considerably affect the firm's performance (Bugandwa et al., 2021).

This research aims to describe control/management practices in African SMEs through a multi-site case study of four SMEs in the city of Bukavu, DR Congo. Specifically, we highlight indigenous control/management practices, which might be specific to the Congolese context and assess their contribution to SMEs' performance. To do so, we present the study context, the research design, the results and discussions, and the conclusion and recommendations for business practice.

The Context

The importance of SMEs in the development process of nations has been established in literature (e.g. Agyapong, 2010; Eniola, 2014; Gyimah, Appiah, & Lussier, 2020). Faced with the financial turmoil that is greatly affecting large public and private companies, SMEs have become a safe haven, a stable foundation for the economies of nations regardless of their level of development (Gherghina, Botezatu, Hosszu, & Simionescu, 2020).

This is particularly the case of Congolese SMEs, which unquestionably play a leading role in the country's economy after the bankruptcy of most large state and private companies due to Zairianization, looting orchestrated by repeated wars that regularly destabilised the country and its governments.[1]

Several reports and economic analyses show that 80% of the Congolese economy is held by SMEs despite the fact that they face enormous difficulties, including the problem of over-taxation, difficult access to bank credit, challenges in supplying inputs and, above all, problems related to their governance and management. Two out of three workers are currently employed by SMEs and represent approximately 52% of the gross domestic product (GDP) of the private sector in Congo, which sufficiently proves that the emergence of (well-managed) SMEs is the answer to the problems of imbalance in the market employment (AfDB, 2012; Ministry of Planning-DRC, 2014). A focus on addressing these challenges would play an important role in the country's economic development process.

The sustainability of the survival of SMEs depends largely on the ability of business leaders to put in place control/management practices capable of dealing with obstacles of various types that hinder development. However, as Avril (2008) pointed out, the idea that the function of management control is only useful to large companies is widespread in the mentalities of the managers of small and medium-sized companies, both African and Congolese. While the establishment of formal control/management practices is often viewed as controversial by many Congolese business leaders, particularly those who have succeeded without using them, it is still relevant to highlight informal, indigenous practices adopted by these leaders, which are likely to have ensured the performance of their organisations. This study is focused on investigating these indigenous practices, using the framework of Congolese SMEs in the city of Bukavu.

Finally, it is important to describe the nature of Congolese SMEs, particularly in comparison with the definition of SMEs in developed countries. In the DR-Congo, SME is defined as 'any economic unit whose actions are in the formal or informal sector, using local raw materials, employing 1 to 200 employees, with the annual turnover equivalent to 400,000 USD in Congolese francs (maximum), as well as investments valued to less than or equal to the total balance sheet of USD 350,000' (SME Charter, 2009). These criteria are different from those used in OECD countries. This might influence the degree of control/management practices implemented within SMEs in the Global North compared to those operating in the Global South. In line with this thought, Torres (2003) suggested that a great diversity of forms of SMEs and the specific behaviours of their managers most often depend on the context and the environment in which they operate.

Methodology

This study utilised interviews coupled with direct and indirect observations. Such techniques fit the requirements of case study research design and, particularly, multiple cases, in line with Yin (1984, 1994, 2003, 2009). In diversifying cases, we ensured we collected data on heterogeneity or homogeneity of control/management practices within SMEs in the city of Bukavu. This approach is recommended, especially when the aim of the research is to allow the emergence of new knowledge and to build new theories from a particular phenomenon (Eisenhart, 1989, 1991).

Selected Companies

The following table depicts the four companies selected, by sector, size and functions of the respondents:

The Table shows that owners/managers and employees with key positions constituted our key informants. However, to corroborate the statements of the targeted actors, we conducted short interviews with other employees.

Criteria for Selecting the SMEs

The following criteria were utilised to determine the inclusion of the case companies in the sample:

A workforce of less than or equal to 200 employees and a turnover excluding tax of less than US$400,000. This choice was made with reference to the 2009 SME classification charter.

Taking into account the criterion of theoretical saturation, our final study was oriented to four companies whose sectors of activity, size and functions of the interlocutors are identified in the following Table 1:

Table 1. Companies in the Sample.

Firms	Sector	Employee Number	Respondent's Function
A[a]	General trade and hotel services	27	Owner-manager, sales manager, Restaurant-bar manager
B	General trade	11	Financial manager and accountant
C	Bakery-pastry	18	Financial manager and accountant
D	Pharmaceutical store	15	Manager-accountant

[a]A, B, C and D are imaginary names for reasons of confidentiality at the request of respondents, as the latter did not want their names to appear in the study.

Have been in sector for at least six years, to take account of experience and sustainability of the control/management practices observed in the firms;

Must be registered in the commercial register: It was important to select companies from the formal sector; and

Managers' willingness to disclose information on their management practices.

Organisation of the Multi-Site Study

As indicated above, we selected four SMEs for our field research. The choice of companies B, C and D was dictated by their managers' willingness to participate in this study; while the choice of company A was motivated by the degree of knowledge one of the authors had about the company, as its external auditor. Therefore, we took advantage of the access granted by these companies to understand certain management realities of the SMEs studied. We also trained and used 'permanent' investigators to collect information through case studies.

The interviews organised with the managers/managers of the four SMEs selected for the case study were scheduled and organised in 'individual negotiation', with the exception of those carried out with company A which were unannounced, unscheduled and organised among a group of workers. The interview guide was built around management control practices in SMEs and with some cultural dimensions of Hofstede (Hofstede, 1980), with reference to certain control levers of Simons' model. Simon's model consists of four types of control which include belief systems, boundary systems, diagnostic systems, and interactive systems (Simon, 1995), which have been given consideration in this chapter.

Analysis of Interviews and Discussions

This section is structured around five themes that emerged from the interviews. These are accounting and finance practices, ownership structure and operations, leadership styles, the influence of national cultures and value systems and the way all these informal practices and cultural values impact the SMEs' performance.

Accounting and Finance Practices

The practices of management control can be categorised into two groups: Management Control Practices 1 (MCP1) and Management control Practices 2 (MCP2). The MCP1 comprises four practices: (i) general accounting, (ii) management accounting, (iii) management information technology and, (iv) auditing, and the MCP2 comprises four practices: (1) the dashboard, (2) financial analysis, (3) budget management and (4) strategic planning.

With regard to the MCP1 group, the firm's managers affirmed that they adapt accounting to their activities. Through our experience in company A, we observed that the cashbook is kept daily by a cashier and regularly monitored by the manager/founder of the company. The manager of the restaurant-bar intervenes daily to establish the cash journal via computer software, for tax purposes and semi-annual control. The managers of the points of sale use 'cash in and out sheets' to justify the report of their cash position, which they are required to present to the cashier at each closing of the day. Stock cards to assess the quantities of items in store – often without any scientifically recognised stock valuation method – are used in the SME and its points of sale. An annual physical inventory is conducted by the manager/founder of the company or members of his family to certify the information from the last half-yearly inspection by the external controller and, as far as possible, to take the necessary decisions.

Similar practices were discovered in companies B, C and D. For the managers of these companies, what matters to them is not having a sophisticated/computerised accounting information system, but rather having a general accounting method capable of meeting their needs. Therefore, it is a question of finding a financial accounting method that makes it possible to monitor cash and inventory movements and meet tax obligations.

Our respondents demonstrated their limits with regard to the use of management accounting, especially the method of rational allocation of cost in the total cost, which they often determine subjectively. How personnel costs, rents (case of A, B, C and D) and depreciation of productive equipment (case of C) are incorporated into the prices is not well disclosed, which creates an ambiguity in the cost calculation. However, they indicated that they include in the price of the goods (case of A, B and D) and materials (C), all the charges resulting from transport, customs clearance, commissions, etc., to determine the cost price and quantify the selling prices. Moreover, the respondents stated that the price determination of their products is obtained either by increasing the cost price by the percentage of the desired margin (case of A, B, C and D) or by aligning themselves with those of the market (case of A, B and D).

Finally, the analyses reveal that there is no visible audit in the SMEs of the city of Bukavu. However, informal practices, similar to those of internal audit, are conducted by company managers/founders who, at certain times, may be mandated by family members (potential heirs) or be assisted by their accounting directors. It is actually a kind of non-formalised internal control based on an informal coordination system (Meyssonnier, 2015; Van Caillie, 2003) led by managers and/or sector managers to reassure themselves of the proper conduct of activities. It is oriented because it generally focuses on cash flow control and stock management.

Consistent with the results of several studies on SMEs in developed countries (Condor & Rebut, 2008; Nobre, 2001; Nobre & Zawadzki, 2013), the chartered accountant often plays the role of the management controller within the Congolese SME. He can give advice, but the final decision is up to the leader, who only adopts those that align with his beliefs.

With regard to the MCP2 group, it is rare to observe clearly visible strategic or operational planning practices in the SMEs considered in the study. In company A, the leader/founder seems to have a long or medium-term planning culture in mind, but this remains vague because it is not formalised and depends on his instinct, his 'moods'. This often causes unwarranted unforeseen situations and hinders the missions of the external controller in the sense that the vision of the company is not clearly defined. This also aligns well with the assertions of other officials interviewed in B, C and D.

The nature of strategic and operational planning of the studied SMEs is not very different from that of their budget management which, in most cases, only exists in the 'heads' of business leaders. Managers interviewed in B, C and D asserted that 'sales and cash budgets exist in their companies but are centralised in the hands of the owners who favour informal modes of evaluation and who care little about the interpretation of discrepancies to correct any deviations'. The case of A is a little different. Indeed, the accounting and financial director works on budget management and firm development but under strict instructions dictated by the entrepreneur, and following the advice of the external controller who has authority to evaluate the achievements and the deviations annually. However, this seems to be a simple formality (case of A) because the suggestions made by the controller in view of the budget evaluation are often not taken into account by the manager/founder of the company, thus favouring informal management mechanisms (Nobre & Zawadzki, 2013).

The dashboard, as well as the financial evaluation (in particular, by the ratios), are also not clearly visible within the studied SMEs. However, within company C, there are specific forms of dashboards based on the result, highlighting the control of production and stock management. Moreover, the statements from the managers interviewed in B and D suggest that these tools are used for the management of (financial) performance without the users necessarily being aware of them. According to these managers: 'Business leaders/founders have results-oriented concerns involving both inventory management, monitoring of sales or expenses and which are tracked on a timely basis'. This reality is not different from the scenario observed in company A.

Taken together, these results highlight that SMEs in the city of Bukavu adopt control/management practices that they consider useful for their objectives, which seem to relate to controlling profitability (Bergeron, 2000; Lavigne, 2002). However, the study did not identify enough formalised practices, rather it observed that within the companies examined, there are indications proving that certain control or management tools are used. While, for example, general accounting is not held to strict compliance with standards in SMEs, there are at least clues that indicate that tools such as books and cash journals, and stock sheets are used.

Although mostly informal, the practices identified in the SMEs in the study take forms that are similar to cost control, inventory management, cash monitoring, financial analysis, budget management and specially shaped dashboards. These exist in the 'heads' of leaders depending on whether they consider them to reflect their strategic concerns without them being visible or popularised in their organisations. They are largely focused on the analysis of results: control of costs, production, stock management and/or supplies. This allows us to suggest that the SMEs examined rather favour financial performance over non-financial performance. This is also consistent with the results of Germain (2006) stressing that the

dashboards of family organisations are centralised, focused on financial performance, integrated into an organisational control device and favour the informal.

Ownership Structure and Organisation of Operations

The companies analysed in this study are family-owned. Their capitals belong
exclusively to the business manager, and his relatives exert the function of control.
Operations are organised in a way to favour the search for financial performance
over non-financial performance. This is consistent with Bergeron (2002), who
argued that SMEs of modest size mobilise rudimentary management tools just to
find out about the company's results. In accordance with Germain (2005), we note
that the governance of these companies is organised via practices far removed
from the logic of management (tools such as type 1 and 2 dashboards), with
techniques focused on providing information about the results of the company.

Consequently, financial performance appears as the component of overall
performance most sought after by the SMEs in the study, with company
managers/founders behaving like 'small impatient capitalists' favouring a
short-term financial vision, centered on maximising their wealth. However, there
is a predominance of informal activities in Congolese SMEs in general and in the
city of Bukavu in particular. Although such activities follow a logic of redistribution rather than that of accumulation (Hernandez, 1997), one cannot confirm
that financial performance is the most prevailing performance dimension for the
surveyed SMEs.

Leadership Style

The employees of the Congolese SME consider the entrepreneur as a protector, a
patriarch on whom they are dependent. The patriarchal style of leadership
(Hernandez, 2000; Razzouki & Benazzi, 2020) makes the entrepreneur a provider
of resources and an insurer of the wellbeing of his subordinates, family members.
They are condemned to obey the principles of their charismatic leader (the
business leader), his beliefs and therefore his traditions. Hernandez (1998) highlights respect for tradition, loyalty to the patriarch and solidarity between
members of the organisation as dimensions associated with the managerial system
of small African organisations.

Most employees of the studied firms being the entrepreneur's family members,
work for the highest interest of the company, motivated by their affection for the
entrepreneur. As a counterpart, they are rewarded through 'informal assistance'
and 'close relationships'. Although staff motivation is not greatly present as a
system in the studied SMEs, observation and analysis of the statements made by
participants in companies A, B, C and D show that there is still within these
companies various 'informal and unplanned' social assistance granted to
employees to encourage the convergence of behaviour. In particular, the leader
provides financial or in-kind help during happy or unhappy events. This creates

team spirit, sense of ownership and strengthens the cohesion among team members while reinforcing their commitment.

Impact of National Cultures and Value Systems

Although the four cases highlight the existence/use of management control tools within SMEs in the city of Bukavu, the question of their formal adoption has remained unanswered. The use of a management control tool does not necessarily translate to a management control practice, but rather refers to the 'formal adoption of a management control tool' (Lorino, 2008).

This finally seems to demonstrate an atrophied diagnostic control, fed by value systems within the Congolese SMEs. Such a system can lead to the translation of 'barriers into critical performance variables while constituting itself a concretisation of these barriers' (Nobre & Zawadzki, 2015, p. 15).

Fig. 1 visually depicts our positive understanding of the levers of control within the Congolese SMEs. It indicates how the lever of control by values would maintain intuitive strategies, which we qualify as 'undisclosed strategies'. Conversely, this intuitive strategy feeds the lever of belief systems (1). The latter affects all other existing levers. The omnipresence of the manager limits the actions of the employees; (2): it then turns out that even the risks that the

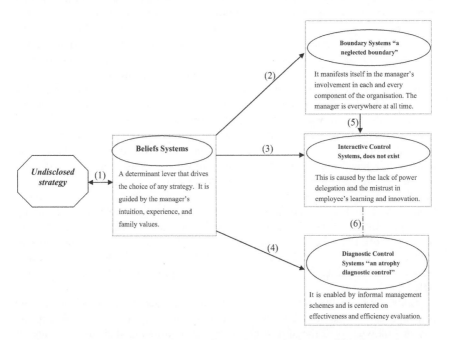

Fig. 1.   A Positive Understanding of Lever's Control in Congolese SMEs (Inspired From the Literature and Observation).

subordinates would be authorised to take are only taken by the omnipresent manager. Respect for ethical principles is also a source of performance in African SMEs (Boubakary & Moskolaï, 2021) and, from this consideration, the manager can assert his omnipresence in the company to ensure compliance with ethical values. As there is no delegation of power or decision (Julien, 1996), this does not promote learning and innovation (3), (5): interactive control is then non-existent. No relation (6) emerges between the interactive control (because absent) and the diagnostic control. This is of the atrophied type because it is fuelled by informal patterns stemming from value systems (4).

As indicated by Speklé, Van Elten, and Widener (2017), balancing the four levers proposed by Simons leads to improved performance. However, the findings of the study point out that within the Congolese SMEs, it is the lever of values that would determine the destiny of the whole organisation [this being the case of most SMEs (Nobre & Zawadzki, 2015)]. The above figure depicts the central role that the lever of beliefs would play in the operationalisation of the other levers and, therefore, in the implementation of management control practices in SMEs in the city of Bukavu. Simons has made a significant contribution by proposing the levers based on a typology of control systems integrating formal and informal practices (Berland, Ponssard, & Saulpic, 2005) for achieving the firm's objectives. Our positive understanding of Simons' control levers, through the results of the study, makes it possible to realise that the management practices implemented within SMEs are those that facilitate managers to act in an optimal way for the company by 'aligning their interests' with those of the 'priority' stakeholders. An SME leader with similar attitudes replaces himself, formally or informally, as a collectivist (Hamel, 2008) and will help his organisation achieve superior performance over the long term, based on financial and non-financial pillars.

In view of the results of the study, should we consider that the leaders of Congolese SMEs think and act according to their socio-cultural contexts generally carried by family beliefs? The affirmative answer seems to outweigh the negative. Indeed, the respondents' statements seem to point to the personality of the leader, his profile (his intellect, his experience, his family culture or clan) as the main contingency factor in the implementation of management strategies and practices within the SME of the city of Bukavu. In line with the management practices adopted, the strategies are also more intuitive and less formalised (Gagné, 2018). The implementation of strategic plans capable of enlightening employees on the direction of the company is not a concern of the leader who trusts his intuitive instinct more. The socio-cultural proximity of managers to their employees allows 'the establishment of uncomplicated internal information systems, while dialogue and direct contact are practiced informally' (Gagné, 2018).

Taking this reality into account, one may be tempted to believe in the convergence of behaviour in terms of the adoption of strategies by SMEs in the city of Bukavu, given the almost homogeneous cultures of their leaders. Such a reflection also fits well with the teachings of Hofstede (1980), arguing that the values, beliefs and behaviours of managers are influenced and shaped by national cultures. The results of several studies underline belief systems as a lever dominating the control systems of small and medium-sized enterprises and that this lever is largely influenced by the leader's family and ethnic culture (Kamdem, 2002). It follows then that the national cultures, the experience, and the manager's profile are contingent on the systems/practices of control and the intuitive coping strategies widespread in Congolese SMEs. This suggests that the intuitive instinct evoked is only a common denominator of the managerial system of the SME, but the informal patterns of activation of management practices and strategies are largely influenced by national cultures, the experience and the personality of leaders.

Informal Practices, Cultural Values and the SMEs' Performance

What is true of management practices should also be true of performance measurement. From the observation made on the SMEs of the study, it seems in light of the teachings of Hofstede, that the Congolese national cultures are more masculine than feminine and even more communal than individualistic, which gives an idea of the nature of the performance that the managers would favour.

The influence of the personality and national cultures of the leader on the control systems and the performance of the SME is summarised in Fig. 2:

It follows from the figure that the values of the manager (his personality, his experience and his culture) influence the control levers widespread in SMEs and determine his performance. This is consistent with the findings of Mayimbi et al. (2021) and those of Boubakary (2016), who argue that the Congolese (and African) company's management is determined by its leader's ethical behaviour, its members' socio-cultural values and the environmental context. The levers of control highlighted here are belief systems and atrophied diagnostic control, the interactive control being absent and the supposed boundary systems affected by

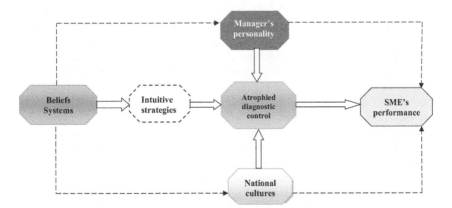

Fig. 2.   Influence of Manager's Personality and Culture on the Adoption of Control Levers and on Performance of SMEs.

value systems. Intuitive strategies are meant to be derived and implemented by both value control systems and atrophied diagnostic control.

Conclusion

This study has evidenced that the governance of Congolese SMEs is characterised by informal management/control and coordination practices, which, however, are likely to positively affect their performance. Five major results have emerged from the analysis and discussion. In terms of accounting and financial practices: there is no accounting system formally adopted or held to strict rigour, both in terms of financial and management accounting. Non-specialised computer software such as Excel is often used to manage financial accounting. Tax reasons are the main driver for holding a kind of accounting. Less formalised management accounting is geared towards controlling costs, but the management of production costs is generally poorly controlled. Dashboards are not used in the studied SMEs, but centralised practices, referring to type 1 and 2 dashboards [in of Germain's (2005) perspective] exist in the 'heads' of managers; meaning that the latter use their own unwritten indicators when it comes to examining their firms' results. Budgetary practices oriented towards sales or cash flow exist in these companies, but they remain centralised in the hands of the managers/founders who use them according to informal management schemes. Managers also use a kind of 'invisible' financial evaluation which makes it possible to assess the level of commercial activity and ensure control of working capital. Strategic planning seems almost non-existent, although the owner-managers seem to be concerned with the sustainability of their businesses over the long term, via 'informal, centralised strategies'.

Most of the businesses in Bukavu town are family-owned; this is the case of the SMEs in this study. Their capital is entirely owned by the business manager. His omnipresence in the company has been seen as an 'informal internal control' and supervision. The manager/founder is often assisted by an external expert in management, taxation or by a chartered accountant. The latter may suggest policies to follow, but the final decision is based on his instincts or on the advice of certain members of his family. Management control is more informal than formal to the point that, most often, the management of the organisation does not realise when it is using it. Business leaders who enjoy formal and symbolic authority centralise decision-making power (Mintzberg, 2002, 2004) while concentrating control on cash monitoring, inventory management, and results. In this sense, the preferred type of leadership is local governance. The daily intervention of leaders in the management of their companies is justified more by their desire to encourage subordinates to converge behaviours.

Through their role as patriarch and protector of employees (generally members of their families), they ensure the redistribution of the wealth created while ensuring that their wealth grows. The values conveyed in the organisation and which guide their local management are based on the personality of the leaders and their families, ethnic or even religious cultures (national cultures). Finally, the personality of the leader (his intuition, his experiences) contributes to the determination of intuitive strategies of adaptation and, in concert with national cultures, it atrophies the diagnostic control lever and affects the performance of his organisation.

The contribution of this study lies in its ability to identify indigenous, less formalised control/management practices common among SMEs in the city of Bukavu and to emphasise that they would likely contribute to both financial and environmental performance. The study also advocates that to encourage the convergence of acceptable behaviour, leaders mobilise 'informal assistance' and 'close relations' in favour of subordinates to informally ensure that their firms are evolving towards high performance. Despite the interesting findings, there are limitations of the study. Three of these are worth mentioning: (i) the methodology used, (ii) the actors surveyed and (iii) the nature of the SMEs considered.

In terms of methodology, this study is conducted via case studies, which implies low external validity. It would have been useful to combine this qualitative approach with a quantitative approach to test the results that emerge. For the actors surveyed, it would have been beneficial to systematically question employees and business leaders within the same company to ensure that the two groups were reporting the same information. Finally, for the nature of the SMEs taken into account in the study, it would have been useful to include the companies which tend to disappear/become bankrupt and those which give off signs of growth in order to ascertain whether the management practices mobilised in these companies are similar. Indeed, we have considered only the companies that showed signs of growth, which could justify why their control/management practices tended to converge towards the same model. In addition, the presence of indications of a management control tool in the company led us to believe that the tool in question was indeed used. These limitations, rather than reducing the quality of our findings, constitute interesting avenues for future research to understand management control in underdeveloped contexts.

From the results, the following suggestions should be made to business leaders to ensure the sustainability of their organisations:

• It is important to consider the formalisation of accounting and financial practices to improve the business profitability (more transparency and best control, best information to obtain funding from financial institutions, etc.).
• In addition to informal assistance, business owners ought to adopt formal motivation (decent wages, formal bonuses...) in order to further transform 'divergent interests' into convergent interests.
• SME managers would strengthen local management and reinforce their image, their figure of patriarch not only with regard to employees who are their family members but also with regard to the minority of non-family members, in order to reduce conflicts and frustration in the firms.
• It would be better to consider the advice of Simons (1994, 1995) to formalise diagnostic control while encouraging learning and innovation. This could make interactive control appear and contribute to the balancing of control levers in

the organisation, the immediate consequence of which would be to improve overall performance.

Case Questions

(1) After reading this text, what are the practices that are different from classical management control systems?
(2) The text illustrates an 'informal internal audit' done by the owner-manager. In your opinion, what problem may arise from it?
(3) What style of leadership is prevalent in Congolese SMEs? What other styles do you know from leadership literature?
(4) What key lessons can African nations learn from the case study?

Note

1. Zaïrianisation is a phenomenon which occurred in the 1970s in the DR Congo, when Mobutu Sese Seko confiscated all enterprises belonging to Belgians and gave them to Congolese elites.

References

AfDB. (2012). *Private investment environment in the Democratic Republic of Congo*, Report presented by the Central Africa Regional Department. 46 p. Retrieved from www.afdb.org

Agyapong, D. (2010). Micro, small and medium enterprises' activities, income level and poverty reduction in Ghana - A synthesis of related literature. *International Journal of Business and Management*, 5(12), 196.

Amanze, R. E., & Nitesh, J. (2012). Contingency theory and management control packages in small firms: Case evidence from India. Retrieved from www.semanticscholar.org

Avril, O. (2008, November). Management control in SMEs: Essential points and objectives. *La Lettre Acting Finance*, (38).

Barbelivien, D., & Meyssonnier, F. (2018). A contribution to the study of the structuring of management control in SMEs: The case of three family and industrial companies of intermediate size. *Revue Internationale P.M.E, 31*(1).

Benaziz, S., & Koubaa, S. (2016). At ENCG-Marrakech, Maroc. Particularity of the concept of governance within SMEs: Proposal of a theoretical framework. International conference "governance and performance", at ENCG-Marrakech, Morocco. International Colloquium on Governance and Performance.

Bergeron, H. (2000). Performance indicators in the SME context, which model to apply? In *21st Congress of the Afc*, May.

Bergeron, H. (2002). Strategic management and measurement of the non-financial performance of SMEs. In *6th International Francophone Congress on SMEs*. HEC Montréal.

Berland, N., Ponssard, J.-P., Saulpic, O. (2005). A typology of control systems inspired by Simons' theoretical framework, hal-00243012.

BIT. (2015). *Working conditions around the world, report.*

Boubakary, B. (2016). Influences of contingency factors on the management of African companies: The case of Cameroon. *African Review of Management, 1*(1), 133–148.

Boubakary, B., & Moskolaï, D. D. (2021, January–June). Leader ethics: Lever of influence? The case of the performance of Cameroonian SMEs. *Congolese Management Review*, (31).

Bugandwa Mungu Akonkwa, D., Lunanga, E., Bahati Mukulu, J., Bugandwa Ciza, T., & Furaha Mwaza, E. (2021). Leadership styles and small enterprises' performance: Is gender an issue? Empirical study from the Democratic Republic of Congo. *Journal of Entrepreneurship and Innovation in the Emerging Economies*, 1–23. doi:10.1177/23939575211044318

Chapellier, P. (1997). Profiles of managers and management accounting data. *Revue International PME, 10*(1).

Chapellier, P. (2003). The contributions of the Internet to the mission of the chartered accountant in small businesses. *Accountancy-Control-Audit, 9*(2).

Condor, R., & Rebut, K. (2008). Determinants and operating methods of management control in SMEs: A comparative qualitative approach. In *CIFEPME Conference*, Normandy School of Management.

Eisenhart, K. (1989). Building theories from case study research. *The Academy of Management Review, 14*(4), 532–550.

Eisenhart, K. (1991). Better stories and better constructs: The case for rigor and comparative logic. *The Academy of Management Review, 16*(3), 620.

Elbousserghini, J., Berger-Douce, S., & Jamal, Y. (2019). The CSR of SMEs: The study of the Moroccan context. *International Review of SMEs, 32*(1).

Eniola, A. A. (2014). The role of SME firm performance in Nigeria. *Oman Chapter of Arabian Journal of Business and Management Review, 34*(2352), 1–15.

Gagné, V. (2018). *Drivers of implementation of sustainable practices by SMEs.* PhD Thesis. University of Sherbrooke and University of Quebec.

Germain, C. (2005). A typology of dashboards implemented in small and medium-sized enterprises. Association FCS, *8*(3).

Germain, C. (2006). Performance management in SMEs in France: A comparison of dashboard practices of family organizations and subsidiaries. *International Journal of SMEs, 19*(1).

Gherghina, S. C., Botezatu, M. A., Hosszu, A., & Simionescu, L. N. (2020). Small and medium-sized enterprises (SMEs): The engine of economic growth through investments and innovation. *Sustainability, 12*, 347.

Giraud, F., Saulpic, O., Naulleau, G., Delmond, M.-H., & Bescos, P.-L. (2004). *Management control and performance management* (2nd ed.). Paris: Business Collection.

Gyimah, P., Appiah, K. O., & Lussier, R. N. (2020). Success versus failure prediction model for small businesses in Ghana. *Journal of African Business, 21*(2), 215–234.

Hamel, G. (2008). The future of management. *Human Resource Management International Digest, 16*(6).

Hernandez, E. M. (1997). *The management of African companies: An essay in development management éd.* Paris: Le Harmattan. Retrieved from https://www.editi ons-harmattan.fr/

Hernandez, E. M. (1998). Human resource management in the African informal enterprise. *French Journal of Management, 119*, 49–57.

Hernandez, E. M. (2000). Africa, the news of the paternalistic model. *French Journal of Management, 128*, 98–106.

Hofstede, G. (1980). Culture and organizations. *International Studies of Management and Organization*, 15–41.

Julien, P.-A. (1996). Entrepreneurship country development and information ownership. *Revue International PME, 9*(3–4), 149–178.

Kamdem, E. (2002). *Management and interculturality in Africa.* Cameroonian Experience Press of the University of Laval. Paris: Le Harmattan. Retrieved from https://www.editions-harmattan.fr/

Lavigne, B. (2002). Contribution to the study of the genesis of accounting information systems in SMEs: An empirical approach. In *Proceedings of the XXIII Congress of the French Accounting Association*, Toulouse.

Lorino, P. (2008). Research methods in management control: A critical approach. *Finance-Control-Strategy, 11*.

Magaji, A., Lawan, Y., & Naziru, S. (2018). Explored and critique of contingency theory for management accounting research. *Journal of Accounting & Financial Management, 4*(5).

Mayimbi, E. N. P., Bolila, L., & Kangela, V. (2021). The determinants of the nature of management control in African SMEs: The case of the Democratic Republic of Congo. *Revue Franççaise d'Economie et de Gestion, 2*(1).

Meyssonnier, F. (2015). What management control for startups? *Accountancy-Control-Audit, 21*(2), 33–61.

Mintzberg, H. (2002). *The daily manager, the ten roles of the manager, New Horizons.* Paris: Editions d'Organisation.

Mintzberg, H. (2004). *Management: Journey to the center of organizations.* Paris: Editions d'Organisation. (Editions d'Organisation).

Ngongang, D. (2007). Analysis of the determining factors of the accounting information system and accounting practices of Chadian SMEs. *The Journal of Management Sciences, Direction and Management*, (224–225), 49–57.

Nobre, T. (2001). The management controller in SMEs. CCA, 129–146; 95.

Nobre, T., & Zawadzki, C. (2013). Analysis of the failure of the introduction of management control in SMEs by the theory of translation: A lack of legitimacy and incomplete moments. *Comptabilité-Contrôle-Audit, 19*(1), 91–116.

Nobre, T., & Zawadzki, C. (2015). A reading of Simons' levers of control by the theory of structuring in an ETI context. In *Accountancy, Control and Audit of the Invisible, the Informal and the Unpredictable.* Toulouse, France.

OECD. (2000). *Small and medium enterprises: Local strength, global action.* Working Paper, Geneva.

OECD. (2002). *High-growth SMEs and jobs.* Paris: OECD Publishing.

Raymond, L., Blili, S., & EL-Alami, D. (2004). The gap between the consultant and the SME: Analysis and perspectives. *Gestion, 28*(4), 52–60.

Razzouki, M., & Benazzi, K. (2020). Management control practices in small Moroccan agrifood companies: Case of the Beni Mellal Khenifra region. *Global Journal of Management and Business Research: An Administration and Management, 20*.

Simons, R. (1994). How new top managers use control systems as levers of strategic renewal. *Strategic Management Journal, 15*, 169–189.

Simons, R. (1995). *Levers of control*. Boston, MA: Harvard University Press.

SME Charter. (2009). Ministry of SMEs. DRCongo, 24 p.

Speklé, R. F., Van Elten, H. J., & Widener, S. K. (2017). Creativity and control: A paradox-evidence from the levers of control framework. *Behavioral Research in Accounting, 29*(22), 73–96.

Torres, O. (2003). Smallness of enterprises and magnification of proximity effects. *Revue Française de Gestion, 3*(144).

Torres, O. (2007). *The French academic research in SMEs: Theses, journals, networks.* Coll. Regards sur les PME, n°14, Observatoire des PME, OSEO.

Van Caillie, D. (2003). The exercise of management control in an SME context. In *Annual Congress of the French Association of Accountancy*, Louvain-la-Neuve.

Yin, R. K. (1984). *Case study research.* Beverly Hills, CA: Sage Publications.

Yin, R. K. (1994). *Case study research: Design and methods* (2nd ed.). Newbury Park, CA: Sage.

Yin, R. K. (2003). *Case study research: Design and methods* (3rd ed.). London: Sage Publications.

Yin, R. K. (2009). *Case study research: Design and methods* (4th ed.). London: Sage Publications.

Part 2
Indigenous Financial Practices

Chapter 7

The Ecosystem of Indigenous Savings and Credit Association in Sierra Leone: Entrepreneurial Success or Nightmare?

Abdul Karim Kafoir and Emeka Raphael Agu

Abstract

Traditional savings and credit associations, also known as 'Osusu' in Sierra Leone, are unions of individuals with common economic goals aimed at reducing poverty and economic vulnerability. The chapter examined the ecosystem of traditional indigenous savings and credit associations, their role as an emerging financial inclusion strategy, and contributions to the socio-economic transformation of business processes in the ecosystem of business operations in Sierra Leone. The chapter adopted the case study method to discuss the Tawoponneh model of ROSCAs in Sierra Leone. The institutional theory provided insight into why individuals join ROSCAs, as well as the resulting outcomes and benefits. Additionally, this chapter discusses the challenges associated with indigenous financial sustainability practices and provides actionable recommendations for joint private and government policy collaboration in supporting traditional entrepreneurial businesses.

Keywords: Savings and credit associations; traditional business practice; economic empowerment; rural dwellers; economic growth; traditional savings

Introduction

The history of savings and credit associations in Africa predates the period of the barter system during colonialism. There is a growing body of research on Rotating Savings and Credit Associations (ROSCAs) in different countries of sub-Saharan Africa (Adeola et al., 2022; Amankwah, Gockel, & Osei-Assibey, 2019; Amankwaha, Osei-Koduahb, & Boahene, 2021; Athieno, Dykstra-McCarthy, Stites, & Krystalli, 2020; Feather Meme, 2018; Frank, Mbabazize, & Shukla, 2015; Green, 2018;

Casebook of Indigenous Business Practices in Africa, 125–140
Copyright © 2023 Abdul Karim Kafoir and Emeka Raphael Agu
Published under exclusive licence by Emerald Publishing Limited
doi:10.1108/978-1-80455-762-420231012

Kabuya, 2013; Lukwa, Odunitan-Wayas, Lambert, & Alaba, 2022; Mbizi & Gwangwava, 2013; Olando, Mbewa, & Jagongo, 2012; Zikalala, 2016). This underscores their relevance to local communities, particularly the rural dwellers who are either financially excluded or unable to access loans from formal financial institutions because of collateral securities and high-interest rates.

ROSCAs serve as a dependable informal institution for tackling the challenges of financial exclusion by providing access to financial services for their members who cannot access financial services from formal financial institutions (Abimbola et al., 2020). ROSCA is often defined as an informal group of individuals who frequently contribute to a shared fund that is subsequently distributed, either fully or partially, among each contributor on a rotating basis (Kabuya, 2015). As one of the emerging markets in Africa, there are various ROSCAs in Sierra Leone providing financial support for the overall wellbeing of their members. The Government of Sierra Leone recognises the potential for economic empowerment of the local communities as well as rural financial challenges by initiating and executing the Rural Finance and Community Improvement Programme (RFCIP) with financial backing from the International Fund for Agricultural Development (IFAD) (Gbakie, Kamara, & Dumbuya, 2018). This has led to the establishment of 17 community financial institutions across the nation to provide access to loans and savings to the rural populace (Gbakie et al., 2018). The United Nations, in collaboration with the Government and citizens of Sierra Leone, is also working to alleviate poverty and inequality and ensure that all Sierra Leoneans can realise their hopes and aspirations (United Nations, 2022). The World Bank has financially supported the Sierra Leonean Government's Social Safety Net Program (SSNP) with a whopping amount of $47 million, which has assisted 68,453 impoverished families and 410,718 people are beneficiaries of cash grants (World Bank, 2022).

Despite these measures, the World Food Programme reported that the level of poverty is on the increase in Sierra Leone, with about 53% of the total population of 7 million living below the income poverty line – US$1.25 per day (World Food Programme, 2022). Thus, a significant proportion of the population (unemployed youths, women, household farmers, local traders, etc.) depend on the ROSCAs for loans to seek economic activities and enhance their capacities to tackle poverty and improve living standards.

Only a handful of studies (i.e. Gbakie et al., 2018; Johnson, 2011; Mahdi, 2018; Sutton, Momo, & Aeckert, 2012) have been conducted to evaluate the impact of these ROSCAs on poverty alleviation, accessibility to loans, financial inclusion, economic wellbeing of the rural populace, and economic growth in Sierra Leone. Some of the studies (i.e. Fraser, 2012; Mahdi, 2016, 2018, and Sutton et al., 2012) focussed on micro-enterprises. To this end, this study aims to fill the gap in the literature by joining the debate on ROSCAs and analysing the effects of their traditional indigenous practices on the economic wellbeing of the local communities in Sierra Leone using the case study approach.

In the remaining parts of this chapter, first, the methodology is presented. Thereafter, we highlighted the traditional indigenous business practices, popularly known as Osusu, in Sierra Leone and discussed the features of these practices. Subsequently, we discussed the theoretical framework for the study and the challenges encountered by ROSCAs in Sierra Leone. In addition, a case study on

Tawoponneh's model of ROSCAs in Sierra Leone was analysed, followed by the discussion of findings, recommendations, suggestions for further studies and conclusion.

Methodology

The case data were obtained from the primary data source. An in-depth interview was conducted to generate data for the study. Four respondents (Wanday Conteh, Manager of Tawoponneh Traders Association (Participant WC/M/TTA), Dr Sheka Bangura, Central Planning and Economic Development, Ministry of Economic Development (Participant SB/CPED/MEE), Miss Fatmata Kamara, Head of Credit Associations, Bank of Sierra Leone (Participant FK/HCA/BS) and Emmanuel Kamara, Education Secretary – Sierra Leone Labour Congress.

Participant EK/ES/SLLC were interviewed within 2 weeks to gain insights on the history, goals and objectives and impact of the Tawoponneh Traders Association on its members and communities. The responses were used to present a case on the Tawoponneh's model of ROSCAs in Sierra Leone.

An Overview of Traditional Indigenous Business Practice in Sierra Leone

Before the advent of the British colonial system in Sierra Leone, there was compelling evidence of economic transactions in the various traditional settings, which included village credit and savings associations, known locally as *Kuma* or the box (Fyle, 1988). Its members ranged from 1 to 100 on a common shared value to maximise welfare solidarity that will promote livelihood and transformation (Fyle, 1988). This was a kind of barter system that focused on anthropological or geological connections – a traditional business process that was practised before the introduction of the financial system (Fyle, 1988). This method is still in existence and has grown in proportion to the high-interest rate imposed by modern microfinance institutions on clients. The negative impacts of these high-interest rates have undermined the intended purpose of poverty alleviation, business growth and transformation in the lives of the poor in emerging economies, like *Kuma* (Fyle, 1988).

In situating the foregoing in its historical context, the financial system was established around 1898 in the colonial epoch (Fyle, 1988). The British West Africa Limited can be traced as far back as the economic period of the barter system when Africans had contact with Europeans. Since the colonial period, formal credit has existed alongside informal credit in West African countries with a long history of entrepreneurship (Fyle, 1988). In Sierra Leone, British colonial rule lasted more than a century and had major impacts, such as the establishment of modern banking, and formal credit systems to enhance economic activities and opportunities in the business environment (Fyle, 1988).

After two years of her independence from British colonial rule, Sierra Leone, in 1963, established the Bank of Sierra Leone (the Bank) through an Act passed by the Sierra Leone Parliament (Fyle, 1988). The Bank is located in Freetown, the capital city of Sierra Leone. The Act empowered the Bank to be the major banker to the Sierra Leonean Government, with the responsibilities of managing the Government's principal accounts and executing all the major banking and foreign exchange transactions (Fyle, 1988). In 1964, the Parliament passed the Banking Act that provided for the regulation of banks and extended the central bank's power of monetary control to allow for closer contact with the banking system (Fyle, 1988).

The Bank of Sierra Leone was also given additional responsibilities to monitor and regulate the Nation's banking system and control the Nation's money supply and foreign reserves (Sierra Leone Trade Journal, 1961). Since its founding, the Bank of Sierra Leone was headed by a British expatriate Governor – Gordon Hall; however, in 1966, a Sierra Leonean, S. B. Nicole-Cole, who had been the bank's Deputy Governor, became the first indigenous Governor of the Bank (Sierra Leone Trade Journal, 1961). The Deputy Governor was another Sierra Leonean – Samuel L. Bangura. Both men were educated in Sierra Leone and Britain (Fyle, 1988). The Sierra Leone Commercial Bank, Standard Chartered Bank, Union Trust Bank, Barclays Bank and the National Development Bank were the major private financial institutions that concentrated on formal credit. Most of Sierra Leone's commercial banks are located in Freetown, and a few major banks have branches in the interior of the Northern, Eastern and Southern provinces of Sierra Leone (Sierra Leone Trade Journal, 1961). The commercial banks' activities include accepting money deposits, operating current accounts for their customers, granting loans and advances and dealing with foreign currencies (Sierra Leone Trade Journal, 1961).

In the past three decades, there has been a growing literature on informal credit in Africa (Abimbola et al., 2020; Amankwaha et al., 2021; Feather & Meme, 2018; and Lukwa et al., 2022). Informal credit refers to loans in cash and kind provided outside formal financial institutions, such as banks. Credit in kind involved items such as rice, cassava and sweet potatoes. It is a complex field of commerce and industry where goods and services are created and distributed in the expectation of profit within the framework of laws and regulations. Situating this to the concept of traditional business processes that have operated in Sierra Leone, it is essential to give the history of savings and credit associations commonly in Sierra Leone. Rotational savings and credit unions are economic institutions founded in the ecosystem of the informal economy that collectively promote the financial wellbeing of its members and seek to reduce poverty in the larger society. Basically, this type of business process constitutes a principal finance resource scheme by people living in a surrounding neighbourhood to provide opportunities for investment, social cohesion and livelihood to members of the credit and savings groups.

The British West Africa Limited was set up primarily to provide banking facilities for British trading companies and colonial administration (Leigh, 2004). As the financial system developed, there was a dire need to set up another financial institution known as the West Africa Currency Board (WACB) in 1912, mainly serving as the Central Bank (Rogers in Sheriff & Quee, 2020). The WACB operated exclusively in London, with satellite stations headed by an Accountant-General from the respective colonies as subsidiaries of the British Headquarters in London (Rogers in Sheriff & Quee, 2020). As the name implies, the currency board was mainly responsible for the buying and selling of currencies required by the colonial administration and its appendage British financial institution (Rogers in Sheriff & Quee, 2020). In the year 1917, there was an increase in the number of commercial banks in the financial landscape of Sierra Leone (Leigh, 2004).

These banking institutions were Barclays Dominion, Colonial and Overseas, and Barclays Bank (DCO). Leigh (2004) highlighted the following limitations of these commercial banks and their implications on the informal financial structure as follows.

First, the banks that existed during the colonial period did not provide credit opportunities for Africans. Second, they did not meet the threshold or appropriate collateral required for loan disbursement. Third, there was the assumption that Africans were inherently unreliable with regard to financial matters. In summary, Leigh (2004), categorically concludes that a greater number of the indigenous population were discriminated against and excluded from what constituted the formal system.

Providing further information on the historical perspective of the indigenous Savings and Credit Association in Sierra Leone, Participant SB/CPED/MEE stated that it started a very long time ago while emerging from the barter system, and in Sierra Leone, it could be traced from the colonial period when they were small communities trading a range of items from salt to other commodities. They also formed village saving organisations known as 'NKUMA', which means box. In these arrangements, they have union leaders who superintended the process of savings and credit. They are rotationally disbursed on weekly basis, and the duration must not exceed one year. The model has thrived and continues to be sustained.

The respondent further stated that another model is the traders union which provides assistance to members in their businesses through loan facilitation from commercial banks and microfinance institutions. The traders' unions may serve as a sort of guarantor which is regarded as a type of collateral. One example is the Teachers Union, which has a strong union and has further established a collaboration with Ecobank to serve the interests of union members.

Theoretical Review

The theoretical framework for this research is based on the institutional theory of saving propounded by Sherraden (1991). The institutional theory of saving states that individuals' and households' savings are facilitated by the institutional operations through which saving transpires. Sherraden's theory underscores the impact of institutions on the acquisition of assets. Sherraden stated that asset acquisitions are basically the outcome of institutionalised techniques involving clear-cut connections, policies, incentives and subsidies. He highlighted the subsidies offered through retirement- and housing-related tax benefits such as discounts for home mortgage and property taxes, employment pension contributions and earnings, etc.

Since these techniques for asset acquisition are subsidised, Sherraden argued that it is logical for individuals and households to explore the opportunities given by these institutions to amass assets. For instance, individuals partake in pension and retirement schemes because of their easiness and traction. This is a clear illustration of how most institutions provide excellent choices for individuals to explore. Hence rational decisions on the best alternatives have been made by the social policy; individuals and households are expected to extensively benefit from the established platforms (Beverly & Sherraden, 1999).

Sherraden claims that the abysmal low saving rates and inadequate access to acquiring and owning assets by low-income individuals and households can be relatively attributed to their inability to access institutions with saving possibilities (Beverly & Sherraden, 1999). This theory is part of a larger body of institutional theory arguing that societal institutions form and pattern individual behaviour. The relevance of this theory is that it explains the imperativeness of financial institutions (ROSCAs) in encouraging savings and investments among individuals and households (Sierra Leone's rural populace). See Fig. 1.

Fig. 1 clearly shows the factors influencing individuals and households to join ROSCAs, such as savings, assets acquisition, business startups, low income, financial exclusion, investment in agriculture, business expansion, the rigidity of

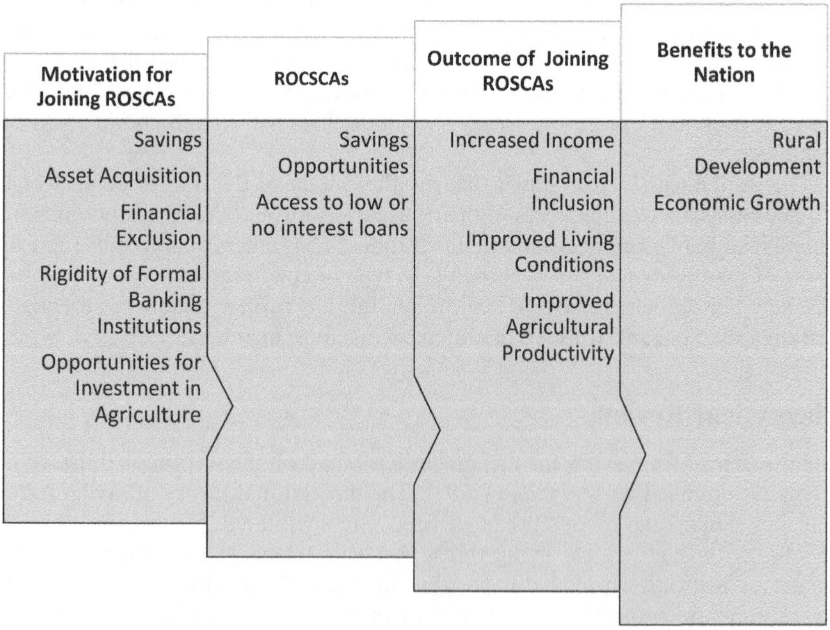

Motivation for Joining ROSCAs	ROCSCAs	Outcome of Joining ROSCAs	Benefits to the Nation
Savings	Savings Opportunities	Increased Income	Rural Development
Asset Acquisition	Access to low or no interest loans	Financial Inclusion	Economic Growth
Financial Exclusion		Improved Living Conditions	
Rigidity of Formal Banking Institutions		Improved Agricultural Productivity	
Opportunities for Investment in Agriculture			

Fig. 1.   Diagrammatic Representation of Motivation, Benefits and Outcomes of Joining ROSCAs in Sierra Leone.

formal banking institutions and solving emergencies. Participation in ROSCAs is expected to create access to savings and obtain loans for solving issues that will result in a better life, improved living conditions, increased income, rural development, improved agricultural productivity, financial inclusion and economic growth. Hence, the chapter argues that the activities of ROSCAs in Sierra Leone can significantly provide access to savings and loan opportunities for the disadvantaged, low-income earners, financially excluded individuals and households in Sierra Leone. By so doing, they can obtain loans and engage in economic activities that will improve their living standard and contribute meaningfully to the Nation's economic growth and development.

ROSCAs Challenges in Sierra Leone

Informal financial institutions (Osusu) exist in different villages in Sierra Leone. These ROSCAs meet to deliberate on savings and loans related issues such as the terms and conditions for a loan, the rate of interest on the loan, the maturity period and measures for defaulters. ROSCAs provide short-term loans and are sometimes plagued with insufficient funds to cater to members' loan requests. Defaulters risk losing their assets, which can breed conflicts and resentments among members of the ROSCAs (Rural Finance and Community Improvement Programme, 2013). There is also an enforcement challenge, a situation where a member stops making a deposit before the end of the payment cycle, or where a member gets an unlucky rank and exits the association before making any payments (Anderson et al., in McNabb, LeMay-Boucher, & Bonan, 2019).

The banking sector in Sierra Leone is composed of 14 commercial banks, 17 community banks, 59 financial services associations, 13 microfinance institutions (MFIs) and 3 mobile money operators (World Bank, 2018). One may argue that these institutions can or cannot adequately meet the financial service demands of the over seven million Sierra Leoneans. But a cursory look at the percentage of people living below the income poverty line and the numbers of unemployed youth, market women, household farmers, local traders, etc., who are either financially excluded or unable to access loans from formal financial institutions, show the level of dependence on the ROSCAs. An increasing number of rural dwellers rely on ROSCAs for opportunities to save and obtain loans.

When these ROSCAs cannot extensively meet the demands of individuals in need of informal financial services, there can be negative public opinion or perceptions of their effectiveness. Participant FK/HCA/BS explained that regulatory frameworks are put in place to ensure that the ecosystem is protected in compliance with rules governing credit unions. According to the respondent:

> In the first place, there is legislation enacted in 2010, referred to as the other Financial Act, which among others, created Credit Unions as the informal economy. It is also a provision for financial inclusion that breaks barriers of the formal institution for access to loans. Also, it created the Credit Bureau Act, of 2016

to mitigate the risk of defaulting clients at the credit unions associations and other Micro Finance Institutions. All these acts are to ensure proper financial operations management and compliance systems.

When asked whether there are measures to help support Credit Unions in their business operations in order to sustain them, she elaborated further:

Yes, chief among is providing awareness and education on financial literacy and management of finances in the ecosystem of saving and credit unions. Secondly, providing training and workshops for the credit unions. Proving leverage for NGOs and INGOs to interface with Credit Unions for bench making of best practices. There are robust reforms underway for a proposed amendment for financial interventions on the Savings and Credits associations.

In addition, Small and Medium-scale Enterprises (SMEs), most times, do not get adequate funds from formal financial institutions to tackle organisational issues hence informal financial institutions are depended on to provide loans (Abimbola et al., 2020). This can significantly reduce the funds in the ROSCAs pool and limit members from accessing loans to enhance their economic activities and tackle emergencies.

Tawoponneh's Model of ROSCAs in Sierra Leone

This section provides an overview of the characteristics, benefits and challenges of the Tawoponneh's Model with excerpts from the interview with the respondents.

Provider of Funds

Informal credit institutions are seen as providers of funds for the rural population by the people (Oleka & Eyisi, 2014). This is the case with Tawoponneh Traders Association. According to Participant WC/M/TTA:

Tawoponneh Traders Association was formed by a group of progressive petty traders drawn from small businesses in the Sierre Leone capital, Freetown, in 2005. This Association was established as a Community- Based Organisation immediately after the end of the eleven (11) years of armed conflict in Sierra Leone by the Revolutionary United Front led by Foday Sankoh. This period under view had caused law and order breakdown and grossly affected the economic activities and business environment. As a result, it pervaded the formation of Tawoponneh – local parlance that implies; 'let embrace ourselves and come together.

Composition

On the composition of the membership of the Tawoponneh Traders Association, the respondent continued:

> The Association comprised a group of thirty (30) members and later transformed into a multi-purpose association. During the period, the association was made of thirty (30) members, it was sub-divided into two (2) groups of fifteen (15) individuals that engaged in rotational savings and credit (monthly contributions and disbursement in an ascending order referred to as **"Ashobie"** Loan Scheme). After they realised that its financial standing is improving and strong, particularly with huge savings and growth in its portfolio, a resolution was passed for it to transform into a cooperative society (Participant WC/M/TTA).

Goals and Objectives

Most informal financial associations have goals and objectives. According to Participant WC/M/TTA, the objectives of the Tawaponneh Traders Association include:

(1) Improving the socio-economic status of its membership.
(2) Poverty reduction and alleviation.
(3) Financial management and business development.
(4) Improving credit management.
(5) To be the first traditional indigenous credit bank

Membership Recruitment

The following criteria guide the membership recruitment process into the Tawopnneh Traders Association but are not limited to the following registration fees, buying of shares, opening an account and depositing an initial amount for servicing the account, and savings, buying of copies of bye-laws of the association as the blueprint for its governance, entrance fees, passbook and the loan policy manual. Membership identification is key for proper documentation and contractual capacity in the recovery processes for money management. Some key information to be supplied include name, business address, next of kin and recommendation (guarantor). These constitute the conditions set by the association for admission.

Services Offered

In terms of services offered, Participant WC/M/TTA stated that Tawoponneh offers a broad range of products and services to its members:

> We give loans, savings, dividends on shares, food, housing, edu-financing, health/medical facilitation, trade facilitation for international trade through emergency loan schemes, weddings, funerals, transportation, agriculture through the availability of the following: fertiliser, seeds, livestock, and business management with the following in view; tailoring, maise milling, business startup capital, liquidity, and microfinancing (Participant WC/M/TTA).

These services have been enhanced through the provision of loan schemes and providing business capital, in order to:

(1) Enhance members' economic activities and improve their living standards.
(2) Empower its membership through edu-financing – a platform that provides access to education from elementary school to university.
(3) Enhance advisory services on agricultural farming processes through agricultural extension programs.
(4) Improve export trade volume in international trade by providing access to emergency loans and fast-track transactions for members (Participant WC/M/TTA)

Meeting the Needs of Members

Also, informal financial associations tend to cater for the wellbeing of their members. Tawoponneh Traders Associatioñ improves the living standard of its members in the following ways:

(1) Better education for their children.
(2) Assist the members in sending their wards abroad for greener pastures.
(3) Most small businesses have been transformed into second-generation investments.
(4) Assist the members in building their houses and reducing the rent burden.
(5) Help to improve members' income generation and improve their lifestyles.
(6) Empower members to shift from subsistence to commercialised farming and improve their farming techniques through extension programmes in partnership with the Ministries of Agriculture, Environment, and Food Security (Participant WC/M/TTA).

Meeting the Needs of the Community

The informal financial institutions, just like their formal counterpart, are always searching for opportunities to expand and meet the needs of people in the communities. Participant WC/M/TTA stated that in 2011, a massive reform was carried out by the Government of the former President of Sierra Leone – Ernest

Bai Koroma on doing business and investment climate. This attracted the interest of the Tawoponneh Traders Association to register as a cooperative society through the Department of Cooperative Society under the Ministry of Trade and Industry in Sierra Leone. As a group, it was restricted only to the members. However, because of its growth and expansion, the membership was open to other interested individuals to join the cooperative society through the purchase of shares at a minimal cost of 100,000 Leones (1,000 SSL) which is equivalent to 10 dollars ($10) as at current exchange rate.

Building a Sustainable Model

In terms of building sustainable models for the interest of the members and local communities, there are laid down criteria to ensure survival, which is achieved through the involvement of stakeholders. Participant WC/M/TTA explained:

> In our association, we use robust loan repayment plans, sales of shares, income generation, the interest rate at 2.5%, and engagement with clients on business development through multi-stakeholders meetings.

Building a sustainable model is beneficial to the economy. Expounding on the impact of savings and credit association as an informal economy, Participant EK/ES/SLLC highlighted the following benefits:

> The Labour Congress made a lot of trade-offs with commercial institutions to improve the business operations of our members in the informal economy to participate in the ecosystem of the traditional business of savings and credit. One of the impacts is that it helps to graduate businesses from the credit and saving association, for example, a daily savings of commercial motor bike to tricycle. The Sierra Leone Labour Congress has entered into an agreement with Ecobank and Union Bank to serve as collateral for its members. This has helped to increase their earnings.

Participant WC/M/TTA suggested the following actionable measures to enhance the effectiveness of the Rotating Credit and Savings Association in Sierra Leona; donor funding, institutional capacity building to the informal sectoral development, reducing rigid bureaucracy on financial access, encouraging financial inclusion of the informal economy for investment, and Government support on poverty reduction financial aid packages.

The Challenges

One of the major challenges identified is the loan recovery process. According to Participant EK/ES/SLLC, there is a huge challenge in loan recovery because, most times onus lies on the union and also slow down loan agreement with commercial banks because of credit risk. However, the Union has established networks to monitor compliance with loan repayment. The saving and credit association is a sustainable model of business process and operation as it has predated the colonial period, and the ecosystem is still growing and has grown. Today, they can be formed into formal institutions if they so desire. They have been sustainable because of the absence of rigorous conditions attached to loans. Also, the conspicuous absence of interest rates in the savings and credits associations has helped its sustainability. As in the case of the formal institution, the effect of markup because the loans do not impact customers owing to high charge of interest. It has the ability to address latent functions like funeral solidarity, school fees for wards and marriage rites.

When asked whether it is advisable for actors to invest in the business processes of traditional business operations, the respondent stated:

> Yes, this is a well-organised ecosystem and has survived its operations for a long period. This niche has a lot of potential if supported by investors and further education is given to them on financial management (EK/ES/SLLC).

Sustainability of ROSCA in Sierra Leone

Despite the challenges and having mentioned the benefits of the indigenous savings practice in Sierra Leone, it is important that we are able to identify ways through which the practice has been sustained over the years. One of the participants mentioned financial literature and collaboration with formal structures.

Financial Literacy

When asked if there is any sustainability in the ecosystem of savings and credits associations one of the participants mentioned financial literacy as a key sustainability factor:

> One of the sustainable models is through financial literacy on saving and credit to do prudent spending and allocation of their savings. Another way of sustainability is using collateral in which the union serves as a proxy for its membership. Donor support for SMEs has also contributed to their sustainability. Supervision and due diligence of the leadership (Participant SB/CPED/MEE).

Collaboration With Formal Institutions

On enquiry about whether there are opportunities for the collaboration of informal and formal institutions for a sustainable savings practice, one of the participants stated:

A clear example is the Teacher Union and Ecobank, which have worked collaboratively through a saving and credit partnership in Sierra Leone and have brought the aspect of financial inclusion to deepen poverty alleviation in the ecosystem of the business processes (Participant SB/CPED/MEE).

Discussions

ROSCAs are regarded as veritable informal financial institutions in Sierra Leone. They cater to the needs of individuals who are financially excluded from formal financial institutions and these financial opportunities are accessible to the poorest member of the local communities. They are also patronised by customers of formal financial institutions who do not want to save with the banks. This is most common among the Muslim population in Sierra Leone, particularly individuals that dislike the banks' interest rates. The ease of doing business with ROSCAs makes it attractive to rural dwellers in terms of reduced bureaucracy and little requirements for financial transactions. ROSCAs are also transparent in their operations and dealing with members. They provide rules and guidelines that guide their operations and relations with members.

ROSCAs provide institutional arrangements that extensively support savings and loan opportunities. This is aptly demonstrated by the institutional theory of saving. Most farmers, unemployed individuals and low-income earners in the local communities are eager to engage in different economic activities but lack the financial resources. ROSCAs provide the platform for assisting individuals, households and businesses to engage in savings and obtain loans. The resultant effects are improved living conditions, increased income, rural development, improved agricultural productivity, financial inclusion and economic growth. However, the ROSCAs in Sierra Leone are currently facing an increasing rate of loan requests from farmers, unemployed individuals and low-income earners. Their inability to cater for these sets of individuals places a negative public opinion and perception on their reputation and effectiveness. In addition, the internal conflicts involving punitive measures breed discontentment and discontinuation of the institution. This shows that there is a need for collaboration between the government, business actors, educators (Madichie & Agu, 2022) and entrepreneurs to investigate how to empower the informal financial sector to achieve set goals.

Conclusion

We conclude by affirming that ROSCAs are essential to achieving economic empowerment, rural development and economic growth in Sierra Leone. The impact of these traditional ROSCAs in sub-Saharan Africa, particularly Sierra Leone, is evident in the saving habit of the people, and opportunities to obtain loans for investment and economic activities. These have enhanced the living standard of the people in the local communities. The social and economic relevance of ROSCAs can assist the Government of Sierra Leone to accomplish some of the United Nations' Sustainable Development Goals of 2030 through the tenets of the institutional theory of savings.

Recommendation for Business Actors in Africa

Our first recommendation is that ROSCAs in Sierra Leone should adopt the Tawoponneh model that emphasises mutual help. The private sector has been instrumental in the growth and development of every developed country. The government must provide conducive environment and sound policies to enable ROSCAs economically empower low-income earners, unemployed individuals, farmers, etc. A significant increase in economic activities in the local communities, in the long run, can culminate in national development.

Entrepreneurship development practitioners, agencies and institutions of higher learning should incorporate the informal African economy in their capacity-building framework, as this will enable the training of individuals on traditional and informal methods of mobilising resources for businesses. Lastly, the government should embark on an intensive cash transfer to vulnerable and disadvantaged members of the local communities and also operate low or no interest loans to the unemployed, farmers, low-income earners and traders to productively engage in economic activities that will improve their living standard and contribute meaningfully to the Nation's economy.

This chapter discussed some of the indigenous business practices of savings and credit associations (Osusu) in Sierra Leone. The chapter sought to discuss the impact of ROSCAs on local communities and the Nation. Future research should empirically evaluate the effects of ROSCAs on the living standard of the rural dwellers, agricultural productivity, rural development and financial inclusion. This can be achieved by conducting quantitative and qualitative research to generate data from samples of different ROSCAs in local communities to ascertain their impacts.

References

Abimbola, A. O., Ben-Caleb, E., Adegboyegun, A. E., Eluyela, D. F., Falaye, A. J., & Ajayi, A. S. (2020). Rotating and savings credit association (ROSCAs): A veritable tool for enhancing the performance of micro and small enterprises in Nigeria. *Asian Economic and Financial Review*, *10*(2), 189–199. doi:10.18488/journal.aefr. 2020.102.189.199

Adeola, O., Adeleye, I., Muhammed, G., Olajubu, B. J., Oji, C., & Ibelegbu, O. (2022). Savings groups in Nigeria. In D. T. Redford & G. Verhoef (Eds.), *Transforming Africa* (pp. 193–216). Bingley: Emerald Publishing Limited. doi:10. 1108/978-1-80262-053-520221015

Amankwaha, E., Osei-Koduahb, E., & Boahene, M. A. (2021). Characteristics of Rotating Savings and Credit Associations (ROSCAs) participants in Ghana:

Evidence from Asunafo North Municipality of Ghana. *International Journal of Arts and Social Science*, *4*(1), 213–229.

Amankwah, E., Gockel, F. A., & Osei-Assibey, E. (2019). *Pareto superior dimension of rotating savings and credit associations (ROSCAs) in Ghana: Evidence from Asunafo North Municipality of Ghana.* Munich Personal RePEc Archive.

Athieno, B., Dykstra-McCarthy, E., Stites, E., & Krystalli, R. (2020). *Youth experiences with and access to savings and credit in Karamoja, Uganda.* Boston, MA: Feinstein International Center, Tufts University.

Beverly, S. G., & Sherraden, M. (1999). Institutional determinants of saving: Implications for low-income households and public policy. *The Journal of Socio-Economics*, *28*(4), 457–473.

Feather, C., & Meme, C. K. (2018). Consolidating inclusive housing finance development in Africa: Lessons from Kenyan savings and credit cooperatives. *African Review of Economics and Finance*, *10*(1), 82–107.

Frank, T., Mbabazize, M., & Shukla, J. (2015). Savings and credit cooperatives (SACCO's) services' terms and members' economic development in Rwanda: A case study of Zigama SACCO Ltd. *International Journal of Community and Cooperative Studies*, *3*(2), 1–56.

Fraser, H. K. (2012). Access to finance: The role of microfinance. *Johnson*, *11*(2), 162–172.

Fyle, C. M. (1988). *History and socio-economic development in Sierra Leone: A reader.* Sierra Leone, Freetown: Sladea.

Gbakie, E. S., Kamara, B., & Dumbuya, P. A. F. (2018). New rural finance institutions in Sierra Leone. In CTA. 2018. Experience capitalization: Insights on rural development in West Africa. *Experience capitalization series 3* (pp. 18–23). Wageningen: CTA.

Green, M. (2018). Scripting development through formalization: Accounting for the diffusion of village savings and loans associations in Tanzania. *The Journal of the Royal Anthropological Institute.* doi:10.1111/1467-9655.12966

Johnson, O. E. G. (2011). *Financial sector reform and development in Sierra Leone.* Working Paper 11/0560. International Growth Centre. (pp. 1–47).

Kabuya, F. I. (2015). The Rotating Savings and Credit Associations (ROSCAs): Unregistered sources of credit in local communities. *IOSR Journal of Humanities And Social Science (IOSR-JHSS)*, *20*(8), 95–98. doi:10.9790/0837-20849598

Leigh, E. S. E. (2004). *The Sierra Leone financial system.* Bloomington, IN: Author House.

Lukwa, A. T., Odunitan-Wayas, F., Lambert, E. V., & Alaba, O. A. (2022). Can Informal Savings Groups Promote Food Security and Social, Economic, and Health Transformations, Especially among Women in Urban Sub-Saharan Africa: A Narrative Systematic Review. *Sustainability*, *14*, 3153. doi:10.3390/su14063153

Madichie, N. O., & Agu, A. G. (2022). The role of universities in scaling up informal entrepreneurship. *Industry and Higher Education.* doi:10.1177/09504222221101548

Mahdi, I. R. E. (2016). *Access to credit, indebtedness, and debt refinancing amongst micro enterprises in Freetown, Sierra Leone: An institutional approach.* Ph.D. thesis, SOAS, University of London.

Mahdi, I. (2018). *Informal finance in Sierra Leone: Why and how it fits into the financial system.* Retrieved from https://www.findevgateway.org/sites/default/files/publications/files/informal_finance_in_sierra_leone-working_paper_i.m_final_160718_1.pdf

Mbizi, R., & Gwangwava, E. (2013). Rotating savings and credit associations: An alternative funding for sustainable micro-enterprise: Case of Chinhoyi, Zimbabwe. *Journal of Sustainable Development in Africa, 15*(7), 1520–5509.

McNabb, K., LeMay-Boucher, P., & Bonan, J. (2019). Enforcement problems in ROSCAs: Evidence from Benin. *European Journal of Development Research, 31*, 1389–1415. doi:10.1057/s41287-019-00215-5

Olando, C. O., Mbewa, M. O., & Jagongo, A. (2012). Financial practice as a determinant of growth of savings and credit co-operative societies' wealth (A Pointer to Overcoming Poverty Challenges in Kenya and the Region). *International Journal of Business and Social Science, 3*(24), 204–219.

Oleka, C., & Eyisi, N. (2014). The effect of informal financial institutions on poverty alleviation in Nigeria. *Journal of Economics and Sustainable Development, 5*(6), 100–107.

Rural Finance and Community Improvement Programme. (2013). *Sierra Leone: Detailed design report.* West and Central Africa Division Programme Management Department.

Sheriff, D. M., & Quee, S. P. (2020). The role of informal financial sectors in domestic fund mobilization in the Eastern region. A case study of Kenema, Kailahun and Kono Districts in Sierra Leone. *Global Scientific Journal, 8*(9), 1252–1263. Online: ISSN 2320-9186.

Sherraden, M. (1991). *Assets and the poor: A new American welfare policy.* Armonk, NY: M.E. Sharpe, Inc.

Sierra Leone Trade Journal. (1961). *Freetown? Ministry of information and broadcasting.* Freetown: Ministry of Information and Broadcasting on Behalf of the Ministry of Trade and Industry.

Sutton, S., Momo, S., & Aeckert, S. (2012). *Social & political perspectives on microfinance (Sierra Leone). Breaking the cycle of political and economic marginalization.* Spanda Foundation Spanda Papers 8, Spanda Publishing, The Hague, pp. 1–24.

United Nations. (2022). The United Nations in Sierra Leone. Retrieved from https://sierraleone.un.org/en/about/about-the-un

World Bank. (2018). *Combined project information documents/integrated safeguards datasheet (PID/ISDS).* Retrieved from http://documents.worldbank.org/curated/en/311571542650741656/pdf/Project-Information-Document-Integrated-Safeguards-Data-Sheet-Sierra-Leone-Financial-Inclusion-Project-P166601.pdf

World Bank. (2022). The World Bank in Sierra Leone. Retrieved from https://www.worldbank.org/en/country/sierraleone/overview#3

World Food Programme. (2022). *Sierra Leone.* Retrieved from https://www.wfp.org/countries/sierra-leone

Zikalala, M. J. (2016). *The role of savings and credit cooperatives in promoting access to credit in Swaziland.* Thesis for the degree of Master of Science in Agriculture (Agricultural Economics) in the Department of Agricultural Economics, Extension and Rural Development, Faculty of Natural and Agricultural Science. University of Pretoria, Pretoria, South Africa.

Chapter 8

Structure of Indigenous Savings Groups in Nigeria: Cases and Implications for Business Actors

Ogechi Adeola, Ifedapo Adeleye, Oserere Ibelegbu,
Babalola Josiah Olajubu and Isaiah Adisa

Abstract

This chapter presents case studies that explore the structures of indigenous savings group practices in Nigeria. Indigenous savings groups in Nigeria can be categorised as either unstructured, semi-structured or structured. These categorisation of savings groups can follow two patterns, which include Rotating Savings and Credit Associations (ROSCAs) and Accumulated Savings and Credit Associations (ASCAs). Through a qualitative case analysis of savings practices in Nigeria, we observed that the indigenous savings groups have similar goals and orientations, though their operating structures differ. The chapter highlighted the relative theme that cuts across these cases, and insightful recommendations are provided for upscaling and adopting indigenous savings groups in Nigeria and Africa. The chapter also discusses the role of government in facilitating savings and credit disbursement to groups. The implications for business actors and the government are highlighted.

Keywords: Indigenous savings groups; rotating savings and credit associations (ROSCAs); accumulated savings and credit associations (ASCAs); Nigeria; Africa; structures

Introduction

The significance of indigenous savings in Africa's informal financial sector and the economy cannot be overemphasised. Savings serve as a source of credit facility, mostly from individuals or groups offering low-risk capital contributions (Adeola et al., 2022). Besides being a source of credit facilities, savings is a scheme that

Casebook of Indigenous Business Practices in Africa, 141–159
Copyright © 2023 Ogechi Adeola, Ifedapo Adeleye, Oserere Ibelegbu, Babalola Josiah Olajubu and Isaiah Adisa
Published under exclusive licence by Emerald Publishing Limited
doi:10.1108/978-1-80455-762-420231015

helps to mitigate poverty and facilitate the growth of indigenous businesses in rural areas (Nnama-Okechukwu et al., 2019). People in rural areas have very limited access to capital from formal financial institutions; a causal factor may be their limited financial literacy (Adeola et al., 2022). In spite of the limitations, there is a need for people to save, particularly indigenous business owners (Iwara, Adeola, & Netshandama, 2021). Herrington and Coduras (2019) and Gyimah and Lussier (2021) highlighted prompt access to finance as one of the major challenges facing indigenous businesses, and this inhibits expansion. Therefore, indigenous savings groups have become essential in meeting this crucial need.

As documented in Adeola et al. (2022), savings groups in Africa existed before the formal financial institutions were introduced. For instance, in Ghana, these groups are referred to as 'Susu' (Gyimah & Boachie, 2018; Nnama-Okechukwu et al., 2019); in South Africa, it is called 'Stokvel' (Iwara et al., 2021), and 'Chama' in Kenya (Sile & Bett, 2015). Savings groups have a systematic structure of operation that is agreed upon by the members (Adeola et al., 2022). The members possess specific attributes and values, which include, but are not limited to, sharing the same faith, engaging in similar occupations, living in the same neighbourhood, working in the same place, or being of the same ethnic group. Monetary contributions are an agreed fixed amount usually paid by members periodically, for instance, weekly or monthly. These savings groups also provide short-term micro-lending to members in accordance with the principles guiding the group (Gyimah & Boachie, 2018).

In Nigeria, savings culture is a common practice that cuts across all ethnic groups with different saving mechanisms (Adeola et al., 2022). History has it that the culture of savings in the country can be traced back to the sixteenth century (Lawal & Abdullahi, 2011). Oranu, Onah, and Nkhonjera (2020) submit that the two most common patterns of savings groups are Rotating Savings and Credit Associations (ROSCAs) and Accumulated Savings and Credit Associations (ASCAs). The difference between ROSCAs and ASCAs lies in their mode of collection and disbursement (Adeola et al., 2022). ROSCA, just as the name implies, involves members contributing a fixed amount either daily, weekly or monthly, and the whole sum is disbursed to one member at the end of each period as agreed by members. Also, the order in which every member gets the large pool of funds is usually based on balloting or by consensus (Osabuohien & Ola-David, 2018). Oranu et al. (2020) highlight short-term forced savings as a major incentive for ROSCA members. Without the existence of ROSCAs, Jerome (1991) emphasises that the poor rural inhabitants would continue to remain at the mercy of moneylenders. Hence, the three major roles ROSCAs play in the rural areas include (i) encouraging savings habits, (ii) mobilising savings from the rural areas and (iii) providing loan facilities to members.

ASCAs, on the other hand, involve members making regular contributions to be kept for an agreed period, which is usually a year. Thereafter, members have the freedom to withdraw and/or keep making deposits until they are ready to quit the group, and this is done voluntarily. In the ASCA arrangement, members can take loans and pay back with interest. Amongst the Yorubas, ASCA is referred to as 'Ajo'. In this case, there is usually an individual known as 'Alajo' (The

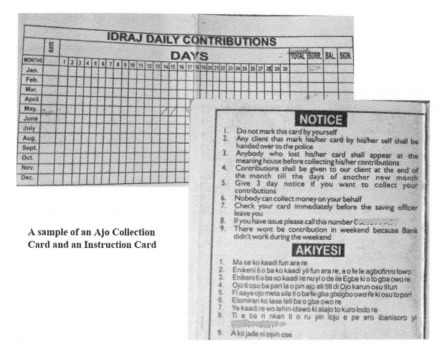

A sample of an Ajo Collection Card and an Instruction Card

Fig. 1.   A Sample of an Ajo Collection Card.

Collector) responsible for the collections. Based on consensual agreement, savers pay a fixed amount to the Alajo at regular intervals, which is usually recorded in the contributor's card (see Fig. 1) and will be withdrawn at the end of an agreed period. The Alajo visits each member's location to collect the contribution on the set days, serving as a form of mobile bank.

ROSCAs and ASCAs have spread from Nigeria to other West African countries, including Ghana, the Democratic Republic of Congo, Liberia (Seibel, 2004), Benin, Burkina-Faso, Cote D'Ivoire, Gambia, Togo, Sierra Leone, Mali, among others (Oranu et al., 2020). ROSCAs have indigenous names in various parts of Nigeria, some of which are in the Southeastern part of Nigeria, mainly inhabited by the Igbos, it is called 'Isusu/oha/ogbo', the Yorubas of the Southwest call it 'Esusu'; in the South-South, it is known as 'Osusu/Asun' in Edo state, 'Etibe' by Ibibio, 'Oku' by Kalabari, and the Hausas/Nupe of Northern Nigeria refer to it as 'Adashi/Dashi' (Adeola et al., 2022; Oranu et al., 2020).

Aside from the ROSCAs and ASCAs categorisation of a savings association (noted as patterns in this chapter), there are different structures that have been identified through serendipity in the process of exploring savings associations in Nigeria. In this chapter, we identify the various structures of indigenous savings groups in Nigeria utilising the case study design. Through the case analysis in this chapter, we identified unstructured, semi-structured and structured savings groups. We also examined the role of government in advancing indigenous savings groups in Nigeria and Africa.

The rest of the chapter is structured as follows. In the next section, we present the case studies on the indigenous savings groups in their various structures as well as the elements that define them. Next, we discuss the similarities and dissimilarities between the three forms of savings groups in relation to identified themes, which include risk, membership, partnership with government/formal financial institution, ease of creation and the pattern. Lastly, we provide the practical implications from the cases, as well as the conclusions.

Case Studies on Indigenous Savings Groups

To conduct this research, the narrative qualitative approach was employed. For each case, a key informant interview is conducted, and the responses used to develop the narrative in the study chapter as well as the informed recommendations for business actors in Africa and across the globe. Cases one and two are unstructured indigenous savings groups, while cases three and four are semi-structured and structured indigenous savings groups, respectively.

Case 1: Neighbourhood Weekly Rotational Savings (Ajo-Etile) in Abeokuta Metropolis

Formation in an Unstructured Savings Group

Mrs Ayedun is a 60-year-old grocery trader who resides in the Abeokuta metropolis. She holds a savings bank account, one current (checking) account, and one microfinance account, and she also contributes to an Ajo-etile (neighbourhood savings group/Ajo). The group consists of 15 members who had agreed on the amount of money to be contributed weekly when the group was formed.

Mrs Ayedun described the steps taken to create this form of savings group:

(1) Members choose a group leader among themselves.
(2) Numbers are written on slips of paper, one or more numbers for each member, depending on how many contributions they make each week. Members draw a number, and that decides the order in which members will receive their contribution. For example, if a person picks number four, he or she will receive the accumulated contribution by the end of the fourth week. If a member draws a number that is not convenient, the member can exchange the number picked with another member who is interested.
(3) Members give their weekly contributions to the group leader before the end of each week.
(4) At the end of the week, the group leader gives the week's accumulated savings to the pre-determined member, whose turn it is to collect the savings.

Money Disbursement Process

Mrs Ayedun explained that when members have two or three slots (i.e. they make two or three contributions per week), they frequently swap numbers in order to make their numbers sequential to receive their 'turns' (weekly savings/payments).

Mrs Ayedun stated that members hope they will not pick the least number because the person to receive last is always at risk since every other person has received their part of the contribution and are less likely to commit to the savings group by turning in their contribution promptly. She explained that this lack of commitment is a serious drawback of the plan, and even when she is not given the last number, she remains anxious until she receives her payment. She shared that she is also less motivated to continue contributing to the group savings after receiving her payment, but she continues with the savings to maintain her integrity as she had agreed to make specific contributions.

The savings group has been Mrs Ayedun's main source of income because she is a retiree. She relies on her Ajo-etile to expand her business and to finance her last child's education in a tertiary institution. Though this method does not include credit facilities, if someone is in urgent need of an amount of money greater than what has been saved, that member can borrow from another member who is able to lend it.

Mrs Ayedun stated that she prefers Ajo-etile to any other Ajo because she knows every member well; hence, she cannot be duped. She shared her previous experiences with dishonest thrift collectors who had cheated her.

Case 2: *Monthly Rotational Savings Among Youth Corps Members in Ibadan*

The National Youth Service Corps (NYSC) initiative of Nigeria's federal government was established on 22 May 1973, to bring Nigerian college graduates from different ethnic backgrounds and geographical locations into contact with other cultures. Its goal is to enhance the exposure and human capacity development of Nigerian youths who have completed their tertiary education before the age of 30. The enroled graduates are generally called youth corps members.

Ms Stephanie, a 29-year-old youth corps member, serving at Oyo State Secretariat, Ibadan claimed to have four savings accounts with different commercial banks. She also belongs to a savings group organised by a fellow corps member. The group consists of 10 members who contribute ₦10,000 ($27.8USD)[1] monthly. She explained that a WhatsApp group was created by a member who emerged as group leader because she initiated the savings group idea. The group leader gave each member a number which served as a 'pointer' to when each member will receive their payment. The group leader took the highest number, making her the last person to be paid, and provided the service for free; the members paid no service charge.

Ms Stephanie said that a requirement for being a youth corps savings group member was to have a bank account that could be accessed through mobile devices. The group leader posts the account number of the person receiving payment for that month on the group's WhatsApp page. Immediately, corps member participating in the savings are expected to send their contribution to the person who will benefit from that month's savings. The beneficiary must, in response, acknowledge every payment received on the group's WhatsApp page.

She stressed that there had been no default issue because every member receives their 'allawee' (allowance) on the same day. The savings group, she said, has provided the needed funds for most of them planning to start a business and has also helped them to cultivate a savings habit.

When asked why she would not prefer to use any of her bank accounts to save money, she explained that she is at risk of careless spending of small amounts of money. Saving with the group motivates her to keep saving until she receives her distribution of ₦100,000 ($277.80USD).[1] Having that large sum of money makes her reluctant to spend it on frivolities.

Outcomes of Unstructured Practices

Most thrift contributors who reside in urban areas are aware of the availability and importance of commercial banks. Nevertheless, they consider Ajo and Esusu as catalysts to expanding their businesses and living a better life. Through Ajo, they are able to save small amounts of money, and at the end of every month or week, they collect their accumulated savings and, perhaps, deposit those savings in a commercial bank to save 'bigger'.

Another advantage of a thrift savings system is that the thrift collector visits the contributing members on a daily basis, which reduces or eliminates the pro-crastination associated with having to go to the bank just to save a small amount of money.

Mrs Ayedun, in the case discussed earlier, agreed that the Ajo/Esusu helps people who urgently need money. In fact, the system saves people the embar-rassment of searching for someone who will lend them the money needed to meet an urgent need. Instead, they turn to either their thrift collector or savings group for assistance.

Despite the advantages associated with savings groups, there are also some disadvantages. As pointed out by Mrs Ayedun, one needs to be cautious when joining a savings group, and it is wise to join a group whose members are well known to you. This familiarity reduces the chances of being duped.

Another risk is that once a member receives their contribution, especially in rotational savings plans, that member may not be motivated to continue saving, a choice that will have a negative effect on other members. Having the last number in a rotational savings plan increases the probability of losing one's savings since many members who have been previously settled might not continue the savings process.

The withdrawal or death of a member in a rotational savings group disrupts the expected contributions and, invariably, the benefits to the remaining members.

Case 3: Association of Thrift Collectors (ATCI) Ibadan, Oyo State, Nigeria

Context of ATCI

The ATCI was established in 1999 for most thrift collectors in Ibadan, though membership is not compulsory. The association is headed by Mr Gbadamosi Eniitan (aka *Baba Aranse*). In an interview with Baba Aranse, he stated that the association was yet to be registered under the Corporate Affairs Commission (CAC) but was recognised by the Ibadan secretariat (regional local government council), which requires payment of certain dues. He explained that since the association's inception, they had sought loans from various banks and micro-finance banks, but all efforts proved challenging. Therefore, the association was formed with the sole aim of pulling resources together to be able to provide loan facilities to its members.

ATCI had 202 members (as of 2019):

- Gender distribution: 57 males and 145 females
- Education: 112, Basic; 64, Junior Secondary School Certificate Examination (JSCE); 26, Senior Secondary School Certificate Examination (SSCE)
- Age: 28–57 years age range with an average of 42.56 years

Fig. 2 describes the relationship between ATCI, the thrift collectors, and the thrift contributors.

An indirect relationship exists when ATCI does not render services directly to thrift contributors; in this case, the contributors are not officially recognised by ATCI. Hence, the contributors relate directly with the thrift collectors. The thrift collectors have a direct relationship with ATCI. ATCI transacts with or renders services to these thrift collectors, officially recognised as members of ATCI. The implication is that with the direct relationship between the thrift collectors and ATCI, thrift contributors only conduct transactions with the thrift collector and not ATCI, though there is an indirect relationship between these contributors and ATCI.

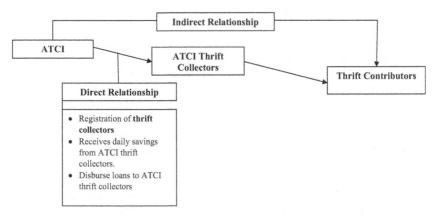

Fig. 2. Relationships between ATCI, Thrift Collectors and Thrift Contributors.

ATCI members visit the head office (the association venue) usually in the evenings at the close of business to deposit contributions meant for accumulating savings. If they are unable to make it to the venue, they have middlemen who are also thrift collectors who receive and make deposit on their behalf. At regular Sunday meetings, they pay a weekly due of ₦200 ($0.56USD[1]) for the administration of the association. New customers (contributors) do not register with the association but register personally with the thrift collectors. Upon registration, a new contributor buys a record card which will be in his/her possession and will be used to record each savings instance, be it daily, weekly or monthly. Contributors choose a rotational or accumulating savings plan. Thrift collectors prefer accumulating savings plans because it is a more effective strategy for people who are close to one another.

After registration, the member decides on the amount to be saved with the knowledge that the amount cannot be changed until savings have been accumulated as agreed. The first contribution is the thrift collector's commission.

Advantages of the Association

If a thrift collector, due to death or disability, can no longer function, their record book is retrieved. The collector's customers are contacted and allowed to choose whether to continue the savings with another collector or collect their money after one month. If the collector is merely incapacitated, he or she returns the contributors' money immediately, depending on the accessibility of funds.

Other advantages include but are not limited to:

* Saving money for members
* Lending a helping hand to members in times of financial crisis
* Providing loans to members for either personal or business purposes

Challenges

Although most members interviewed agreed that thrift collection depends on trust on the part of the collector, the contributor and the association, they also believed that risk is part of the game of every business venture.

Majority of the thrift collectors interviewed described the experience of having a contributor default on a loan. The number of worst-case scenarios experienced by thrift collectors depended on how long they had been in the business. Some thrift collectors even reported that they had to change their location frequently because once someone defaults on a loan, it negatively affects two or three and sometimes four other contributors. If the collector cannot get assistance from the association (which is very rare), they had to 'dodge' the affected contributors to prevent embarrassment. Some contributors recounted experiences of being duped. Nevertheless, in instances where the collectors belong to an association such as ATCI, collectors duping contributors have fewer incidents.

Most thrift collectors reported that they have only personal bank accounts and no special accounts for their businesses since all they have to do is get their contributors' money to the association's head office, where it is banked. The association itself has only a single association account with three banks (undisclosed). The only business they conduct with the bank is saving and withdrawal of funds. They have no credit relationship with these banks because they could not meet the criteria for obtaining a loan.

Other challenges faced by the Association include:

- Some members of the Association default on loans, though infrequently
- A huge loan default at the Association level can affect every member of the organisation
- Thrift collectors are an easy target for thieves; virtually every collector reported having been attacked by thieves as many as three times.
- Some thrift collectors, due to robbery or contributors' loan defaults, have experienced health issues (e.g. depression, anxiety, high blood pressure)
- Some contributors have reported being duped by collectors. However, the bone of contention seems to be that some or most of these contributors continued saving with the collector that once duped them. The reason for their loyalty is that some of the collectors who have once duped them have also helped them resuscitate their crumbling business. On the other hand, some contributors believe 'God understands' (*Oye Olohun*).

Assessing ATCI's Relationship With Formal Financial Institutions

When asked if they had a bank account with a formal financial institution, 50% of the thrift collectors and thrift contributors responded that they had accounts with a formal financial institution, but they differed in the types of financial institutions they chose. While the thrift collectors mostly had accounts with commercial banks, a large number of thrift contributors mostly chose microfinance banks and cooperative societies. The reason for these choices seems to be that most thrift collectors have formal education and are knowledgeable about processes in commercial banks, but many thrift contributors are without formal education; thus, the rigour of filling out the forms to open accounts or deposit/withdrawal slips or even communicating in languages different from their indigenous languages discouraged them from patronising commercial banks.

Most thrift contributors who patronised formal financial institutions, especially microfinance banks, did so because they were able to access loans. Nevertheless, some thrift contributors may not apply for microfinance bank loans because of the embarrassment they would likely experience if they defaulted. While some of the respondents could access loans from microfinance banks, most were unable to access loans from commercial banks.

Thrift collectors and contributors prefer their savings group – the 'poor people's bank' – to other formal financial institutions, citing numerous benefits of the groups:

- Easy access to zero-interest loans.
- Convenience. Thrift collectors visit members' homes, shops, or workplaces to collect their savings, eliminating the need to go to the banks.

- No language barriers or problems filling out forms. Most collectors are able to communicate with their contributors in their indigenous languages.
- Collectors give gifts to their contributors at the end of the year in appreciation for their membership and contributions.

Assessing Economic Outcomes

Based on association records and data, from June 2018 to January 2019, the association receives an average contribution in millions from members participating in the accumulated savings plan (non-rotational funds) retained in the accumulated savings plan are only for the benefit of customers who maintain membership in the plan. The association prefers contributions from accumulated savings because it has a longer maturity span of at least one month and at most one year, which facilitates the capacity to disburse loans. Generally, most customers prefer collecting their savings at the end of the year. Baba Aranse, one of the thrift collectors, interviewed, stressed that:

> ... thrift collectors risk losing customers if they are not buoyant enough to offer loans, to which every member is entitled, therefore a good pool of funds at their disposal is advantageous.

From the association's records, the largest loan that has been offered to a single individual was ₦2million ($5,555.00USD[1]) which was to be paid back repaid in six months. Loans are given to customers based on the amount and consistency of their savings, and the borrower must have been a customer for at least eight months. It is, therefore, easy to obtain loans from thrift collectors as it attracts no interest, no collateral, and no guarantor. The only condition attached is that the borrower must have a fixed location like a shop or house known to the association.

Most thrift contributors would rather save with their thrift collectors than with commercial banks. Most thrift collectors prefer depositing savings contributions with the association on a daily basis rather than saving with other financial institutions. Nevertheless, thrift collectors generally conduct other financial transactions, including personal savings accounts with commercial banks.

In summary, this case study has defined the limits of formal financial institutions when compared to ATCI, which has effectively provided members with interest-free loans, motivated members to save, and rendered convenient financial services to members.

Case 4: The Trust Fund Model and Savings Group Under the Agricultural Credit Guarantee Scheme

Context of Trust Fund Model

This case investigates the role of the government in facilitating savings and credit for the agricultural sector using a Trust Fund Model (TFM) that encourages small group savings by farmers and identified stakeholders and provides funding interventions to these small groups. The crucial role of regulatory authorities in encouraging savings by providing a platform for oil companies, state/local governments and non-governmental organisations (NGOs) to participate in a TFM is also discussed.

Establishment

The government established the Agricultural Credit Guarantee Scheme Fund (ACGSF) in 1977 to guarantee bank loans advanced to the agricultural sector (Olaitan, 2006). Over the years, ACGSF adopted various models to ensure the sustainable operation of its programme, including the Self-Help Group Linkage Banking, Interest Draw Back, Refinancing, and Rediscounting Facility and, more recently, the Trust Fund Model (Olajide & Aderolu, 2017). To encourage group savings, the Self-Help Group Linkage programme, launched under the ACGSF in 1991, became operational in 1992. According to the Central Bank of Nigeria (CBN) website, farmers are advised to form groups of between 5 to 15 people that agree on a common purpose, to encourage and cultivate a consistent saving habit with any bank of their choice. After six months, the group or cluster may apply for a loan from their preferred bank.

The primary aim of the self-help group is to instil a culture of savings, encourage banking services amongst group members, and enable them to finance farm projects. In essence, group members are better placed to leverage savings accumulated over the previous six months and qualify for a partner bank loan, which is different from typical bank loans. It is a scheme designed to make farmers more productive (CBN, 2019a).

The CBN, however, expanded the Self-Help Groups Linkage Banking by introducing the Trust Fund Model to accommodate participants, which include State Governments and blue-chip companies willing to provide funds for farmers within their catchment areas or in the host communities where they operate (CBN, 2019b; Olaitan, 2006). TFM also seeks to encourage savings mobilisation through groups and associations to enable the latter to have access to loans. The main objective of TFM is 'to assist farmers access loans, create a good credit history, induce savings culture, help in creating enterprise and also incentive-based if repayment of facility is made promptly within the agreed period. This arrangement was intended to help in ameliorating the problem of collateral requirements by commercial banks' (Olajide & Aderolu, 2017, p. 40).

Dr Garzali Muhammed of CBN Development Finance Department provided more insight into the reasons for the TFM, particularly concerning savings and loans:

> The need to encourage lending to the agricultural sector was the prime objective of the scheme. The project rationale is a consideration of the fact that micro-entrepreneurs require credit facilities to finance their business. Additionally, the need to create an ecosystem that's beneficial to stakeholders, where farmers mobilise some form of savings for their business and the banks have some contingency (collateral) for their agricultural lending

(Interview with *Dr Garzali Muhammed*, Development Finance Department of the Central Bank of Nigeria).

The Trust Fund Model framework was developed in 2005 under the Agricultural Credit Guarantee Scheme Fund (ACGSF) to facilitate credit provision to the agricultural and real sectors in response to the changes in the money market occasioned by the deregulation of the economy. With the deregulation of the economy and increased competition since 1986, banks exhibited greater flexibility to channel their resources to investment options offering the highest returns and minimal risks.

Just as agriculture had inherent risks, agricultural financing also was characterised by specific inherent risks. In the face of such risks, the volume of new loans dropped, and the number of banks operating under ACGSF fell drastically from 34 in 1989 to 6 by mid-2000 (Olaitan, 2006). The peasant, and unsophisticated farmers, with no collateral to secure bank loans, were even more adversely affected. Even the meagre savings of the groups of self-help farmers, accepted as collateral at the time by some banks, became unattractive. Consequently, the TFM was developed. The TFM combines the cost-effective group-lending approach with the availability of readily realisable cash security that reduces the credit risks of the lending banks.

Features of the Model
Under the TFM, oil companies, state/local governments, and NGOs place funds in trust with the lending bank to augment the small-group savings of the farmers in their states or area of operation. Under the arrangement, the TFM secures 25%, or more of the intended loans of the prospective borrowers, the farmers' savings secure another 25%, and ACGSF guarantees 75% of the remaining 50%. This leaves the lending banks with only 12.5% risk exposure, a feature that has proven very attractive to the banks. Therefore, the amount of a loan each individual farmer group can obtain depends on the amount of their savings, the expected cost of the proposed project, and the size of the trust fund available from the state/local government, oil company, or NGO.

Modalities
Implementation of a TFM loan requires the following steps:

- The state government makes adequate preparation and agrees to commit funds in demonstration of the government's resolve to improve the fortune of the rural farmers and alleviate poverty. Those funds are deposited with the lending banks to establish credit capacity under the programme to support the funding needs of farmers in the state.
- A bank's interest in participating in the programme includes an initial meeting with the state, after which the government will identify and select banks that are suitable to participate in the Trust Fund Model.

- The programme manager of the State Agricultural Development Program (ADP) initiates the process of identifying, screening, and organising the farmers into groups. The farmers are encouraged to begin saving with the designated banks since group savings such as cash security is an important component of the model.
- These important steps are then followed by a tripartite meeting of the state government, the lending banks, and the Central Bank of Nigeria, leading to the execution of a memorandum of understanding (MOU) by all parties involved.
- Finally, the state government would deposit the agreed-upon trust funds with the partner banks to signal the launch of the programme.
- The mode of application process is essentially the same as those under ACGSF.

As noted earlier, the amount of credit each farmers group can access would depend on the level of savings the farmer can muster, the cost of the proposed project, and the availability of trust funds. However, the senior Central Bank official stressed that the state government, taking into consideration the capacity of the poor farmers in the state, can decide to increase its stake beyond 25% in order to assist farmers who may be unable to provide sufficient savings to qualify for an adequate loan. The pre-condition for this variation of the lending rules, however, is that farmers should mobilise savings in groups, which itself has inherent challenges. To ameliorate this problem, farmers utilise the self-help groups of 5–15 members to achieve the requisite threshold of saving 25% of the loanable funds, which makes up their contribution.

Impact of TFM
On the impact of the TFM, Dr Garzali Muhammed stressed that:

> TFM's role in financial mediation in agricultural lending had recorded some successes. For instance, in the Niger-Delta area, the Shell Petroleum Development Company (SPDC) adopted this agricultural finance model in favour of farmers in their host communities. A memorandum of understanding (MOU) between the partners (Shell, Lending Banks and the CBN) specifying the duties and obligations of each of the parties was signed, and the program was code-named Micro Credit Scheme for Agricultural Development (MCSAD). The Agip Oil Company in a similar move also signed an MOU for its program, code-named Green Card.

Some state governments have also adopted this model to improve the fortunes of their rural farmers and alleviate poverty in the states. The Katsina State Government raised a Rural Development Loan from the International Fund for Agricultural Development (IFAD) and placed a part of it with a partner lending bank to enable the effective disbursement of credit facilities to the rural farmers.

Under this arrangement, the farmers' savings groups secured 25% of the loans, the TFM secured 25%, and ACGF guaranteed 75% of the balance of 50% of the loan.

The strategy has also been used by other state governments and local government councils to re-position farmers to enable them to gain access to credit from banks. The Jigawa State Government Trust Fund for Agricultural Development invested about ₦50million (about $139,000USD[1]) in the project. Cross River State, with the goal of enhancing agriculture, requested all the local government areas to contribute ₦2million (about $5,556USD[1]) each to the State Trust Fund for agricultural finance intermediation.

Encouraged by inquiries about being registered on the programme, the CBN intends to pursue replication of the model in all the states of the federation to enhance credit purveyance to the agricultural sector. Despite the successes, there are some drawbacks. According to a senior Central Bank official:

> The farmers usually find it challenging to raise the 25% individually; therefore, group savings are encouraged.

Olajide and Aderolu (2017), in their research on the effect of TFM on the welfare of farmers' households in Oyo State of Nigeria, found that administrative bottlenecks in funds disbursement, including delays in the disbursement of approved loans and lack of awareness of the programme, were amongst the major disincentives of the Fund (Olajide & Aderolu, 2017).

Future Outlook

Olajide and Aderolu (2017) found that most beneficiaries of TFM in their survey of 134 farmers were adult males, with a male to female ratio of 85%–15%. There is a need to encourage greater participation amongst women to enhance inclusiveness. Increasing awareness of the fund, removing administrative bottlenecks related to funds disbursement, and an increase in the availability of loan funds, are important challenges to resolve. Self-help savings group formation should be encouraged to improve savings opportunities amongst the farmers. Incentives for increased participation by stakeholders, particularly the state governments, should be considered. In futuristic terms, the senior executive was confident that the state government's provision of the 25% collateral requirement would increase the scheme's patronage.

Discussion

Some distinguishing factors across the structures identified in all the cases include the method of operation, relationship with formal financial institutions, availability of parent association, risk and method of funds disbursement. For example, the unstructured savings groups association (either rotative or accumulative) has a higher level of risk for contributors if the collector dies or a contributor defaults in repayments, unlike the semi-structured and structured where there is an association to protect the funds of contributors and provides risk management outcomes. However, the unstructured savings group provides benefits for rural dwellers, the less educated and those in small communities who wish to access loans and contributions faster to meet their financial needs. With less formality and ease of formation, unstructured savings has thrived in the low-income environment and has enhanced social cohesion among community members.

What differentiates the semi-structured and the structured is the partnership with a government institution, formal financial institutions, the target audience, and the contributory nature of contributors that is present in the latter but absent in the former. Semi-structured savings group provides associations that will regulate the actions of a thrift collector towards protecting the contributors. The semi-structured savings scheme will also encourage relationships with the formal financial institution to the thrift collector so as to reduce the risk associated with holding cash in a highly unsecured social environment. Table 1 shows the differences and similarities among the three structures.

The overarching narrative for all the three structures is that they all provide a systemic savings culture that allows members to experience the ease of financial accessibility towards meeting their personal and business needs. However, despite the success of the various savings groups identified, there is room for upscaling towards a better performance.

Implications for Business Actors

The structure of indigenous savings groups should be of interest to business actors wishing to obtain finance for their businesses and also to financial institutions that give loans to target customers, particularly small and medium-scale enterprises (SMEs). Access to business funding or capital has always been challenging for SMEs in Africa. Additionally, access to finance is one of the biggest obstacles for SMEs identified in 71% of countries in Africa, according to a World Bank report (World Bank Ghana Office, n.d.). In the report, 20% of SMEs mentioned that access to finance is a major constraint to their business, with commercial banks declining to offer loans to businesses that do not fit their models (World Bank Ghana Office, n.d.). Rather than waiting for banks with stringent collateral requirements and huge interest rates, SMEs in Africa with limited access to loans from commercial banks and other formal lending institutions can:

i. *Create Associations to Pool Financial Resources*
    SMEs can incorporate lessons from the ATCI by creating an association that will pool resources together from members' contributions for members who need financial aid for their business activities. Having a business association should not be for regulating members' activities alone but also meeting the financial needs of members. The challenges of accessibility to loans which SMEs are plagued with in Africa will gradually be eased if SMEs can create a savings scheme among its members that enables the provision of loans

Table 1. Cross-Cases Analysis of the Similarities and Differences in the Indigenous Savings Structures.

Themes	Unstructured	Semi-structured	Structured
Risk	High level of risk	Regulated risk by the association	Regulated risk by government and financial institution
Membership	• Less educated • A sense of community relationship • Ease of membership	• Characterised by more educated elites • Regulated membership process	• Focused on farmers • Membership in groups for targeted project
Partnership with government/ formal financial institution	No government partnership or financial institutions	Partnership with financial institutions through the collector and the association	Partnership with government and financial institution
Ease of creation	Easy to establish	Regulated establishment process by the association	Established to carry out an agricultural project
Pattern	Can be both rotative and accumulative savings patterns (ROSCA and ASCA)	Mostly accumulated savings pattern (ASCA)	Contributory accumulative pattern (members contribute 25% of total savings)

Source: Authors' compilation.

according to your contribution. Just as the practice of all savings groups, the members can freely withdraw from the association, in as much as such member has no debt to pay. Also, making credit facilities available to members of existing SMEs association or establishing a new venture that focuses on this will improve financial availability for SMEs in Africa.

ii. *Partner With Government and Financial Services*
Lessons must be learnt from the relationship between farmers, the CBN and the government, as discussed in this chapter. The relationship allows the farmers to form groups and contribute 25% of their financial needs while the

government and financial institutions provide the rest. However, the caveat remains – forming a group and having a target project. SMEs can also learn from this initiative by coming together, identifying their separate business goals, create a proposal that will allow for an evaluation of business intentions which will be screened in accordance with the expected financial aid. SMEs should, through their association, build a relationship with the government and suggest this model, which is in practice for farmers, for favourable financial support for their businesses.

On the other hand, there is the need to preserve these savings structures for continuity and improve on recognisable gaps.

iii. *Incorporate Indigenous Financial Practices in Schools' Curricula*
To sustain knowledge, it should be passed from generation to generation. Hence, the structures and patterns of indigenous savings (ROSCA and ASCA) identified in this chapter can be taught in schools by incorporating them into the educational curriculum. Beginning from primary education to tertiary institutions, pupils should be taught how to generate financial capital through existing indigenous knowledge. The dependence on commercial banks for financial loans would gradually be eased, and the availability of finance for capital will improve progressively in Nigeria and also, in the continent.

iv. *Formulate Policies and Insist on Indigenous Financial Associations*
The ATCI provides actionable lessons for reducing risk in indigenous financial services. A significant challenge of indigenous financial methods is the risk of losing funds due to the carelessness of a thrift collector or a selfish member who collects and disrupts the rotative process; most times, the contributors bear the risk – especially in the case of the sudden death of the thrift collector. Hence, formulating policies for a thrift collector to belong to an association will prevent the loss and mitigate this kind of risk. This will also promote the confidence of the public in participating in thrift activities.

This arrangement is important because when a thrift collector belongs to an association, it will provide financial security for members and their contributors when there are issues of fraud, death, or other identifiable risks. Though this is limited to semi-structured savings associations, it would also benefit unstructured systems if thrift collectors can join the association or create a system that helps to manage risks associated with death and loss of funds.

v. *Lobbying of Government for the Establishment of an Agency for Savings Groups*
Having an agency that regulates the activities of savings groups with requirements for creation, dissolution, reconciliation, disagreement and responding to legal issues that might occur from savings relationships will systematically institutionalise the savings model in Africa. Also, this will increase the number of savings groups and the rate of participation among those without formal

education as well as those regarded as the high-class citizens. Government regulating savings activities will instil confidence in contributors, enhance a savings culture and promote financial inclusion in Nigeria and Africa. These suggestions are for business actors (government, SME leaders/owners, educators and the general public), and their adoption has a significant implication for sustaining indigenous financial values in Africa.

Conclusion

Financial practices represent an integral aspect of economic prosperity; the regulation and management depict the standard of living of a particular nation. The suggestion in this chapter is valuable to all African countries and other developing nations, especially as SMEs hold an integral part in the quest for sustainable development. This would require sustainable savings practices and scaling up the practices of indigenous savings groups, as discussed in this chapter. The informal economy, through the encouragement of indigenous savings groups, can result in a boom in the overall economy particularly if the government and other business actors allow savings groups to thrive successfully.

****Note:* All names mentioned in the case studies apart from Case 4 are fictitious.

Acknowledgements

The research was conducted under SG4Africa, a pan-African research project which seeks to illuminate the phenomenon of Savings Groups across the continent. The project culminated in the publication of the book, Redford, D. T., & Verhoef, G. (Eds.). (2022). Transforming Africa: How Savings Groups Foster Financial Inclusion, Resilience and Economic Development. Emerald Publishing Limited. This chapter contains some more insights from the Nigeria team.

Note

1. US dollar rate as of the year 2019.

References

Adeola, O., Adeleye, I., Muhammed, G., Olajubu, B. J., Oji, C., & Ibelegbu, O. (2022). Savings groups in Nigeria. In D. T. Redford & G. Verhoef (Eds.), *Transforming Africa* (pp. 193–216). Bingley: Emerald Publishing Limited. doi:10.1108/978-1-80262-053-520221015

CBN. (2019a). Self help group linkage banking. Retrieved from https://www.cbn.gov.ng/devfin/selfhelp.asp

CBN. (2019b). The trust fund model. Retrieved from https://www.cbn.gov.ng/devfin/trust.asp

Gyimah, P., & Boachie, W. K. (2018). Effect of microfinance products on small business growth: Emerging economy perspective. *Journal of Entrepreneurship and Business Innovation*, 5(1), 59–71.

Gyimah, P., & Lussier, R. N. (2021). Rural entrepreneurship success factors: An empirical investigation in an emerging market. *Journal of Small Business Strategy*, 31(4), 5–19.

Herrington, M., & Coduras, A. (2019). The national entrepreneurship framework conditions in sub-Saharan Africa: A comparative study of GEM data/National Expert Surveys for South Africa, Angola, Mozambique and Madagascar. *Journal of Global Entrepreneurship Research*, 9(1), 1–24.

Iwara, I. O., Adeola, O., & Netshandama, V. O. (2021). Traditional savings association for entrepreneurial success in Africa: A case study of rotative Stokvel enterprise. *Academy of Entrepreneurship Journal*, 27(2), 1–15.

Jerome, T. A. (1991). The role of rotating savings and credit associations in mobilizing domestic savings in Nigeria. *African Review of Money Finance and Banking*, 2, 115–127.

Lawal, W. A., & Abdullahi, I. B. (2011). Impact of informal agricultural financing on agricultural production in the rural economy of Kwara State, Nigeria. *International Journal of Business and Social Science*, 2(19), 241–248.

Nnama-Okechukwu, C. U., Okoye, U. O., Obikeguna, C., Onalu, C. E., Agha, A. A., Eneh, J., ... Okunsanya, T. (2019). An impact study of the village savings and loan association (VSLA) in Nigeria. *African Population Studies*, 33(2), 4901–4912.

Ola-David, O., & Osabuohien, E. S. C. (2018). Esusu – Global encyclopaedia of informality. In A. Ledeneva (Ed.), *Global encyclopaedia of informality* (Vol. 2, Chapter: 5). London: UCL Press.

Olaitan, M. A. (2006). Finance for small and medium enterprises: Nigeria's agricultural credit guarantee scheme fund. *Journal of International Farm Management*, 3(2), 30–38.

Olajide, B. R., & Aderolu, M. A. (2017). Effects of trust fund model credit intervention on welfare of farmers' households in Oyo State. *Agrosearch*, 17(2), 38–50.

Oranu, C. O., Onah, O. G., & Nkhonjera, E. (2020). Informal saving group: A pathway to financial inclusion among rural women in Nigeria. *Asian Journal of Agricultural Extension, Economics & Sociology*, 38(12), 22–30.

Seibel, H. D. (2004). *Microfinance in Nigeria: Origins, options and opportunities*. Koln: University of Koln.

Sile, I., & Bett, J. (2015). Determinants of informal finance use in Kenya. *Research Journal of Finance and Accounting*, 6–19.

The World Bank Ghana Office. (n.d.). Access to finance for small and medium enterprises in Africa. Access to finance for SMEs. Retrieved from http://www.acetforafrica.org/acet/wp-content/uploads/publications/2016/03/Access-to-Finance-for-SMEs-Paper.pdf

Chapter 9

Exploring the Financial Literacy of a Chama Women's Group in Rural Western Kenya

Lillian Zippora Omosa

Abstract

Chama microfinance models continue to be a safety net for many rural women in Kenya; however, their financial literacy remains largely unexplored. This study sought to explore the financial literacy of women entrepreneurs who are also members of Chama groups in rural Western Kenya, examine the specific indigenous practices and values that educators could draw upon to support and enhance the teaching of financial literacy to women, and also highlight the potential outcome of integrating indigenous knowledge and pedagogies to financial literacy. The study adopted critical participatory action research and African womanism methodology to centre learning on the experiences of rural Chama women. Based on in-depth interviews of six women in Western Kenya, the study found that the women's financial literacy can be explained and demonstrated through their relationships, connections and identity. On specific indigenous practices and methods the study found community engagement, centred learning and discovery learning, as relevant ways of engaging with the women. Integrating values, practices, and methods to inquire about the financial literacy from the Chama women's perspective cultivated an environment that encouraged mutual respect, sharing, participation and learning. Within the context of the findings, the study suggests that it is best to understand the women's financial literacy from their perspective. This study also contributes to knowledge on critical participatory action research and financial literacy from an Africana womanist perspective.

Keywords: Financial literacy; Chama women's groups; pooling of resources; Africana womanism; indigenous financial knowledge; Chama microfinance

Casebook of Indigenous Business Practices in Africa, 161–181
Copyright © 2023 Lillian Zippora Omosa
Published under exclusive licence by Emerald Publishing Limited
doi:10.1108/978-1-80455-762-420231016

Introduction

Chama is a Swahili word meaning group, and a majority of the Chama groups in Kenya engage in microfinance practices both formally and informally, where formal Chamas are regulated by the Ministry of Social Services, and informal Chamas are regulated by members and primarily operate on trust (Gichoi, Karara, Kanyi, Raichura, Wameyo, & Waweru, 2014). Lending and borrowing within the majority of informal Chamas involve small amounts, usually not attached to collateral and the loan, in many cases, is interest-free if repaid within the agreed period (Egbide, 2020; Thomas, 1988). There has been a marked increase in the use of informal microfinance services like Chama, and this is largely attributed to a demand for relevant financial products and services. Literature cites that the rural economy in many parts of Africa is gradually shifting from mainly subsistence farming to a more market-based system (Wentzel, 2016). The pooling of resources has been and continues to be an activity done by people acting as a group; it is practised among various communities in Africa and is mainly referred to as *Chama* in Kenya, *Upatu* in Tanzania, *Susu* among the Akan of Ghana, and *Esusu* among the Yoruba of Nigeria (Dei, 1994; Gichoi et al., 2014). The groups often exist to provide financial safety nests, especially for the economically marginalised where such supports are not provided by the State (Egbide, 2020; Gichoi et al., 2014). Once basic needs are met, the pooling and sharing of resources extend to other unmet needs, including acquiring household items, investments to support businesses, school fees, savings and many other needs. This phenomenon, also referred to as *table banking*, involves the organised collection of money from members, the development of lending processes and rules, and the lending of money to members, usually in a *merry-go-round* way, from one member to the next (Gichuki, Mulu-Mutuku, & Kinuthia, 2015; Tiwari, Schaub, & Sultana, 2019). The lending and repayment of pooled money continue until each member has received and repaid within the agreed cycle.

Empirical and theoretical studies have been done on Chama groups in Kenya, most often focused on performance as defined by traditional Western notions of 'success' without regard for local views; further literature suggests that many informal entrepreneurs are mainly under-resourced (Aterido, Beck, & Iacovone, 2013; Olando & Kimuyu, 2019; Takayanagi, 2016).

Further, numeracy, literacy and digital finance skills, which are the focus of financial literacy conceived from Western perspectives in addition to the cultural context that informs financial literacy, remain unscrutinised (Tiwari et al., 2019). Pre-colonial Indigenous financial management practices are prevalent, especially in areas of pooling of resources, credit management, and investing practices (Ojera, 2018). However, the practices, except mainly in informal microfinance groups, have largely been relegated, and in some cases, represented as subordinate to Western financial practices (Bray & Els, 2007; Ojera, 2018). Most users of informal ways of financing remain necessity entrepreneurs, and rural Chama women's financial literacy remains largely unexplored. Financial literacy, when approached from Western understanding, is concerned with having the right knowledge, attitude and skills in context to enable relevant decision-making about the acquisition and management of financial resources, including engaging in income-generating activities, saving, credit or debt management and retirement planning (Lusardi, 2015; Lusardi & Mitchell, 2014; OECD, 2018).

Like many social and economic institutions in Kenya, informal rural women entrepreneurs are at a crossroad as the income gap continues to grow, especially between informal and formal entrepreneurs. This is happening despite an increase in state-led and market-led initiatives towards strengthening small-scale businesses. These programs are simply not taken up by most informal Chama members, often due to the lack of recordkeeping and other requirements. From an imperialistic perspective, some argue that these 'deficiencies' signal poor financial literacy. Studies have found that financial literacy is relevant to the transformation of women-owned and managed enterprises (Wangui, 2018). This study argues for relevant financial literacy and consequently aims to contribute to the knowledge by inquiring about the financial literacy of rural Chama women in Kenya.

In development work, Western pedagogical practices that request Indigenous learners to adapt to received knowledge and expectations are all too commonplace (Assie-Lumumba, 2016; Tran & Wall, 2019). To rely only on the Western universalist understanding of financial literacy could result in the faulty or mistaken evaluation that groups like rural Chama women entrepreneurs in Kenya have low financial literacy.

The approach taken in this study responds to the call to reclaim the African educational space by constructing educational systems that are culturally and intellectually meaningful to African learners (Assie-Lumumba, 2016; Bray & Els, 2007; Keane, Khupe, & Seehawer, 2017). From the preceding argument, this study explored Indigenous beliefs, values, traditions, and pedagogies that potentially inform the financial literacy practices of rural Chama women to facilitate learning. There have been arguments for integrating financial literacy into the Kenyan school's curriculum, which is in progress (Alex & Amos, 2014; D. Ngugi, personal communication, October 28, 2020; Githui & Ngare, 2014). Detailed in the chapter is a discussion on pooling of resources, Chama groups, financial literacy and Indigenous financial knowledge. This is followed by an analysis of interplays between financial literacy and informal Chama groups, state-led and market-led interventions, then methodology, findings, recommendations and conclusion of the chapter.

Pooling of Resources

Pooling is a complex term used in resource management to define the grouping together of resources, including assets, personnel and equipment, to maximise benefits while minimising risk (Oghojafar, Alaneme, Kuye, & Latef, 2013; Zhong, Zheng, Chou, & Teo, 2018). Pooling of resources is a way of managing supply and demand in an organisation, noted Zhong et al. (2018) and Chama groups have certainly drawn upon the practice. The approach of pooling resources has been widely practised by the Indigenous communities of Africa and continues to play a vital role today through organised groups (Maina, 2013a, 2013b; Omosa, 2017). Pooling resources has been described as a pro-social behaviour directed at helping one another and society as a whole and is a sharing behaviour that fosters social connection (Archambault, Kalenscher, & Laat, 2020; Ojera, 2018). Chama, especially Chama women groups, has been described as a strategy for capacity building and economic transformation; it is a way of addressing challenges associated with an evolving economy (Thomas, 1988). The process of pooling was traditionally organised by members of most communities living close together, which involves pooling labour and other resources, like tools to support one another, mainly during high planting and harvesting seasons (Maina, 2013a, 2013b; Ndeda, 2019; Were & Nyamweya, 1986). Even though the pooling of resources in communities can include labour and goods, in this study, it refers to money. This method of pooling and managing efforts is related to the resource-based theory of strategic partnerships, where firms pool their resources as a way of seeking a strategic fit between their internal and external environment (Das & Teng, 2000). The argument for a resource-based view of strategic partnerships, notes Das and Teng, is that firms use partnerships to gain access to other firms' valuable resources, especially when they are in need of resources or when they are in a strong financial and social position and can share their resources. Money, like labour and goods, is essentially rooted in a sociocultural context, notes Archambault, Kalenscher, and Laat (2020), which also influences its arrangements, its use, and certainly its value and how society organises around its use. The practice of pooling resources is established as a way of life in Kenya. Maina (2013a, 2013b) discusses the practice of pooling resources among the Kikuyu of Kenya, where it ranges from women fetching water together for one family at a time to harvesting corn, one farm at a time, through the pooling of labour. Women combined their efforts until each household had filled its granaries with enough food for the season, work that otherwise required weeks to complete with the monetary exchange was accomplished in a few days and the work compensated in kind (Maina, 2013a, 2013b). Maina also suggests that Chama groups evolved out of Indigenous practices within communities in Kenya, all aimed at pooling resources to satisfy two main purposes: economic and social. The processes of organising and working cooperatively and establishing of pooling processes were part of the education process (Bogonko, 1996; Were & Nyamweya, 1986).

Chama Groups

Chama groups are made up of women-only, men-only and mixed-gender collectives in urban and rural Kenya (Gichoi et al., 2014). The groups are formed with the aim of collectively addressing social and economic issues that members face, including gaps left by mainstream banks and formal microfinance services. The main objective is for members to pool their money to provide financial products, including savings, loans and insurance, to improve the members' material and social conditions (Bhatt & Tang, 2001; Gichoi et al., 2014; Maina, 2013a, 2013b).

Chama essentially describes a microfinance approach practised in Kenya. Microfinance refers to a range of banking products directed at low-income populations that are either underemployed or unemployed (Christen, Lyman, & Rosenberg, 2003). These low-income populations are usually without access to mainstream financial and microfinance products, to facilitate their daily livelihood activities such as mining, buying and reselling of agricultural products, raising, and selling of poultry, livestock, and other products to generate income (Kinyanjui, 2013; Tiwari et al., 2019). Microfinance products include but are not limited to savings, loans, insurance, and payment services. The products may be initiated by community-led groups like Chama, state initiatives aimed at improving the lives of consumers, market-based lending institutions or non-profit microfinance organisations (Gichoi et al., 2014; Natile, 2020). However, state-led, market-led and even many not-for-profit initiatives have been criticised for offering expensive loans, and at times shifting resources away from much-needed services like education and healthcare, further marginalising the poor (Natlie, 2020; Tiwari et al., 2019).

Informal Chama Women's Groups (ROSCA)

This study's focus is Chama groups referred to as a Rotating Savings and Credit Association (ROSCA), also commonly known as the merry-go-round (Egbide, 2020; Kenya F.S.D., 2015; Gugerty, 2007). ROSCA is mostly informal, and members contribute an agreed amount either on a weekly, bi-weekly or monthly basis. When resources have been pulled together, the members take turns in collecting the money (Ademola et al., 2020; Omosa, 2017). ROSCAs explicitly serve the purpose of saving and investing, but some groups also offer an insurance option where members contribute as agreed by all, basically, for the welfare care of members, especially, in the case of emergencies (Ademola et al., 2020; Egbide, 2020; Gugerty, 2007). This kind of Chama offers the advantage of equal ownership by members. Commitment is argued as an important rationale for participation and simplicity in terms of record keeping; however, it is not without its own challenges including that a member cannot increase contributions if others are not ready to do so. Also, if one member misses a payment, the effect is felt by all (Gichoi et al., 2014; Gugerty, 2007; Omosa, 2017). Members are required to wait for their turn to receive the pooled resource and are unable to access funds otherwise. Although there are various ways of operations that define Chama, what is common among the groups is the culturally organised approach of transacting, as most Chamas form based on previous relations and shared values, beliefs and practices (Gichoi et al., 2014). Chama groups that fall within the ROSCA category can be formal or informal based on their registration status. This study is about the financial literacy of informal Chama women's group members whose main characteristics falls within that of a Rotating Savings and Credit Association (ROSCA). The women that prefer ROSCA or the merry-go-round tend to look for flexibility in terms of how much will be contributed and how often the contribution is to be made. This is because, and in some cases, all members are self-employed in emerging business sectors which can be highly unpredictable (Gichoi et al., 2014; Morgan & Olsen, 2011). Despite the challenges they are constantly faced with, many of them strive to overcome and are able to expand their business activities, which often qualify them to apply and to access loans from formal microfinance banks.

Informal Chama groups engage in microfinance activities by financing small business activities. Informal Chamas operate based on traditions and communal norms of the group (Kinyanjui, 2012, 2013). Chama groups are associated with indigenous ways of financing business enterprises. Various scholars including Olarewaju, Sunday, and Olusoji (2018) have noted that this approach could be adopted to fit diverse contexts. Operating as an informal savings group has its strengths, which includes independence and group-reliance, the building of local financial networks that tend to be deep-rooted and stable, and sustaining practices that are built on social communal norms relevant to members (Maina, 2013a, 2013b; Shipton, 2010). However, most informal Chamas face challenges associated with operating in a pluralistic economy where public resources are heavily directed towards the formal sector. Nonetheless, Chama remains an important resource in communities where formal financial institutions, including microfinance, are weak or non-existent (Ademola et al., 2020).

Even more, social and economic transformation through state-led and at times, market-led programs, argued Natile (2020) has consequences. These consequences include shifting government funding from social welfare programs, contributing to further unfavourable conditions for those living along the margins economically (Natile, 2020).

Informal Chama groups have constitutions in place, whether documented or otherwise, that govern their activities, including the aims and objectives used to achieve expressed purposes (Gichoi et al., 2014). Included in these constitutions are criteria for vetting members seeking entry into the group, which is mainly based on character, principles regarding individual and collective responsibility concerning savings and lending, guidelines stating how members access and repay loans and accountability regarding the use of a loan (Gichoi et al., 2014; Shipton, 2010, 2017). Shipton acknowledges that the repayment of loans have been assessed favourably, especially in women groups, and this is mainly attributed to prior relations, peer pressure, tying loans to pooled savings and rotating the funds among group members (Shipton, 2017, 2019). The system and activities of the groups, such as requiring savings as a prerequisite for loans, give participants an ownership stake and allows them to play a key role in screening out non-committed borrowers (Gichoi et al., 2014; Shipton, 2010). The process of initiating and managing informal Chama microfinance groups is a way of knowing that is connected to financial literacy, and the success rate of rural Chama entrepreneurs is highly linked to social ties significant in solidarity groups in rural regions (Gichoi et al., 2014; Lopez & Winkler, 2018; Shipton, 2010). This solidarity is an asset and argued as otherwise not easily reproduced in many urban and formal financing mechanisms. The solidarity of women's groups like Chama in rural Kenya can mainly be attributed to the prevailing ideas and ideals specific to a community, which Ubuntu and Africana womanism advance: the centrality of culture, family and community, as well as a collective consciousness of the goal of everyone's survival (Hudson-Weems, 2005, 2020; Ntiri, 2001). Ubuntu describes how people should interact in community based on the view that 'a person is a person through other people' (Taylor, 2014; Tutu, 1994). According to Assie-Lumumba (2016), Khoza (2006), and Mahaye (2018), the word Ubuntu derives from the Nguni of Southern Africa's Indigenous language and has a shared meaning with various Bantu-speaking communities, including those in Western Kenya. Ubuntu is an African word derived from *ntu* and translates in the English language as 'humanness' or being human; the word Ubuntu is the essence of being human (Assie-Lumumba; 2016; Mahaye, 2018; Mukuni & Tlou, 2018; Oviawe, 2016). Hence, Ubuntu implies the acts or behaviours that are associated with ethical practices in community (Asamoah & Yeboah-Assiamah, 2019). The core meanings embedded in Ubuntu are argued as significant in various social landscapes including at the workplace, and have been associated with management and ethical business practices (Molose, Goldman & Thomas, 2018; West, 2014). Consequently, the survival and longevity of Indigenous ways of microfinancing through pooling of resources is an argument for the view that there are relevant processes, whether documented or not, that govern the groups; and of relevance is how the groups have interacted with received sites and knowledge on financial literacy and the broader implications.

Financial Literacy

Relevant financial literacy for women-owned and managed groups, including informal Chamas, is important for the economic transformation of the groups (Gichoi et al., 2014; Messy & Monticone, 2012; Tiwari et al., 2019). Financial literacy is a complex phenomenon whose understanding is as diverse as its users and their knowledge, skills, attitudes, and context where practised (Lusardi, 2015; Lusardi & Mitchell, 2014; OECD, 2018).

Financial literacy from the Western perspective is explained as one having the right knowledge, attitude and skills in context to enable relevant decision-making about the acquisition and management of tangible and intangible assets, including engaging in income-generating activities, savings, credit or debt management, and retirement planning (Lusardi, 2015; Lusardi & Mitchell, 2014; OECD, 2018).

Financial literacy rests on the notion that an individual equipped with the right knowledge, skill and attitude about money and transactions, planning and management in context will engage in activities that account for and document the use of resources against the consumption of resources, with the aim of saving and investing to support future activities (Lusardi, 2015; Lusardi & Mitchell, 2014; OECD, 2018).

Indigenous Financial Knowledge

Finance is understood as the skill involved in managing money and various assets. When referencing the knowledge, skills and attitudes associated with financing within a frame of a financial system whose origin and development are traced to a specific location, culture and tradition of a group of people, Bray and Els (2007) and Ojera (2018) have referred to views and perceptions associated with the processes as Indigenous financial knowledge systems (IFKS). Ojera (2018) and Bray and Els (2007) have identified pre-colonial Indigenous financial management practices in Africa, prevalent especially in areas of financing trade, credit management, investing practices and accounting processes. The practices are connected to the customs and locations of the indigenes. However, colonialism and associated knowledge did not institute proper mechanisms for recognition of indigenous ways of knowing, and hence are gradually becoming obsolete, and in some cases, represented as subordinate to Western financial practices (Bray & Els, 2007; Inyang, 2008; Ojera, 2018; Roe, Nelson, & Sandbrook, 2009). Studies cite that the pre-colonial African market was mainly influenced by values and not price, creativity and innovation were mainly motivated by respect and admiration, redistribution, and exchange within the community (Eze, 1995; Ojera, 2018). Even more importantly, the scholars note that African production and enterprises revolved around family and community work, they were informal, and involved the exchange of goods or services for other goods and services (Eze, 1995). The scholars argue that there is a need for restoring context-specific financial ways of knowing and associated practices (Bray & Els, 2007; Ojera, 2018). Promotion and protection of Indigenous knowledge globally have been argued for by various disciplines, including education, Assie-Lumumba (2016), research, Khupe and Keane et al. (2017) and Tuhiwai-Smith (2012), languages, Aylward (2010) and Thiong'o (1998). Authors such as Ojera (2018) and Olarewaju et al. (2018) suggest that Indigenous financing in Africa is viewed from the perspective of customary funding practices which are founded on clan or communal norms, and are particularly based on beliefs, values, and practices of a society. The norms inform terms of engagement, including ways of financing and are rooted in various African views, including Ubuntu, a humanistic philosophy that espouses values anchored on the view that the well-being of a person is connected to the community that the person belongs to. Further, research indicates that a society's ability to build and make useful knowledge or human capital like financial literacy is as critical as the availability of tangible assets like money in improving a society's quality of life (Bray & Els, 2007; Ojera, 2018). Relevant financial literacy is indicated for the growth of enterprises, especially those on the margins of the economy. There is the possibility of continued building upon Indigenous financial knowledge through creativity, including reflecting on the knowledge, current practice, and context and this study makes important contributions in this regard.

The Interplays Between Financial Literacy and Informal Chama Groups

Financial literacy practices, as understood in wider academia, are now becoming pervasive in rural Africa. This is attributed to the diffusion of financial products and associated services conceived elsewhere; these products and services are, to a larger extent, reluctantly received at the sites in countries like Kenya, Uganda and South Africa (Chowa, Ansong, & Despard, 2014; Wentzel, 2016). With continued penetration into rural regions, evidence suggests that financial literacy efforts may not result in their intended outcomes unless programs are designed to complement a pluralistic economy, an economy that is characterised by the existence of two sectors separated by levels of 'development', use of technology, and patterns of relating within a country (Wentzel, 2016). This study argues for financial literacy that is culturally relevant to Chama women in rural Kenya.

A World Bank (2016) survey submits that 80% of the worldwide poor live in rural areas, and an estimated two-thirds of the poor are women, are self-educated, live in larger households and are usually under-employed in the agricultural sector. Further, the survey found that more than half (50.7%) of the global poor are in African countries, mainly South of the Sahara, although some of the countries are rich in minerals, oil and other natural resources. Women, according to Corus and Ozanne (2011) and Houh and Kalsem (2015), bear most of the consequences of poverty, given systemic inequities in education, employment, asset allocation and unpaid responsibilities, including the care of children and ageing parents. Women, therefore, potentially make up two-thirds of the global rural population that lacks resources including relevant financial literacy skills. Relevant financial literacy for Chama women in rural Kenya has the potential to narrow the poverty gap. Corus and Ozanne (2011) and Takayanagi (2016) note that literacy is indicated in women's economic outcomes, and studies still reveal an ongoing ill-equipped adult population lacking relevant skills to navigate the ever-changing financial landscape (Page, 2020). And this lack of financial literacy continues to exacerbate inequality. Consequently, relevant knowledge and skills in addition to economic opportunities are urgently needed for women's well-being.

Formal microfinance services have emerged in many rural regions in Kenya but have failed to be sustainable, with many exiting the villages. Such challenges to microfinance are not specific to Kenya; but as pointed out by Lopez and Winkler (2018) and Shipton (2010), microfinance banks in rural regions generally face challenges in terms of penetration due to high operating costs. Chama groups have formed vehicles for saving, investing and borrowing in Kenya, and they serve as both formal and informal microfinance banks where practised (Gichoi et al., 2014; Shipton, 2010; Tiwari et al., 2019). Rural women are key participants in Chama groups. Gaining a deeper understanding of the women's financial literacy levels and incorporating women's practices into a financial literacy curriculum has the potential for impacting the economic well-being of rural Chama women and possibly relations with microfinance banks and other partners attempting to penetrate the sector.

While a considerable number of urban dwellers in African countries may have access to income from employment, save through formal banks and pension plans, and access credit through home mortgages and credit cards, many have different experiences (Chowa et al., 2014). This is particularly significant for the majority in rural regions, especially Chama women. Many rural dwellers in

Kenya and neighbouring countries are unemployed, under-employed or self-employed. They save, invest, and build up assets through self-employment by utilising natural resources like land and associated resources involved in mining, fishing, and agricultural activities, including livestock. Most rural dwellers accumulate lump sum money to invest, often through family and friends organised into formal and informal Chama microfinance groups and their savings are mostly in livestock and other agricultural products (Chowa et al., 2014; Tiwari et al., 2019). Studies conducted in various contexts find financial literacy relevant to decisions about money, including investing (Riepe, Rudeloff, & Veer, 2020). The studies suggest that financial literacy is a determining factor in investing behaviours including the risk of both the employed and self-employed. Literature about Chama women's groups points to a segment of women in rural Kenya that engage in informal financial services. A review of financial literacy concurs and suggests that low participation of women in formal financial services in rural areas is primarily due to a lack of collateral, lack of financial institutions compatible with the needs of the women, and a lack of or low demand for formal financial services, resulting in high operating and transaction costs (Corus & Ozanne, 2011; Lopez & Winkler, 2018; Shipton, 2010, 2017; World Bank, 2016). Therefore, there is an urgent need for customised financial literacy that is conceived within the appropriate context.

Even more, studies about Chama women's groups in underdeveloped regions, including in Kenya, suggest that capital alone, whether in the form of a loan or a grant, is not enough to grow women-owned livelihood businesses, many women who take up loans tend to use the proceeds for their sustenance and eventually end in bigger debts (Buvinić & Furst-Nichols, 2016). Financial literacy geared towards rural Chama women can address some of the challenges to growth. There is a sense of urgency for relevant financial literacy in developing economies given that, to a larger extent, under-employment and unemployment are high and most individuals are engaged in informal labour markets, therefore, they are charged with managing their own financial planning in many ways (Lusardi & Mitchell, 2008, 2014; Ondiba & Matsui, 2019).

Studies conducted on factors affecting women's enterprises especially found inconsistencies in terms of income, wealth and education to be a major hindrance to the growth of the enterprises in Kenya and among various countries in East, Central, and Southern Africa (Messy & Monticone, 2012; Olando & Kimuyu, 2019). The inconsistencies are attributed to low economic and human capacity development, low school enrolment, and high unemployment and under-employment, resulting in increased poverty, unpredictable labour markets and low financial literacy (Aterido et al., 2013; Dupas, Green, Keats, & Robinson, 2012; Messy & Monticone, 2012). Studies done in Northern Kenya and in Kakamega County found circumstances related to low human capacity development and unpredictable income to be relevant (Ondiba & Matsui, 2019; Tiwari et al., 2019). This study aimed at inquiring whether Chama women entrepreneurs face similar challenges. Chama women's groups emerge at the village level in rural Kenya and have the potential to influence economic growth if the barriers are addressed (Gichuki, Mulu-Mutuku, & Kinuthia, 2014; Kiragu & Sakwa, 2013).

Chama is conceptualised within the community's values, beliefs and practices which is a useful model of empowerment in various ways including through the promotion of community entrepreneurship. Studies indicate that social networks including Chama groups play a significant role in supporting entrepreneurial activities (Ondiba & Matsui, 2019). The practice is significant to the women's way of life (Maina, 2013a, 2013b; Parwez, 2017). Chama groups that continue to operate informally and on the honour system are unique and have a built-in strength that contributes to the value of the microfinance sector. However, given the evolving economic landscape that Chama operates in, there is a need to explore alternatives that allow informal groups to maintain significant values while building on their financial literacy to grow and offer transformative opportunities to members (Gichoi et al., 2014; Tiwari et al., 2019).

It is argued that most of the poor are in rural regions and one of the ways to support rural populations to come out of economical struggles and poverty is through economic growth. However, the income gap between formal and informal groups and gendered enterprises continues to grow (Buvinić & Furst-Nichols, 2016; Ondiba & Matsui, 2019; World Bank, 2016). Though there are as many female-owned businesses as male-owned ones in rural regions, studies indicate that women-owned businesses are not expanding compared to men-owned businesses (Buvinić & Furst-Nichols, 2016; Maru & Chemjor, 2013; Ondiba & Matsui, 2019). The growth and income disparities between formal and informal and gendered enterprises are attributed to various reasons, including low school enrolment, high school pushouts, income disparities, social constraints and social programmes that are not designed to meet the needs of the very poor rural women (Buvinić & Furst-Nichols, 2016; Maru & Chemjor, 2013). There is the possibility for informal rural women to benefit from social programs offered by formal microfinance groups and state-led programs to tap into the informal sector if programs, including a relevant financial literacy programme, are designed to meet the needs of the unbanked poor.

State-Led and Market-Led Interventions

The Kenyan government, through microfinance programs like the Women Enterprise Fund (2007) and the Uwezo fund (2014), offers targeted programs to qualified groups like Chama women's groups. While not suggesting these to be appropriate to the needs of all Chama women's groups, and the only interventions, the opportunities do present a pathway to improving women-owned enterprises and related income if properly managed. Majority of rural dwellers especially women who participate in informal business activities, tend to be economically marginalised, and disconnected from formal programs (Buvinić & Furst-Nichols, 2016; Tiwari et al., 2019). This is not necessarily because the women lack motivation, but is mainly caused by the lack of knowledge, skills and practices that appear inconsistent with formal state and market-led programs and financial institutions' requirements. Therefore, the institutions even though eager to tap into the social capital present in most rural regions remain inoperative while state and market-led programmes continue incentivising offers hoping to attract the population (Aterido et al., 2013; Lopez & Winkler, 2018; Ondiba & Matsui, 2019; Tiwari et al., 2019).

Alongside state-led microfinance programs like Women Enterprise Fund, a mobile money transfer platform was introduced into Kenya in 2007. The platform is a mobile phone-enabled transfer system commonly known as M*Pesa* (M for mobile and *Pesa* is a Swahili word for money). The idea of mobile-enabled money transfers emerged from the practice of sending airtime to friends and family by transmitting prepaid airtime from one phone line to another, and it has transformed financial literacy and inclusion to a significant extent in Kenya (Leydier, 2016; Natile, 2020). With the introduction of the M*Pesa* platform, the number of people with access to formal financial services, including mobile money transfer, increased (Leydier, 2016; Natile, 2020). The increase in use suggests improvements in financial literacy, but it is unclear whether the increase in participation is in urban Kenya or both urban and rural Kenya. Additionally, studies indicate that financial exclusion, especially among women, remains problematic (Gichuki & Mulu-Mutuku, 2018). M*Pesa* has been widely recognised as a successful digital financial inclusion platform; however, just like many state-led and market-led approaches to financial planning and development, it has been criticised for promoting Western capitalistic interests, which are far from the interests of those economically along the margins (Natile, 2020). Further, Natile (2020) and Tiwari et al. (2019) observe that the opportunities and benefits of programmes such as M*Pesa*, like banks, are largely opportunistic and the profits move towards the provider. Profits from mainstream banks and services are rarely redirected in any meaningful way towards the unbanked poor, including women in rural areas, to enable them to fully benefit from utilising the resources. Financial products, and especially those that utilise digital platforms, have added costs. In addition to recurring transaction fees, there are other associated costs like literacy and the cost of acquiring new technology to access the M*Pesa* service, including phone and airtime. For a woman struggling to access mainstream financial services from banks, the cost of using the M*Pesa* money transfer platform can be prohibitive (Natile, 2020; Tiwari et al., 2019).

Methodology

This study adopted critical participatory action research (CPAR) method. To conduct the study, the researcher purposefully selected women in rural Western Kenya through referrals, therefore incorporating an element of snowballing. The study selected women who had the potential to contribute to our understanding of their financial literacy practices and the conditions under which they are conducted (Kemmis, McTaggart, & Nixon, 2014; Merriam & Tisdel, 2016). The researcher engaged six Chama women who were also livelihood business owners and who were willing to (1) talk about issues facing women, finance, and the community; (2) participate in training in financial literacy; (3) engage in a conversation collectively and individually; (4) have been members of a Chama for at least six months; and (5) give consent. Between December 2018 and May 2019, the researcher met with six Chama women who lived and conducted their livelihood businesses in rural Western Kenya. The women were between the ages of mid-twenties to lower sixty, mothers and one grandmother, the highest level of formal education attained by two of the women was secondary school, and they were all engaged in micro-business for sustenance.

This study was conducted in three phases. The first phase involved the introduction of the study, signing of consent forms, completing a demographic questionnaire to assess co-participants' financial literacy, holding individual conversations to clarify information on the questionnaire, and planning our following meetings. The second phase involved individual and group interviews with training on identified gaps. The third phase was a follow-up on participants' views of the study, where the researcher also shared emerging findings with co-participants to clarify interpretations and, at the same time, to identify any assumptions or misunderstandings of what the researcher heard or observed.

To gather data, the study engaged in a collective self-reflective inquiry guided by a structured demographic questionnaire, semi-structured and unstructured interview questions, following up on the questions with probes, held individually and in group settings while facilitating learning (Hudson-Weems, 1997, 2005, 2020; Kemmis et al., 2014; Merriam & Tisdel, 2016). The study used a journal, field notes and audio recording to gather and record conversations, observations and reflections on a regular basis in the field.

The study commenced data analysis and management simultaneously with data gathering. After each session of data gathering, the study manually transcribed, translated and constructed categories of co-participants' narratives, and compared to the researcher's perceptions and observation notes. The study accomplished this by writing notes, comments and questions in the margins of interview transcripts then the study further compared emerging themes generated from the transcribed data, field notes and journaled notes to the theoretical framework (Merriam & Tisdel, 2016). The researcher continued with this process until all sub-categories were grouped into a manageable number of overall categories then proceeded with classifying, interpretation and dissemination.

Ethical Considerations

This study was carried out according to Acadia university Research Ethics Board TCPS2 (2014) policy, CPAR group protocols, and NACOSTI Kenya requirements.

The study took into consideration strategies that could help increase the credibility and reliability of the research by employing reflexibility, and triangulation of data (Merriam & Tisdel, 2016). Regarding external validity, the findings from the study can contribute to knowledge but may not be generalised to other individuals or groups (Herr & Anderson, 2015; Merriam & Tisdel, 2016).

Findings

Financial Literacy of the Women's Chama Group

The study found that without careful consideration of the women's context, their financial literacy can be misinterpreted and misunderstood; to rely only on historic western notions would result in the evaluation that the women have low financial literacy. Our findings suggest that this is not the case. The women demonstrated knowledge and skills in context-specific financial literacy amid their activities of pooling, loaning and investing; the knowledge possessed by the women did transform their activities, but not to the extent of impacting profit. The study found that the women practice a form of financial literacy which mainly relies on mental bookkeeping, learning through others, and through activities.

Altogether, the Chama women expressed interest in further expanding their knowledge and skills in financial literacy. Co-participants agreed to practice documenting transactions even though they indicated that not all members were ready to patronise formal financial institutions. Consequently, continuous practice and document activities were directed towards the benefit of expanding while maintaining current ways of funding co-participants' activities. Co-participants were of the view that building upon what they know, and practice would increase awareness about resources and opportunities available in the wider landscape and in this regard, the women would have the freedom to decide what works best in their circumstances.

Secondly, the study found that co-participants gather and do much more than pool and loan money. They share practical information on accessing the products they trade in, where given products are in demand, and especially about pricing and markets.

Indigenous Pedagogies With the Potential to Support the Learning of Financial Literacy

The study found that the system and principles for working and carrying out activities together exist within the group. It is upon this basis that I negotiated space with Chama members and incorporated CPAR and Africana womanism to collaborate and learn about the financial literacy practices and found the method appropriate for learning.

The study found community engagement, a method that describes Chama women's ways of working together an appropriate one for facilitating learning of financial literacy, it is a method through which the women organise to address and transform challenges. Community engagement is described as a method for learning, voicing members' concerns as well as for collective action and transformation (Raja, 2019; Takayanagi, 2016).

Findings from the study also pointed towards well-thought-out processes through which the women have drawn out knowledge and transferred it to new situations.

The Chama women's narrations about how they formed the group, their actions, processes, and activities can be explained as discovery learning (Knowles, Holton, & Swanson, 2015). Chama women were actively involved in the learning process as they negotiated ways of solving problems within the group, with customers and traders, or when calculating sales and change due to a customer by memory.

Chama members drew upon experiences gained along their journey as they confronted new problems. This exemplifies not only methods associated with discovery learning, but also key characteristics of Africana womanism, including self and collective determination, identifying, and naming one's challenges, planning and putting the plan into practice to solve the problem (Hudson-Weems, 1997, 2020).

The study found community engagement, centred learning and discovery learning relevant methods for engaging the women. Integrating values, practices and methods to achieve inquiry about financial literacy from the Chama women's perspective cultivated an environment that encouraged mutual respect, sharing, participation and construction of knowledge.

CPAR is a method that shares attributes with most subjugated knowledge, as explained by Houh and Kalsem (2015). Notwithstanding the paucity of literature on CPAR and gender or race perspectives, where it has been adopted, the method spontaneously pairs with the knowledge theoretically and methodologically; and this study indicates that CPAR shares various features with Africana womanism.

Recommendations

One of the main contributions of this study is drawing from the margins and bringing to the centre the experiences of rural Chama women entrepreneurs in Western Kenya, concerning their financial literacy practices, and adding to knowledge from the women's perspectives.

This is significant given that knowledge attributed to groups like rural Chama women is considered subjugated knowledge and has to contend with dominant business theories and associated interpretations of the world (Bray & Els, 2007; Collins, 2009; Hudson-Weems, 2005). Consequently, mainstreaming the experiences of rural entrepreneurs not only gives voice to their experiences about financial literacy, but presents the opportunity to discover gaps in financial literacy to guide the designing of a training manual. This study's findings suggest that attempting to improve upon the financial literacy of marginalised rural Chama groups can engender greater benefits if relevant learning methods are incorporated and training is designed from the learner's perspectives. Consequently, this study recommends that educators, practitioners and policymakers adopt a learner-centred approach when designing financial literacy programmes intended for socially and economically marginalised entrepreneurs.

Conclusion

This study's findings suggest the possibility of building on the financial literacy of rural Chama women in western Kenya from a culturally relevant perspective.

This approach can provide some leverage in advancing financial literacy by increasing the understanding of lending models, borrowing, and saving from the women's perspective.

Many informal rural Chama women mainly operate from the margins of the economy. To a large extent, they are poor and improving their financial literacy from their perspective presents the likelihood of a better understanding of the economic context and sustainable ways that the women can employ to facilitate their economic transformation. The study also found that a rural informal Chama woman's ability to organise and apply appropriate financial knowledge to a situation is as important to improving their livelihood as is having access to capital. Consequently, increasing knowledge on the diversity of programs and products available to Chama women and accessibility is equally significant to improving the women's economic well-being.

Case Discussion Questions

(1) Chama is viewed by various scholars as a method that evolved out of Indigenous African values on pooling resources and is now considered a vehicle for raising money to invest in micro, small, and even medium enterprises in Kenya. Chama is now mainly viewed as a microfinancing entity; what are some of the ways of building upon the concept to meet the needs of many more entrepreneurs who, for various reasons, are often overlooked by conventional banks?

(2) In which way is the pooling of resources by Chama members and within Chama groups related to the resource-based theory of strategic partnerships?

(3) Scholars have argued that there is a need for restoring context-specific (African) financial knowledge and associated practices. Discuss the implication of this to society and the economy.

References

Asamoah, K., & Yeboah-Assiamah, E. (2019). "Ubuntu philosophy" for public leadership and governance praxis: Revisiting the ethos of Africa's collectivism. *Journal of Global Responsibility*, *10*(4), 307–321.

Ademola, A. O., Egbide, B.-C., Adegboyegun, A. E., Eluyela, D. F., Falaye, A. J., & Ajayi, A. S. (2020). Rotating and savings credit association (ROSCAs): A veritable tool for enhancing the performance of micro and small enterprises in Nigeria. *Asian Economic and Financial Review*, *10*(2), 189–199.

Alex, K., & Amos, A. (2014). The role of financial literacy in promoting children & youth savings accounts: A case of commercial banks in Kenya. *Research Journal of Finance and Accounting*, *5*(11), 106–110.

Archambault, C., Kalenscher, T., & Laat, J. (2020). Generosity and livelihoods: Dictator game evidence on the multidimensional nature of sharing among the Kenyan Maasai. *Journal of Behavioral Decision Making*, *33*(2), 196–207.

Assie-Lumumba, D. T. (2016). The Ubuntu paradigm and comparative and international education: Epistemological challenges and opportunities in our field. *Comparative Education Review, 61*(1).

Aterido, R., Beck, T., & Iacovone, L. (2013). Access to finance in sub-Sahara Africa: Is there a gender gap? *World Development, 47*, 102–120.

Aylward, M. L. (2010). The role of Inuit languages in Nunavut schooling: Nunavut teachers talk about bilingual education. *Canadian Journal of Education, 33*(2), 295–328.

Bhatt, N., & Tang, S. Y. (2001). Delivering microfinance in developing countries: Controversies and policy perspectives. *Policy Studies Journal, 29*(2), 319–333.

Bogonko, S. N. (1996). Grazing grounds and Gusii indigenous education. *Education in Eastern Africa, 6*(2), 191–206.

Bray, R. J. C., & Els, G. (2007). Unpacking 'ethno-finance': An introduction to indigenous 'financial' knowledge systems. *South African Journal of Information Management, 9*(1), 1–10.

Buvinić, M., & Furst-Nichols, R. (2016). Promoting women's economic empowerment: What works? *The World Bank Research Observer, 31*(1), 59–101.

Chowa, G., Ansong, D., & Despard, M. R. (2014). Financial capabilities: Multilevel modelling of the impact of internal and external capabilities of rural households. *Social Work Research, 38*(1), 19–35.

Christen, R. P., Lyman, T. R., & Rosenberg, R. (2003). *Microfinance consensus guidelines: Guiding principles on regulation and supervision of microfinance.* Washington, DC: © CGAP and World Bank. Retrieved from http://hdl.handle.net/10986/16958 License

Collins, P. (2009). *Hill. Black feminist thought.* New York, NY: Routledge.

Corus, C., & Ozanne, J. L. (2011). Critical literacy programs: Can business literacy be a catalyst for economic and social change? *Journal of Macromarketing, 31*(2), 184–198.

Das, T. K., & Teng, B. S. (2000). A resource-based theory of strategic alliances. *Journal of Management, 26*(1), 31–61.

Dei, G. J. (1994). Afrocentricity: A cornerstone of pedagogy. *Anthropology & Education Quarterly, 25*(1), 3–28.

Dupas, P., Green, S., Keats, A., & Robinson, J. (2012). *Challenges in banking the rural poor: Evidence from Kenyan's western province.* Working Paper No. 17851, National Bureau of Economic Research. Retrieved from http://www.nber.org/papers/w17851

Egbide, B. C. (2020). Rotating and savings credit association (ROSCAs): A veritable tool for enhancing the performance of micro and small enterprises in Nigeria. *Asian Economic and Financial Review, 10*(2), 189–199.

Eze, N. (1995). *Human resource management in Africa: Problems and solutions* (Vol. 1). Lagos: Zomex Press.

Gichoi, M., Karara, P., Kanyi, S., Raichura, S., Wameyo, P., & Waweru, Z. (2014). *Kenya association of investment groups: The Chama people* (2nd ed.). Nairobi: Raspberry, Haven Ltd.

Gichuki, C. N., & Mulu-Mutuku, M. (2018). Determinants of awareness and adoption of mobile money technologies: Evidence from women micro entrepreneurs in Kenya. *Women's Studies International Forum, 67*, 18–22.

Gichuki, C. N., Mulu-Mutuku, M., & Kinuthia, L. N. (2014). Performance of women owned enterprises accessing credit from village credit and savings associations in Kenya. *Journal of Global Entrepreneurship Research*, (1), 1–13.

Gichuki, C. N., Mulu-Mutuku, M., & Kinuthia, L. (2015). Influence of participation in "table banking" on the size of women-owned micro and small enterprises in Kenya. *Journal of Enterprising Communities*, 9(4), 315–326.

Githui, T., & Ngare, P. (2014). Financial literacy and retirement planning in the informal sector in Kenya. Retrieved from http://erepository.uonbi.ac.ke/handle/11295/65614

Gugerty, M. (2007). You can't save alone: Commitment in rotating savings and credit associations in Kenya. *Economic Development and Cultural Change*, 55(2), 251–282.

Herr, K., & Anderson, L. G. (2015). *The action research planner: A guide for students and faculty* (2nd ed.). Washington, DC: SAGE Publications, Inc.

Houh, E. M. S., & Kalsem, K. (2015). Theorizing legal participatory action research. *Qualitative Inquiry*, 21(3), 262–276.

Hudson-Weems, C. (1997). Africana womanism and the critical need for Africana theory and thought. *The Western Journal of Black Studies*, 21(2), 79.

Hudson-Weems, C. (2005). Africana thought-action: An authenticating paradigm for Africana studies. *Western Journal of Black Studies*, 29(3), 622–628.

Hudson-Weems, C. (2020). *Africana womanism: Reclaiming ourselves*. New York, NY: Routledge.

Inyang, B. J. (2008). The challenges of evolving and developing management indigenous theories and practices in Africa. *International Journal of Business and Management*, 3(12), 122–132.

Keane, M., Khupe, C., & Seehawer, M. (2017). Decolonising methodology: Who benefits from indigenous knowledge research? *Educational Research for Social Change*, 6(1), 12–24.

Kemmis, S., McTaggart, R., & Nixon, R. (2014). *The action research planner: Doing critical participatory action research*. New York, NY: Springer.

Kenya, F. S. D. (2015). FinAccess business supply bank financing of SMEs in Kenya.

Khoza, R. J. (2006). *Let Africa lead: African transformational leadership for 21st century business*. Johannesburg: Vezubuntu.

Kinyanjui, M. (2012). *Vyama: Institutions of hope: Ordinary people's market coordination and society organisation: A Kenyan case study*. Oakville, ON: Nsemia Inc.

Kinyanjui, N. M. (2013). Informal garment traders in Taita Taveta road, Nairobi: From the margins to the center. *African Studies Associations*. doi:10.1017/asr.2013.83

Kiragu, E. M., & Sakwa, M. (2013). Effect of group lending mechanism enterprise development of rural women in Kenya. A survey of Kenyenya District, Kisii County, Kenya. *Interdisciplinary Journal of Contemporary Research in Business*, 4(12), 556–576.

Knowles, S. M., Holton, F. E., & Swanson, A. R. (2015). *The adult learner: The definitive classic in adult education and human resource development* (8th ed.). New York, NY: Routledge.

Leydier, B. (2016). *Technology and financial inclusion: An analysis of mobile money usage and savings behaviors in Kenyan households*. Unpublished Doctoral Dissertation. Georgetown University.

Lopez, T., & Winkler, A. (2018). The challenge of rural financial inclusion – Evidence from microfinance. *Applied Economics, 50*(14), 1555–1577.

Lusardi, A. (2015). Financial literacy: Do people know the ABCs of finance? *Public Understanding of Science, 24*(3), 260–271.

Lusardi, A., & Mitchell, O. (2008). Planning and financial literacy: How do women fare? *The American Economic Review, 98*(2), 413–417.

Lusardi, A., & Mitchell, O. S. (2014). The economic importance of financial literacy: Theory and evidence. *Journal of Economic Literature, 52*(1), 5–44.

Mahaye, N. E. (2018). The philosophy of Ubuntu in Education. *Research Gate, 3*, 167.

Maina, F. (2013a). Vyama, institutions of hope: Ordinary people's market coordination and society organization. *African Journal of Business Management, 7*(14), 1100–1102.

Maina, F. (2013b). Vyama, institutions of hope: Ordinary peoples market coordination and society organization. In M. N. Kinyanjui (Ed.), Oakville, ON: Nsemia Inc.

Maru, L., & Chemjor, R. (2013). Microfinance interventions and empowerment of women entrepreneurs in rural constituencies in Kenya. *Research Journal of Finance and Accounting, 4*(9), 2222–2247.

Merriam, B. S., & Tisdel, J. E. (2016). *Qualitative research: A guide to design and implementation* (4th ed.). San Francisco, CA: Jossey-Bass.

Messy, F., & Monticone, C. (2012). *The status of financial education in Africa, OECD working papers on finance, insurance, and private pensions.* Working Paper No. 25. doi:10.1784/5k94cqqx90w/-en

Molose, T., Goldman, G., & Thomas, P. (2018). Towards a collective-values framework of Ubuntu: Implications for workplace commitment. *Entrepreneurial Business and Economics Review, 6*(3), 193–206.

Morgan, J., & Olsen, W. (2011). Aspiration problems for the Indian rural poor: Research on self-help groups and micro-finance. *Capital & Class, 35*(2), 189–212.

Mukuni, J., & Tlou, J. (2018). The place of Ubuntu in global education. In B. Bizzell, R. Kahila, & P. Talbot (Eds.), *Cases on global competencies for educational diplomacy in international settings* (pp. 223–248). Pennsylvania, PA: IGI Global.

Natile, S. (2020). Digital finance inclusion and the mobile money "social" enterprise. *Historical Social Research/Historische Sozialforschung, 45*(3), 74–94.

Ndeda, M. A. J. (2019). Population, movement, settlement, and the construction of society to the East of Lake Victoria in pre-colonial times: The Western Kenya Case. *The East African Review, 52*, 83–108. Retrieved from http://journals.openedition.org/eastafrica/473

Ntiri, D. (2001). Reassessing Africana womanism: Continuity and change. *Western Journal of Black Studies, 25*(3), 163–167.

OECD. (2018). OECD/INFE Toolkit for measuring financial literacy and financial inclusion.

Oghojafar, B., Alaneme, E., Kuye, G., & Latef, O. (2013). Indigenous management thought, concepts, and practices: The case of Igbos of Nigeria. *Australina Journal of Business Management and Research, 3*(1), 8–15.

Ojera, P. (2018). Indigenous financial management practices in Africa: A guide for educators and practitioners. *Indigenous Management Practices in Africa, 20*, 71–96.

Olando, O. C., & Kimuyu, M. (2019). Community based financial practices for the proliferation of access to higher education in Kenya's ASAL regions: A pointer to enhancing peace in the region. *Universal Journal of Educational Research, 7*(2), 609–623.

Olarewaju, A. D., Sunday, A. A., & Olusoji, G. J. (2018). Indigenous African financing strategies as a unique engine for entrepreneurship growth. *Indigenous Management Practices in Africa, 20*, 147–166.

Omosa, Z. L. (2017). 'Exploring the financial literacy of Chama women's groups in rural Kenya' work and play in the Tidal Zones: Gender and diversity. Paper presented at the *Atlantic School of Business Conference at Acadia University*, Wolfville, NS, 29th September 2017.

Ondiba, H. A., & Matsui, K. (2019). Social attributes and factors influencing entrepreneurial behaviors among rural women in Kakamega County, Kenya. *Journal of Global Entrepreneurship Research, 9*(1), 1–10.

Oviawe, J. O. (2016). How to rediscover the Ubuntu paradigm in education. *International Review of Education, 62*, 1–10.

Page, P. M. (2020). *Parents' perceptions of financial technology to support financial socialization and literacy levels*. Doctoral dissertation, Walden University.

Parwez, S. (2017). A systems view across time and space. *Journal of Innovation and Entrepreneurship, 6*(14). doi:10.1186/s13731-017-0074-

Rajah, S. S. (2019). Conceptualizing community engagement through the lens of African indigenous education. *Perspectives in Education, 37*(1), 1–14.

Riepe, J., Rudeloff, M., & Veer, T. (2020). Financial literacy and entrepreneurial risk aversion. *Journal of Small Business Management*, 1–20.

Roe, D., Nelson, F., & Sandbrook, C. (Eds.). (2009). *Community management of natural resources in Africa: Impacts, experiences, and future directions, Natural Resource Issues No. 18*, International Institute for Environment and Development, London, UK.

Shipton, P. M. (2010). Self-help with help banking between charity and usury. In *Credit between cultures* (pp. 179–209). New Haven, CT: Yale University Press.

Shipton, P. M. (2017). Self-help and the underground individual incentive and the group guarantee. In *Credit between cultures* (pp. 156–178). New Haven, CT: Yale University Press.

Shipton, P. (2019). The rope and the box: Group savings in the Gambia. In *Informal Finance in low-income countries* (pp. 25–41). New York, NY: Routledge.

Smith, L. T. (2012). *Decolonizing methodologies: Research and indigenous people*. New York, NY: Zed Books Ltd.

Takayanagi, T. (2016). Rethinking women's learning and empowerment in Kenya: Maasai village women take initiative. *International Review of Education, 62*(6), 671–688.

Taylor, D. F. (2014). Defining ubuntu for business ethics-a deontological approach. *South African Journal of Philosophy= Suid-Afrikaanse Tydskrif vir Wysbegeerte, 33*(3), 331–345.

Thiong'o, N. (1998). Decolonising the mind. *Diogenes, 46*(184), 101–104.

Thomas, B. P. (1988). Household strategies for adaptation and change: Participation in Kenyan rural women's associations. *Africa, 58*(4), 401–422.

Tiwari, J., Schaub, E., & Sultana, N. (2019). Barriers to last mile financial inclusion: Cases from Northern Kenya. *Development in Practice, 29*(8), 988–1000.

Tran, L. T., & Wall, T. (2019). Ubuntu in adult vocational education: Theoretical discussion and implications for teaching international students. *International Review of Education, 65*(4), 557–578.

Tutu, D. (1994). *The rainbow people of god: The making of a peaceful revolution.* New York, NY: Doubleday Books.

Wangui, K. J. (2018). *Financial literacy amongst women entrepreneurs in Kenya: A value-added product for economic empowerment.* Doctoral dissertation, University of Zululand.

Wentzel, A. (2016). Financial literacy in South Africa. In C. Aprea, K. Breuer, P. Davis, & S. Lopus (Eds.), *International handbook of financial literacy* (pp. 329–339). Long Beach, CA: Springer.

Were, G. S., & Nyamweya, D. (1986). *Kisii district socio-cultural profile.* Nairobi: Government Printer.

West, A. (2014). Ubuntu and business ethics: Problems, perspectives and prospects. *Journal of Business Ethics, 121*(1), 47–61.

World Bank. (2016). *Poverty and shared prosperity 2016: Taking on inequality.* Washington, DC: World Bank.

Zhong, Y., Zheng, Z., Chou, M. C., & Teo, C. P. (2018). Resource pooling and allocation policies to deliver differentiated service. *Management Science, 64*(4), 1555–1573.

Chapter 10

Rotating Stokvel Model for Entrepreneurial Success in South Africa: Validation of Constructs from a Case Study

Ishmael Obaeko Iwara and Ogechi Adeola

Abstract

Stokvel is an African traditional credit system with initiatives that are typically situated in the informal economy and are easily accessible to alleviate financial challenges associated with micro and small enterprise financing, networking and product marketing. A wealth of research has provided an understanding of the entrepreneurial imperatives in this regard; however, knowledge of processes of setting up a successful Stokvel model to achieve this overarching benefit of scaling the initiative is still lacking. This study consolidates and examines the application and distribution of the model's four-building constructs established in a previous case study in a broader spectrum, providing requisite knowledge for its adoption in the contemporary entrepreneurial economy. Using a sample of 418 valid responses from the rural and urban areas of Limpopo Province of South Africa, findings reveal that the four building constructs (formation, operation, financial segment and disciplinary measures), are conformant to the study area, with no statistical evidence to support a difference between the ratings of the categories of location. This implies that Stokvel practices across areas of the province are similar, and a proper understanding of the building blocks that sustain its operations can enhance its applicability in other parts of South Africa, as well as other regions. The study, therefore, lays a foundation that can be used to develop a typical rotating Stokvel model for entrepreneurial success in Africa and beyond.

Keywords: Afrocentric models; indigenous entrepreneurship; local economy; informal credit systems; rotating Stokvel model; digital Stokvel

Casebook of Indigenous Business Practices in Africa, 183–201
Copyright © 2023 Ishmael Obaeko Iwara and Ogechi Adeola
Published under exclusive licence by Emerald Publishing Limited
doi:10.1108/978-1-80455-762-420231018

Introduction

This chapter builds upon an existing work by the authors, which laid the foundation for traditional Stokvel standardisation for mainstream entrepreneurship and proposed four building constructs for its successful adoption and implementation. Stokvel is an arrangement wherein a group of like-minded individuals convene to interact entrepreneurially, financially and socially to contribute to informal savings and credit associations for their mutual benefit. The current study mainly resulted from the fact that there is a considerable discussion about Stokvel and entrepreneurship, as well as their significant contribution to socio-economic development (Matuku & Kaseke, 2014; Menze & Tsibolane, 2019). However, the pathways through which the initiative can be institutionalised in the mainstream economy for policy and practice is still under-researched. Building on the study of Iwara, Adeola, and Netshandama (2021) titled 'Traditional savings association for entrepreneurial success in Africa: a case study of rotating Stokvel enterprise', this chapter further resonates the advantages of Stokvel and, more importantly, explores the modalities for its standardisation. Iwara et al.'s (2021) study highlighted a step-by-step approach to successfully establishing a rotating Stokvel based on the lived experience of 47 key informants drawn from the Thulamela local municipality. This chapter tests the generalisability of the suggested models by applying the building blocks to other localities of Limpopo Province in South Africa.

Four recurrent building constructs with their associated initiatives were derived from the empirical study that culminates with practical implications for further research and policy decision in South Africa. While this has provided insights into the need to implement a successful traditional Stokvel initiative within the locality, it is unclear whether the four constructs are applicable to other areas of South Africa and beyond. This knowledge gap leaves researchers with questions regarding the model's adaptability and integration into the mainstream economy. Thus, the current exploratory study was carried out to examine the four building constructs on a broader scale for validity, predominantly utilising quantitative methods. The rationale for this study is premised on the fact that Thulamela, where the initial study was performed, is only a Local Municipality out of 225 others in South Africa. Due to the variability of the country's municipalities and cultural dynamics, the sample used may not present sufficient evidence to generalise the findings, even within its host District, Vhembe, which has four other local municipalities. This motivated the need to cross-examine the building constructs in different locations, both rural and urban areas of Limpopo Province, to demonstrate conformity or no conformity and the benefits to business actors. The study's objective is twofold: (1) To determine the applicability of the building constructs in the study area and (2) To examine the distribution of the building constructs across categories of location.

Stokvel Model: Critique and Discourse

In South Africa, Stokvel initiatives are present in the informal economy, operating across urban, peri-urban and rural areas, easily accessible and flexible to various groups of individuals. This South African traditional initiative for entrepreneurial practice (originally 'stock fairs') emerged in the nineteenth century (Lukhele, 1990) as a business model through which certain farmers in the country convene to auction off their goods (Irving, 2005), exchange entrepreneurial ideas and gambling as part of livestock entrepreneurship in the informal economy. This practice has, in recent times, broadened and gained relevance; individuals from all walks of life, specialisation, profession and qualifications play Stokvel for both economic and social reasons. Households, especially people in rural areas, use the Stokvel model as a capital and revenue stream, as well as a critical financial resilience mechanism (Bophela, 2018). Overall, through its different segments, people interact both financially and socially to earn a living and build a cohesive society.

Stokvel models, in South Africa, especially the rotating structure which is predominant, provide platforms where a network of like-minded individuals or community members with common goals agrees to trade and/or contribute certain resources to actualise their shared vision (Lappeman, Litkie, Bramdaw & Quibell, 2020; Iwara et al., 2021). There exist several rotating forms of the model, such as farming Stokvel. In this category, group members collectively work on each other's farmlands every season. This practice relatively reduces the cost of hiring labour and likewise encourages expanded farming. Similarly, Building Stokvel involves members working as a team to map resources within their network and buy or put up a structure for each other, one after another. Property Stokvel is a practice that enables members to save money and purchase material items worth a certain amount for one member at a time. This approach is similar to grocery Stokvel, while a funeral Stokvel helps the bereaved receive a gift or lump sum from members.

In this current study, the focus is on rotating credit Stokvel, also called rotating budget Stokvel. While the other types of rotating Stokvel mentioned earlier, characterise a wide range of events which sometimes compel participants to be collectively involved in an agreed physical activity, procure material items for members and even contribute to show empathy, the latter (rotative credit/budget Stokvel) is limited to financial transactions on a rotational basis. As a result, it is classified as rotating credit Stokvel system. Rotating credit Stokvel model comprises a sizeable number of people where members contribute a fixed premium, specifically money, which makes a lump sum to a central fund weekly, monthly or quarterly depending on members' collectively agreed turnaround time. The lump sum that accrues from each settlement lag is handed to one member at a time, and the exercise continues until everyone in the circle benefits. Selecting this type of Stokvel as a case analysis in this study is based on the fact that it can become a source of financial strength for grassroots entrepreneurs lacking access to business capital.

Studies have shown that commercial banks rarely encourage the financial inclusion of micro and small enterprises, especially those operating in rural areas and/or managed by less-privileged and uneducated individuals (Moliea, 2010; SEDA, 2016; Verhoef, 2020). Similarly, scrounging business start-up capital from personal savings can be challenging for many. In addition to the time, it takes to ramp up, the lack of savings ethics and discipline are common obstacles that confront potential entrepreneurs. Although some individuals believe in the idea of saving money to raise business start-up capital, these limitations often jeopardise their business dreams, ideas and goals. In contrast to personal savings, individuals can contribute a small amount of their income to Stokvel credit systems to enable them to generate a business start-up lump sum over time. The idea of contributing a fixed premium, which makes a lump sum to a central fund, makes the model critically imperative for business start-up capital mobilisation. Ideally, deepening the knowledge of the model can reinforce the understanding of how the marginalised can independently mobilise business capital.

The knowledge this study provides is essential and would enable business actors in the study area to navigate alternative informal channels of resource mobilisation. Like many other developing economies in the world, the South African entrepreneurship landscape is compounded by several complexities that militate business entry and survival. For instance, a lack of financial information, as well as inaccessible funding and loans from the formal sector (Lekhanya & Mason, 2014) which emanate from cumbersome security requirements (SEDA, 2016; Bomani & Derera, 2018), poor financial literacy, and limited financial awareness programs (Mishi, Vacu, & Chipote, 2014). Research has shown that funding challenges are a major reason why local businesses in the country struggle to compete with global counterparts and maintain an upward trajectory (Mukwarami, Mukwarami, & Tengeh, 2020). This constraint is linked to the country's high enterprise failure rate (Fatoki, 2021; Yeboah, 2021). The argument above echoes the fact that entrepreneurial funding, particularly to small- and micro-scale enterprises in rural areas, is complex and chaotic. However, Stokvel plays an alternative role, similar to formal financial institutions, serving as a resilient factor for the growth of the informal economy, especially in rural areas. "Stokvel has evolved to become the primary mechanism to save money, access credit, obtain micro-loans for individuals and small businesses, reduce economic vulnerability, create social capital and provide mutual support for the vast number of the economically marginalised" (Menze & Tsibolane, 2019).

Stokvel's role in the local economy generally cannot be overemphasised. Its appreciation in this regard is justified by the increasing number of enrolments across board. In 2020, for instance, the National Stokvel Association of South Africa (NASASA) reported an average of 810 000 active Stokvel groups consisting of about 11 million South Africans; collecting an estimated R50 billion annually (NASASA, 2020). Nearly 50% of the country's adult population has a stake in at least one form of Stokvel initiative for livelihood. Iwara et al. (2021) further speculated that, in reality, the figure supersedes the estimated population, holding that many groups exist in silos. South Africans from diverse spheres of life and in different sectors are involved in Stokvel to address socioeconomic issues.

In the tourism sector, South Africans confront barriers to increasing domestic leisure travel, exacerbated by a decrease in earnings among a sizeable portion of the country's population amidst the COVID-19 pandemic. According to Adinolfi, Harilal and Giddy (2021), saving travel Stokvel contributes to keeping the country's tourism industry afloat; hence, it should be encouraged. This form of the Stokvel initiative provides residents with affordable payment options, one of which is to contribute a certain premium to a pull which makes a sum over time for leisure travel.

Recently, a diffused version of the model has emerged that allows for online engagements using platforms such as Facebook and WhatsApp. Similar to many other forms of digital financial transactions, credibility and quality assurance are still subject to further debate; however, research shows that the system provides exciting and innovative ways to raise business start-up capital and promote youth entrepreneurship in the country (Kariuki & Ofusori, 2017). According to Iwara (2022), university students harness digital savings and rotating Stokvel channels not only for business capital mobilisation but also to network and interact entrepreneurially, as well as market products. Beyond economic benefits, the increased use of Stokvel in different entrepreneurial spheres attests that African traditional informal business models are critical in stimulating the continent's enterprise capacity; they can exist as well as operate successfully in a developed and digital future. However, the application of Stokvel models in other parts of Africa could be stalled by weak knowledge of its building blocks. Against this premise, the application of four fundamental building constructs necessary for the rotating credit Stokvel initiative is investigated across areas of Limpopo province. This includes – the formation process, operational plan, financial management and disciplinary measures – see Table 1.

Four Constructs of Stokvel Operations and Performance

Stage One

The first construct is labelled the formation stage. It encompasses ideation and sharing of thoughts with individuals for implementation. Ideally, starting up any traditional rotating Stokvel begins with the idea of a need for development, which is then deliberated with a close friend, relative or colleague to augment for spin-off into a successful venture. Thereafter, it is made open to incorporate people into a significant but manageable number. Typically, Stokvel members convene monthly, fortnightly or weekly, with each group averaging 20 individuals. Enrolment of people into the group is based on the recommendation of those who started the initiative. Usually, people attract those close to them to participate and benefit from the venture as this makes it easy to connect, interact financially and manage the circle. More people can be involved using the networks of the enroled members. It operates like a snowball sampling technique where one known contact with unique attributes could refer to another until a saturation point is derived. In the end, traditional rotative Stokvel becomes a chain of a network of known people as each member is known and connected to at least another. Entry into the Stokvel is free, and so also is an exit – a reason we see most groups being careful about people to recruit to mitigate involving antagonists. Arguably, a non-entry fee reduces members' obligation to remain; hence, some members can easily pull out to the detriment of others. This is demonstrated in Code 1:4 – Admission criteria, where members strive to enrol like-minded and trustworthy people within their social and economic clusters.

Table 1. Self-Consolidated Rotating Credit Stokvel Key Attributes Derived From Literature.

Sl N	Key Attributes	Factors					
1	Stage 1: Formation process	*1.1 Ideation* The Stokvel starts with self-ideation and subsequently, focus group debriefing with interested peers	*1.2 Enrolment* Enrolment of new members into the group is based on recommendations of those who developed the idea	*1.3 Expansion* More members can be involved using contact through existing members	*1.4 Admission criteria* Enrolment into the group is based on trust, social status and economic class	*1.5 Familiarisation* Each member is known to at least one member	*1.6 Enrolment fee* Entry into the Stokvel group is free, so also is exit
2	Stage 2: Setting operations standards	*1.7 Operation plan* All members convene and debrief a suitable operation plan	*1.8 Inception* The Stokvel founders decide the venue and dimension of the group's first meeting	*1.9 Meetings* Stokvel meetings are hosted and rotated among members	*1.10 Leadership* Positions are elected based on trustworthiness and economic and social standing	*1.11 Profile* All members' information such as address and contact details are documented	
3	Stage 3: Financial management	*1.12 Records* All financial transactions are recorded in a ledger	*1.13 Contribution methods* Premiums are collected by one of the members	*1.14 Financial record* Chairperson is responsible for the financial administration	*1.15 Payroll* A balloting system is used for pay-out	*1.16 Exemptions* People with pressing needs are prioritised	*1.17 Dividends* All members equally benefit from the Stokvel profit

| 4 | Stage 4: Disciplinary measures | *1.18 Fines* Late coming, absence, squabbles and theft attract financial penalties | *1.19 Traditional authority* The involvement of traditional leaders in dispute resolution | *1.20 Prohibition* Frowning, shaming and discriminating against non-complying defaulters |

Source: Iwara et al. (2021).

Stage Two

Setting up operation standards, the second building construct, requires a meeting with all members who would have indicated an interest in the Stokvel to map out the dimension of initiatives as well as terms and conditions. The venue of the first meeting (usually a physical platform) is based on the discretion of the principal Stokvel initiator(s). Subsequent sessions can be rotated amongst members' residences or places of choice, depending on the collective agreement at the inception. In most cases, meetings are held in the initiator's house. With exceptions to some groups, hosts are obliged to cater for refreshments at the end of each meeting for members to enjoy in a relaxed manner and socialise, having engaged financially. This provides platforms to familiarise and establish more bonding that stimulates social ties, trust and networks and even determines the selection of people into key positions. The chairperson, secretary and treasurer, among other portfolios, are elected during the meeting based on a person's trustworthiness, behaviour and social standing in society.

Stage Three

The financial segment is the third building construct. This deals with the overall management of Stokvel's finances. Firstly, members attend each meeting with an agreed premium, which makes a sum for one of the members. However, some additions are also made for the group's running costs and short-term investments, such as lending, which generate revenue for the members. The agreed premium from all members is payable in cash to a designated member, who then consolidates for further action. In recent times, physical payment methods have been complemented by digital methods wherein members transfer money directly from their account to a designated account, making it more convenient and secure to engage financially. Nonetheless, groups strive to record financial transactions in a ledger for future reference. Group Chairperson oversees the administration of finances, except when directed to another member. The pay-out of a lump sum follows a balloting system. This mitigates potential bias as well as favouritism and potential rift or conflict among members. In some cases, exceptions are made for people with pressing needs who have discussed their situation with the group and agreed to terms or for those who are voluntarily exchanging turns.

Stage Four

Disciplinary, the last building construct, explains measures enacted to limit misconduct among members. For instance, lateness to meetings, absenteeism, fights and theft are serious offences that attracts fines. Hesitancy to take on responsibility is a punishable offence. Failure to pay the agreed premium, having received a lump sum from other members, is a serious offence that is often dealt with using local authorities or other traditional methods. Generally, defaulters, especially the non-complying members, are duly sanctioned and admonished to preserve the sanctity of the agreement.

To standardise these measures for adoption in Limpopo, South Africa, and beyond, this study proposes a test of measurement under different circumstances. The following null hypotheses were formulated to test the assumptions:

H1. The distribution of the Stokvel formation construct is the same across categories of location.

H2. The distribution of Stokvel operation standards is the same across categories of location.

H3. The distribution of Stokvel financial management is the same across categories of location.

H4. The distribution of Stokvel disciplinary measures is the same across categories of location.

Methodology

The illustrative case study was ideal for the study. It is a descriptive type of case study that enables the use of one or more instances (examples) to describe a phenomenon with the primary aim of making what is considered unfamiliar familiar (Harrison, Birks, Franklin, & Mills, 2017). This case study enables building inferences more broadly, based on findings of already best-established Stokvel foundations in one local area, thereby, deepening the understanding of how the model applies to a wider spectrum. In doing so, Stokvel members from five rural villages and five townships were conveniently selected in Limpopo Province (see Fig. 2). Guidelines for classifying rural areas, in line with Mudimeli (2019), were adopted. This includes distance (50 kilometres away) from basic services and infrastructure, considerable absence of shopping centres, inequitable spatial planning and lack of land use management. Limpopo Province is one of the nine in South Africa and the country's northernmost province, which shares borders with Botswana, Mozambique and Zimbabwe. The province has five district municipalities that contribute about 9.8% of the country's 59,62 million population (Stat SA, 2020a). Named after the great Limpopo River that flows along its northern border, this province is rich in agriculture, wildlife, spectacular scenery and a wealth of historical as well as cultural treasures. However, the province is still grappling with the triple challenge of unemployment, inequality and poverty. This constitutes part of the reason many people resort to Stokvel activities for social and economic upliftment.

Distribution of Samples by Location

At present, statistical records showing the distribution of Stokvel membership for each province in South Africa are inaccessible. As a result, the country's estimated 11,000,000 average Stokvel membership population from NASASA was disaggregated across the nine provinces to derive a suitable population. This aided derivation of the actual sample size in Limpopo Province (Table 2). Using the percentage population distribution for each province, it is estimated that

Table 2. Estimated Stokvel Membership Distribution.

S/N	Province	Population (%)
1	Gauteng	15.5 million (26.0%)
2	KwaZulu-Natal	11.5 million (19.3%)
3	Western Cape	7.05 million (11.8%)
4	Eastern Cape	6.73 million (11.3%)
5	Limpopo	5.85 million (9.8%)
6	Mpumalanga	4.68 million (7.8%)
7	North West	4.10 million (6.9%)
8	Free State	2.93 million (4.9%)
9	Northern Cape	1.29 million (2.2%)
	Total	59.62 million (100)

Source: Author's consolidation based on data derived from STATS-SA (2020a) and NASASA (2020).

Limpopo Province accounts for about 1,000,000 to 1,100,000 of the total Stokvel membership, which then serves as the total population for the current study.

The statistical formula ($n = N/1 + N(e)2$) based on Yamane (2021) is adopted to determine the actual sample size from the estimated 1,100,000 Stokvel membership in Limpopo Province.

n = required or actual sample size from the population under study
N = population that is under study
e = precision or sampling error (usually 0.01, 0.0.05 or 0.10).

This would hence be: $n = N/1 + N(e)2$
$N = 1,100,000$; $e = 0.1$; $e2 = 0.01$
$n = 1,100,000/1 + 1,100,000 (0.1)2$
$n = 385 \cong 400$.

Therefore, a sample size of 400 respondents out of the population of 1,100,000 would be the lowest acceptable number of responses to maintain a 95% confidence level in this study. The Snowball sampling technique, with the support of key informants, enabled the selection of participants, mainly South Africans, involved in rotating Stokvel initiatives. Generally, Stokvel groups meet periodically in convenient areas to interact on financial matters, making it difficult to sample participants randomly; thus, a non-probability sampling technique was ideal. In line with the four re-occurring building constructs, a self-developed 5-point Likert-type scale wherein '1' is the least agreed, while '5' represent the strongest agreed decision was distributed to Stokvel members who consented to participate in the study. The questions were designed to enable participants to rank the extent to which the initiatives in each Stokvel building construct apply to their land-scape. To ensure variation and data validity, 500 participants were targeted; however, 473 completed the survey and 55 were void – summing up to a 94.6% (418) response rate. This response exceeded the estimated 400 sample size threshold for the study. Thus, the 95% confidence level is maintained.

In total, participants from the township accounted for 49.8%, while the rural villages constituted 50.2% of the valid sample. The female tallied at 53%, while their male counterparts accounted for the remaining 47% (Fig. 1). The majority of the participants (42.4%) had no formal education (Fig. 2). This is relatively high when compared to those with high school and university education, which contributed about 15% thus raising the assumption that level of education may have a significant influence on intentions to Stokvel. Poverty and unemployment margins in South Africa are significantly high amongst the those with little or no formal education (Stats SA, 2020b) – justifying their increasing involvement in Stokvel as an alternative revenue stream and means of survival.

The data from a Likert-type scale were recalibrated into the four Stokvel building constructs and fitted into the IBM Statistical Package for Social Sciences

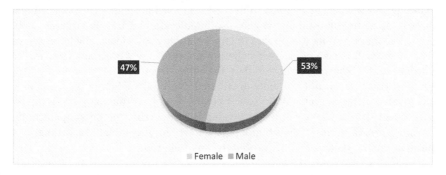

Fig. 1.   Distribution of the Participants by Gender.

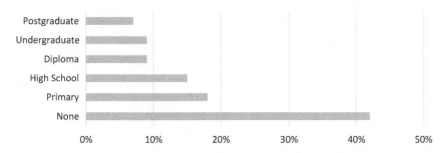

Fig. 2.   Distribution of the Participants by Qualification.

(SPSS) version 27 for analysis. Firstly, the Kolmogorov–Smirnov test and the Shapiro–Wilk test were carried out for data normality which then suggests the adoption of a non-parametric analytical method. Secondly, One-Sample Wilcoxon Signed Rank Test was performed to determine the extent to which the four Stokvel building constructs apply to the study area, using a test value of 4.0. Lastly, an Independent-Samples Mann–Whitney U Test was carried out to examine the distribution of the Stokvel building constructs between rural and urban areas. This test compares the number of times a sample's score is ranked higher than a score from another sample in each of the four constructs and further determines whether there is a significant difference between the means of the two groups.

Result and Discussion of Findings

Test of Normality

Table 3 presents the results from two tests of normality – the Kolmogorov–Smirnov Test and the Shapiro–Wilk Test performed on the four rotating Stokvel building constructs. The Shapiro–Wilk Test examined normality for small sample sizes (<50 samples), although it can also handle sample sizes as large as 2000, while the Shapiro–Wilk test applies to larger sample sizes. Hence, the latter serves as a numerical means of assessing the normality of the 418-sample size in the current study. The test indicates that the data structure for the four Stokvel building constructs is not normally distributed. Normality assumptions are that if the p-value of the Shapiro–Wilk Test is greater than 0.05, the data are normally distributed. In the event where the p-value is below 0.05, the data significantly deviate from a normal distribution, as shown in the table. Accordingly, a non-parametric data analytical procedure was followed.

Table 3. Test of Normality ($n = 418$).

Tests of Normality

	Kolmogorov–Smirnov[a]			Shapiro–Wilk		
	Statistic	**df**	**Sig.**	**Statistic**	**df**	**Sig.**
Formation	0.166	418	0.000	0.897	418	0.000
Operation	0.156	418	0.000	0.888	418	0.000
Finance	0.129	418	0.000	0.928	418	0.000
Disciplinary	0.187	418	0.000	0.891	418	0.000

[a]Lilliefors Significance Correction.

Application of Stokvel Building Constructs in the Study Area

Fig. 3 illustrates the mean scores obtained from One-Sample Wilcoxon Signed Rank Test for the Stokvel building constructs, while Table 4 presents the statistically significant levels. On average, the observed means scores for the Formation (F1 = 4.3, p = 0.00), Operation (F2 = 4.4, p = 0.00), Finance (F3 = 4.2, p = 0.00) and Disciplinary (F4 = 4.3, p = 0.00) significantly exceed that of the hypothesised mean score (4.0) at 5% statistical level of significance. This implies that the majority of the participants believe that the examined constructs apply strongly to the study area.

Distribution of the Stokvel Building Constructs Across Categories of Location

A Mann–Whitney U Test subsequently confirmed the mean scores and low standard deviation, indicating that one of the data for the four constructs is clustered about the mean. On average, the distribution of the Stokvel formation construct in the rural area (Mean *Rank* = 219.74) exceeded that of the urban area (Mean *Rank* = 199.16); however, there is no evidence to support a difference between the ratings of the two locations (U = 19,689.000, z-1.76, p = 0.077, two-tailed) (Table 5). Similarly, there is no evidence to support a difference between the ratings of the two locations for operation construct (U = 20,233.000, z-1.312, p = 0.189, two-tailed), financial segment (U = 20,587.000, z-1.020, p = 0.308, two-tailed) and disciplinary measures (U = 20,168.000, z-1.379, p = 0.168, two-tailed). Therefore, the null hypothesis that the distribution of the four-building construct is the same across categories of location is retained.

Based on the findings of this study, it can be inferred that the four constructs for building a successful Stokvel are consistent across areas of Limpopo Province. This argument finds legitimacy in the observed Mean Ranks of the constructs, which move towards 4.5 on a 5-point scale, where 1 is the least. Accordingly, there was no statistical evidence to support a difference between the ratings of rural and urban areas. The fact that other forms of Stokvel, especially the digital approach, which contrast significantly from the traditional concept, are emerging, thus partly responsible for the diffusion of people's orientation, and this could account for the remaining 0.5 that skewed towards 3, 2 and 1 of the ratings. However, the contribution is not statistically significant. In addition, there is a considerable transformation of the traditional Stokvel. For instance, physical cash transactions and home saving, which are central to traditional Stokvel, are gradually being complemented with digital transfers and formal banking, mostly in urban areas (Biyela, Tsibolane, & Van Belle, 2018; du Pisanie, 2018; Menze & Tsibolane, 2019). Research reveals that the digital Stokvel system is convenient, effective and minimises the risk of attacks/theft of physical cash in transit (Thomas, 2015; van Wyk, 2017); likewise, irregularities, mismanagement of members' resources and embezzlement resulting from inadequate managerial skills and inappropriate record keeping. Thus, it is appropriate to believe the

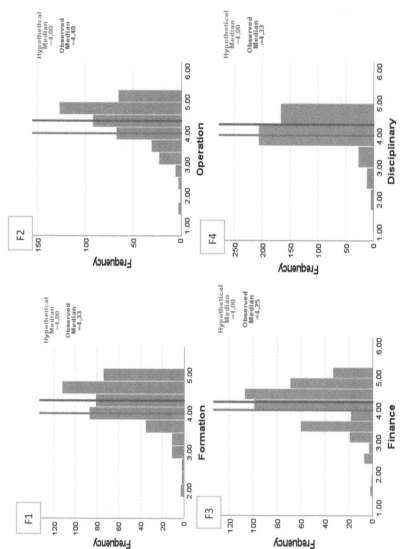

Fig. 3.　One-Sample Wilcoxon Signed Rank Test (Observed and Hypothetical Means).

Table 4. One-Sample Wilcoxon Signed Rank Test Summary.

	Test Statistic	**Standard Error**	**Standardised Test Statistic**	**Asymptotic Sig. (2-Sided Test)**
Formation	52527.000	1942.198	10.502	0.000
Operation	53424.500	2089.415	8.698	0.000
Finance	47387.000	2050.724	6.373	0.000
Disciplinary	48808.000	1914.320	8.899	0.000

The significance level is 0.050.

evolution of other forms of Stokvel and the gradual transformation of the existing ones may amount to misconceptions.

In a typical Stokvel setup, various disciplinary measures exist. The use of indigenous measures such as peer pressure and the commitment of traditional authority (Iwara et al., 2021), involvement of the taxi drivers (van Wyk, 2017), social exclusion (Forkuoh, Affum-Osei, & Quaye, 2015) and discrediting (Thomas, 2015) believed to have a significant disciplinary implication. The fact that the world is revolving and Stokvel is gradually transforming from a rural-based, women-oriented initiative to a common practice widely embraced by many individuals across societies and distinct cultural backgrounds (Kok & Lebusa, 2018; Iwara, 2022), may have diffused its traditional status quo in some contexts. In comparison with customary judicial methods, urban residents would rather resort to conventional legal systems for Stokvel conflict resolution, which is indicative of how people in different areas perceive disciplinary measures.

Conclusion

The current study was carried out to examine the rotating credit Stokvel model applicability in Limpopo Province, laying the foundation for its adoption in other provinces of South Africa and beyond. The model's four building constructs adopted from Iwara et al. (2021) – formation, operation, financials and disciplinary – serve as proxy for the measurement. Two main objectives were considered: (1) To determine the applicability of the Stokvel building constructs to the study area and (2) To examine the distribution of the building constructs across categories of location. Data obtained from participants reveal a strong alignment of the constructs in the study area, and there is no statistically significant evidence to support a difference between the ratings of the rural and urban locations in the province. This leads to the conclusion that traditional rotating credit Stokvel practices are similar in areas of Limpopo and possibly across South African provinces. However, an observable trend from the literature points to the continuous transformation of the model, for instance, complementary online transactions amongst certain Stokvel groups. Similarly, the digital forms of the Stokvel are evolving. In contrast with the traditional system, the latter operates

Table 5. Independent-Samples Mann–Whitney *U* Test.

Descriptive Statistics

	N	Mean	Std. Deviation	Minimum	Maximum
Formation	418	4.3082	0.56212	2.00	5.00
Operation	418	4.2694	0.64050	1.60	5.00
Finance	418	4.1623	0.59017	1.50	5.00
Disciplinary	418	4.2624	0.60990	1.33	5.00
Location	418	1.50	0.501	1	2

	Location	Mean Rank	Sum of Ranks
Formation	Urban	199.16	41425.00
	Rural	219.74	46146.00
Operation	Urban	201.77	41969.00
	Rural	217.15	45602.00
Finance	Urban	203.48	42323.00
	Rural	215.47	45248.00
Disciplinary	Urban	201.46	41904.00
	Rural	217.46	45667.00

Test Statistics[a]

	Formation	Operation	Finance	Disciplinary
Mann–Whitney U	19689.000	20233.000	20587.000	20168.000
Wilcoxon W	41425.000	41969.000	42323.000	41904.000
Z	−1.768	−1.312	−1.020	−1.379
Asymp. Sig. (2-Tailed)	0.077	0.189	0.308	0.168

The significance level is 0.050.
[a]Grouping Variable: Location.

more conveniently on online platforms with a large number of members (sometimes over 100). This is beginning to reshape how people approach the model.

Insight for Business Actors

In South Africa and Africa, business capital mobilisation through formal financial institutions is a major challenge for entrepreneurs, especially those operating micro- and small-scale enterprises in rural areas. The step-by-step approach to setting up successful rotating credit Stokvel provides entrepreneurs with an alternative informal and reliable capital mobilisation channel. In this case, a sizable number of people who share similar goals can contribute a fixed premium which makes a lump sum to a central fund weekly, monthly, or quarterly, depending on members' collectively agreed turnaround time, and then handed to one member to start up or expand their businesses.

Acknowledgements

This study extends on 'Traditional Savings Association for Entrepreneurial Success in Africa: A Case Study of Rotative Stokvel Enterprise' which was carried out in Thulamela Local Municipality. We are indebted to the grassroots Stokvel members in Limpopo Province who willingly participated in this study.

References

Adinolfi, M. C., Harilal, V., & Giddy, J. K. (2021). Travel Stokvels, leisure on lay by, and pay at your pace options: The post COVID-19 domestic tourism landscape in South Africa. *African Journal of Hospitality, Tourism and Leisure, 10*(1), 302–317.

Biyela, N., Tsibolane, P., & Van Belle, J. P. (2018). Domestication of ICTs in Community Savings and Credit Associations (Stokvels) in the Western cape, South Africa. In *International Development Informatics Association Conference*, Cham (pp. 35–47). Springer.

Bomani, M., & Derera, E. (2018). Towards developing a strategic framework for stimulating rural entrepreneurship in KwaZulu-Natal, South Africa: A case study of three municipalities. *International Journal of Economics and Finance Studies, 10*(1), 150–166.

Bophela, M. J. K. (2018). *The role of Stokvels in the economic transformation of Ethekwini municipality*. Doctoral dissertation, University of Kwazulu-Natal.

du Pisanie, K. (2018). Stokvel empowers young farmers. *Stockfarm, 8*(10), 18–19.

Fatoki, O. (2021). Access to finance and performance of small firms in South Africa: The moderating effect of financial literacy. *WSEAS Transactions on Business and Economics, 8*, 78–87.

Forkuoh, S. K., Li, Y., Affum-Osei, E., & Quaye, I. (2015). Informal financial services, a panacea for SMEs financing? A case study of SMEs in the Ashanti region of Ghana. *American Journal of Industrial and Business Management, 5*(12), 779–793.

Harrison, H., Birks, M., Franklin, R., & Mills, J. (2017). Case study research: Foundations and methodological orientations. *Forum Qualitative Sozialforschung/ Forum: Qualitative Social Research, 18*(1), 1–17.

Irving, M. (2005). *Informal savings groups in South Africa: Investing in social capital.* Working Paper Number 112. Centre for Social Science Research, University of Cape Town.

Iwara, I. O. (2022). Digital informal credit system for student entrepreneurship promotion in higher learning-the case of South Africa. In *Digital service delivery in Africa* (pp. 163–186). Cham: Palgrave Macmillan.

Iwara, I. O., Adeola, O., & Netshandama, V. O. (2021). Traditional savings association for entrepreneurial success in Africa: A case study of rotative stokvel enterprise. *Academy of Entrepreneurship Journal, 27*(2), 1–15.

Kariuki, P., & Ofusori, L. O. (2017). WhatsApp-operated stokvels promoting youth entrepreneurship in Durban, South Africa: Experiences of young entrepreneurs. In J. Gil-García & T. A. Pardo (Eds.), *Proceedings of the 10th International Conference on Theory and Practice of Electronic Governance* (pp. 253–259). ACM.

Kok, L., & Lebusa, M. (2018). *The Savings Associations Clubs (Stokvels) in South Africa: The Stokvels as an informal way to finance Black entrepreneurship in South Africa.* London: LAP Lambert Academic Publishing.

Lappeman, J., Litkie, J., Bramdaw, S., & Quibell, A. (2020). Exploring retail orientated rotating savings and credit associations: Festive season 'Stokvels' in South Africa. *International Review of Retail Distribution & Consumer Research, 30*(3), 331–358.

Lekhanya, L. M., & Mason, R. B. (2014). Selected key external factors influencing the success of rural small and medium enterprises in South Africa. *Journal of Enterprising Culture, 22*(03), 331–348.

Lukhele, A. K. (Ed.). (1990). *Stokvels in South Africa: Informal savings associations by Blacks for the Black community.* Johannesburg: Amagi Books.

Matuku, S., & Kaseke, E. (2014). The role of Stokvels in improving people's lives: The case in Orange farm, Johannesburg. *South Africa Social Work, 50*(4), 504–519.

Menze, A., & Tsibolane, P. (2019). Online Stokvels: The use of social media by the marginalized. In *CONF-IRM 2019 Proceedings* (p. 26).

Mishi, S., Vacu, N. P., & Chipote, P. (2014). *Impact of financial literacy in optimising financial inclusion in rural South Africa: Case study of the Eastern Cape Province.* Retrieved from https://www.econrsa.org/system/files/workshops/papers/2012/mishi-financial-literacy.pdf

Moliea, H. (2010). *Stokvels as alternative microfinance institutions: Conversations with women from Venda.* Doctoral dissertation, University of Pretoria.

Mudimeli, R. N. (2019). *Determining the functionality of traditional leadership council as agent of rural development in Vhembe district, South Africa.* Doctoral dissertation, University of Venda, Thohoyandou.

Mukwarami, S., Mukwarami, J., & Tengeh, R. K. (2020). Local economic development and small business failure: The case of a local municipality in South Africa. *International Journal of Business and Globalisation, 25*(4), 489–502.

NSASA. (2020). Statement on measures to prevent COVID-19 coronavirus transmission. Retrieved from https://nasasa.co.za/

SEDA. (2016). The SMME sector of South Africa. Research Note, 2016. Bureau of Economic Research. Retrieved from http://www.seda.org.za/Publications/

Publications/The%20Small,%20Medium%20and%20Micro%20Enterprise%
20Sector%20of%20South%20Africa%20Commissioned%20by%20Seda.pdf

Stat SA. (2020a). *South Africa – Mid-year population estimates 2020.* Retrieved from
http://www.statssa.gov.za/publications/P0302/P03022020.pdf

Stats SA. (2020b). *Quarterly labour force survey – Quarter 4: 2020.* Retrieved from
http://www.statssa.gov.za/publications/P0211/P02114thQuarter2020.pdf

Thomas, A. (2015). Revolving loan scheme (ESUSU): A substitute to the Nigerian
commercial banking? *Journal of Business and Management, 17*(6), 62–67.

Verhoef, G. (2020). Stokvels and economic empowerment: The case of African women
in South Africa, c. 1930–1998. In *Women and credit* (pp. 91–114). London:
Routledge.

van Wyk, M. M. (2017). Stokvels as a community-based saving club aimed at erad-
icating poverty: A case of South African rural women. *The International Journal of
Community Diversity, 17*(2), 13–26.

Yamane, T. (2021). *Statistics: An introductory analysis* (3rd ed.). New York, NY:
Harper & Row.

Yeboah, M. A. (2021). Determinants of SME growth: An empirical perspective of
SMEs in the cape coast metropolis, Ghana. *The Journal of Business in Developing
Nations, 14*, 1–31.

Part 3
Conclusions and Recommendations

Chapter 11

Internationalisation of Indigenous Agribusiness in Africa: The Case of JR Farms in Rwanda and Zambia

Belinda Nwosu and Edidiong Esara

Abstract

The agribusiness ecosystem in Africa is shaped by a myriad of complex and interwoven issues. Navigating these complexities and growing sustainable businesses with high social impact value is usually the outcome of a sustained effort to succeed. The knowledge of the African business context, the ability to identify opportunities and the willingness to learn from experience constitute a veritable means for any entrepreneur seeking to scale up an Indigenous agribusiness in Africa. This chapter presents JR Farms as a case study of one of such Indigenous agribusinesses that has successfully expanded within the African market. The case examines the trajectory of JR Farms from its beginnings in Nigeria to its definitive establishment in Rwanda and Zambia. Through the lens of a qualitative case study approach, we write a narrative of the vision, strategies and decisions that transformed JR Farms into a multi-million-dollar development partner for the communities where it operates. Finally, we reflect on these experiences in making recommendations for growing agribusinesses in Africa.

Keywords: Agribusiness; Indigenous business; coffee value chain; internationalisation; Africa; Rwanda; Zambia

Introduction

The African Development Bank (AfDB) has as its primary strategy to transform agriculture in Africa into a globally competitive, inclusive and business-oriented sector (AfDB, 2022). The bank estimates that 3.6 million people benefitted directly from improvements in agriculture in 2021 alone. However, on a continent with close to 1.4 billion inhabitants, this remains a modest figure (AfDB, 2022).

Casebook of Indigenous Business Practices in Africa, 205–223
Copyright © 2023 Belinda Nwosu and Edidiong Esara
Published under exclusive licence by Emerald Publishing Limited
doi:10.1108/978-1-80455-762-420231019

One of the identifiable benefits of developing agribusiness in Africa is its potential to unlock sustainable growth for promoting economic growth, food security and poverty reduction (Ademola, Manning, & Azadi, 2017). The following case study provides an overview of the transformation of JR Farms from an Indigenous small-scale cassava-processing initiative to a multi-million-dollar multinational agribusiness. By building on the experiences of its founder, this case demonstrates the contributions of Indigenous knowledge and experience of local context in growing a sustainable agribusiness in Africa.

Country Context

Zambia is a landlocked country located in South-central Africa. The country is bordered in the north by the Democratic Republic of Congo and Tanzania, to the west by Angola, to the east by Malawi and Mozambique, while Namibia, Botswana and Zimbabwe border the south. According to ZambiaInvest (2022), agriculture plays a critical role in the Zambian economy, contributing 2.7% to the country's gross domestic product (GDP) in 2020. Government strategies to position agribusiness as a key economic sector are evidenced by the scale of investments currently underway. For instance, in June 2022, Zambeef Products PLC, a key player in agribusiness in Zambia announced that it had invested US$100 million in boosting its row cropping capacity and production efficiency (Market Watch, 2022) (Table 1).

Table 1. Rwanda and Zambia Country Data.

	Rwanda	**Zambia**
Land Mass	26,338 sq km	752,618 sq km
Population (est 2022)	13.2 million	19.6 million
Population growth (est 2022)	1.74%	2.9%
Real GDP (est 2020)	US$27.2 billion	US$60.1 billion (est 2020)
Agricultural products	Bananas, sweet potatoes, cassava, potatoes, plantains, beans, maize, gourds, milk, taro	Sugar cane, cassava, maize, milk, vegetables, soybeans, beef, tobacco, wheat, groundnuts
Export commodities (est 2019)	Gold, refined petroleum, coffee, tea, tin	Copper, gold, gemstones, sulphuric acid, raw sugar, tobacco

Sources: The African Union (www.au.int); The World Factbook https://www.cia.gov/the-world-factbook/

Rwanda is a hilly and richly fertile country located in the heart of central Africa. Also landlocked, Rwanda is bordered by the Democratic Republic of Congo to the west, Tanzania to the east, Uganda to the north and Burundi to the south. The Rwanda Development Board (2022) estimates that the agricultural sector contributes 31% to the country's GDP. Given that close to 61% of the landmass in the country is fertile, agribusiness has been positioned as a strategic economic sector (*ibid.*). Consequently, the RDB has made several incentives available for investors in the sector, for example, a seven-year tax holiday for export-oriented registered investment projects (*ibid.*) (Fig. 1).

Methodology

The case study investigated the vision and strategy of an Indigenous agripreneur to provide a chronicle of agribusiness expansion in Africa. An in-depth interview with the protagonist constituted the primary data source. Data were also collected from secondary sources, namely, company and media publications. The interview transcript was reviewed and analysed to derive themes. The different data sources were then integrated and interpreted to form the framework of the case narrative. Transparency was achieved by reviewing the case findings with the protagonist.

Fig. 1.   Map of Africa: Rwanda and Zambia.

The Beginnings at JR Farms

The founder and CEO of JR Farms, 33-year-old Olawale Rotimi Opeyemi (Wale for short), had been exposed to agriculture since his teenage years. As a pastime in his rural homeland in Oyo State, South-western Nigeria, he helped his uncle in a Garri (cassava flakes) processing factory and observed daily routines at a family friend's piggery. This was after oil in commercial quantities had been discovered, and agriculture had ceased to be the mainstay of Nigeria's economy (Ani, Nnanwube, & Ojakorotu, 2018). Still too young to have experienced Nigeria as a thriving agricultural economy, Wale was keenly aware that there was a strong case for agribusiness in the country. In 2012, he started publishing articles about agribusiness, which got him noticed in the media. He wished to do more than just advocacy, so he got into agribusiness that year, including running a farmers' co-operative. Unfortunately, this initiative failed two years later. In 2014, Wale and his wife started JR Farms, specialising in agro-consultancy and Garri-processing (Figs. 2 and 3).

Wale's interest in agribusiness grew, and he actively participated in several industry meetings. 'As time went on, our attendance at those meetings made people see what we had to offer, and they started inviting us to these conferences, sponsoring us, and this graduated to partnerships', he recounted. He

Fig. 2.   JR Farms Receives Cassava Supplies From Farmers in Oyo State, Nigeria.

Fig. 3.   JR Farms' CEO Olawale With Local Garri Traders in
Gambari Food Market, Oyo State, Nigeria.

brainstormed with stakeholders at these conferences, including the 2015 African
Development Bank annual meeting in Ivory Coast, where he shared his ideas
regarding the food future of Africa.

Venturing Into Rwanda

During these engagements, Wale identified opportunities in different parts of
Africa and sought to expand beyond the shores of his homeland. He understood
that in Africa, the role of the government in shaping policies for sustainable
agribusiness was critical. Rwanda, for one, showed enterprise-friendly indicators.
Rwanda Vision 2050 had Agriculture for Wealth Creation as one of its pillars, as
approximately 70% of the population in Rwanda earned their livelihoods from
agriculture (RMFEP, 2015). The vision was to develop a market-led and
high-tech agricultural sector driven by professional farmers, thereby placing the
private sector at the forefront of commercialisation and value chains. This
repositioning would be financed through greater Foreign Direct Investment. In
effect, Rwanda intended to adapt to the changing environment by transforming

the sector to become modern and innovative, while also promoting local and home-grown solutions.

Wale took advantage of the opportunities he identified in the coffee value chain in Rwanda. Coffee looked good for business. He found that big organisations preferred to buy coffee from foreign companies. Although coffee originated in Africa, the coffee beans were roasted in Europe or America and then exported back to Africa. One of the reasons for this common practice was logistics-related, and the other was the cost of production in many parts of Africa. JR Farms knew they had to invest in quality production and good packaging to compete with Western markets. It was imperative that young African entrepreneurs acquired the know-how necessary for manufacturing products to international standards.

In 2017, JR Farms moved to Rwanda to focus on beverage processing and the exportation of roasted coffee beans. However, this required funding. Reliance on family social capital for starting up businesses in Africa is typical. African societies, being highly collectivist, suggest that family and community are central to the growth and development of businesses of young entrepreneurs, especially where an institutional support structure found in more developed economies is absent (Jongwe & Sono, 2022). Banks and would-be investors typically wanted to see results before partnering or putting in their funds. This challenge was foreseen by the Rwanda Vision 2050, which acknowledged the reluctance of banks and private sector players to invest in agriculture due to perceived high risks and high transaction costs. Wale turned to his family and used this as a launching pad for this move into commercial coffee production. For Wale, an important contributor to the success of JR Farms' operations in Rwanda was the start-up funding provided by the family.

Partnerships and Value Addition

As JR Farms started to expand its operations, Wale began to appreciate the importance of partnerships in creating more value for the farmers and communities. Here was an opportunity to stimulate private sector engagement in the African agribusiness ecosystem. However, Rwanda's agribusiness sector was mostly populated by micro-enterprises that partnered with smallholder farmers. In some cases, these partnerships formed relational contracts, whereby trading partners cooperated in facilitating mutually beneficial outcomes (Gerard, Lopez, Kerr, & Bizoza, 2021). Partnerships became the core of JR Farms' operations, which involved working with institutional partners who were reliable and organised. They collaborated with sectoral agencies/associations such as Coffee Exporters and Processors (Fig. 4).

According to Wale, JR Farms is '...a leading agribusiness determined to transform agriculture in Africa by undertaking opportunities for growth and business that will engender sustainable food production and increased incomes for farmers'. In 2018, JR Farms Africa signed a partnership agreement with Rwanda Farmers Coffee Company which allowed them to work with thousands of coffee

Fig. 4.   JR Farms Renews Its Partnership With Rwanda Farmers
Coffee Company.

farmers in Rwanda, roast specialty coffee, and package and export to various
markets. Through this partnership, JR Farms exported to eight countries (JR
Farms, 2020) (Fig. 5).

They also worked with global organisations like Food and Agriculture Organization (FAO), International Labour Organization (ILO) and other development
agencies. Since the focus of the development plans in Rwanda projected agriculture
as one sector that would provide productive employment, initiatives that supported
young people interested in farming were encouraged (Fig. 6).

Organisations such as the Rwanda Youth in Agribusiness Forum (RYAF)
offered a platform for business linkage opportunities and orientation to agriculture for scores of young entrepreneurs.

Describing their business model, Wale said:

> We focus on the value addition side of things. We have a lot of
> partnerships across the value chain. We don't farm. We have a
> cassava factory, but we don't own a cassava farm; we process in
> our coffee factory, but we do not own any coffee farm. We work
> with a network of farmers. So, partnership is one key thing in our
> business model. We position ourselves at the forefront of the value
> chain; then we connect with partners behind and around the chain
> – logistics partners, farmers, labour etc. Also, our business model
> is assets-driven; we build many assets – owning land, building
> factories, owning machinery. If a business goes wrong, we have
> something to hold on to, which helps mitigate our risks.

Fig. 5.   JR Farms' Coffee Processing Factory in Rwanda.

Fig. 6.   JR Farms Hosted by International Labour Organization
Regional Office for Africa in Abidjan, Côte d'Ivoire.

The goal was to achieve decent job creation, food security and improved living standards for Africans. JR Farms believed that these would not be achieved only by planting and harvesting crops, but especially in value addition. Hence, they tried to reverse the dependence on goods exported into the continent by setting up structures for processing coffee in Africa, hoping to push down the international price of the commodity and earn more money for locals. In addition, emphasis was made on improving branding and product quality to justify the premium pricing of Rwandan coffee in the global market. As the volume of coffee exported from Rwanda by JR Farms continued to increase, farmer revenue receipts continued to rise. Farmers sold their coffee at fair rates, which translated to higher revenue for the national economy and more employment for citizens.

Piloting on a Small Scale

From experience, JR Farms understood the purpose of pilot programmes when addressing gaps within the agribusiness ecosystem in Africa. For one, it was an essential first step in managing available resources, identifying challenges and finding the right solutions. Wale knew that projects launched without a pilot scheme tend to fail due to a lack of understanding of the cultural, social and even political dynamics within the communities where JR Farms worked. With this foresight, JR Farms led an initiative called the Green Agribusiness Fund (GAF, 2020) in collaboration with Generation Africa and the FAO. The primary aim of this initiative was to invest in youth-led agribusinesses that addressed issues of rural development, sustainability and decent jobs for women and youth across Africa. After a long-drawn design phase, the initiative was piloted, and a US$30,000 fund to support six youth-led agribusinesses was launched.

The six beneficiaries had to undergo various due diligence processes to be held accountable for their projects. The success of this pilot scheme allowed the GAF initiative to eventually scale up and open an academy where 200 participants were assisted in making their businesses investor-ready over a period of eight weeks. In addition, the Young Farmers' Green Hangout, a forum of intensive and solution-oriented conversations with experts from various sectors, was held periodically as a contribution to the goals of the GAF initiative. Eleven agri-businesses from Rwanda, Uganda and Nigeria were shortlisted as finalists for the 2022 cohort.

In effect, JR Farms' efforts aimed at addressing the challenges faced by agribusinesses in Africa by means of home-grown solutions.

Wale recalled,

> We designed propeller-driven machines that could work without electricity when it became difficult for JR Farms to compete in the Nigerian Garri market because of the high production costs due to scarce electricity from the national grid. The results of this pilot scheme in Oyo paid off as JR Farms now supplies an average of 35 tonnes of Garri to the local market.

Leveraging Government Policies

Wale's first attraction to Rwanda stemmed from easy access to investment information on the Rwanda Development Board (RDB) website, especially regarding the country's Agribusiness Investment Promotion Strategy. He was amazed at how quickly he could register a business online, free of charge, and have his certificate of registration issued in six hours. Setting up and transacting business – including tax payment and litigation – was possible online. Rwanda also had an investment code that entrenched equal treatment for foreigners and nationals in some business operations, facilitated the free transfer of funds and compensated against expropriation.

Leveraging the digitalisation drive contained in the Rwanda Vision 2050, JR Farms utilised technology to fast-track its operations. They deployed an app to interact with farmers and track products in different locations. These initiatives were innovative as JR Farms brought technology to the heart of the African rural farmstead. It was now possible for the agribusiness ecosystem, which demanded market-driven technology for sustainable value creation, to embed Indigenous farming practices that had existed for decades in the region.

Wale also found appreciable infrastructural support and an enabling environment that made it easy to forecast the future of the business in Rwanda. First, there was relatively stable electricity which the government planned to upgrade to meet the country's power generation needs. Another advantage was access to the East African Community (EAC) and the Common Market for Eastern and Southern Africa (COMESA), where there were untapped investment opportunities in agribusiness for approximately 600 million consumers. Rwanda was one of the first countries to ratify the African Continental Free Trade Area (AfCFTA) agreement in 2018. This agreement was vital for enhancing and fast-tracking trade, easing procedures, reducing the time and cost of maritime trade, and exporting and importing tariff-free agricultural products. Through AfCFTA, opportunities to move into other countries on the continent opened for JR Farms.

Being landlocked, Rwanda faced significant logistics challenges. Air travel had its limits regarding haulage as many African airports had no cargo planes. Consequently, cargo had to travel through several regional airports to reach the destination country. Road travel was also a challenge in many African countries. The lack of adequate road infrastructure created bottlenecks along the supply chain. But this proved to be the best option for JR Farms to reach its intended goal of becoming a major regional player in agribusiness. Consequently, Wale and his team brainstormed and devised the idea of setting up an internal logistic supply chain whereby several minivans were purchased and used to convey products by road. This arrangement worked better than articulated lorries, which were more difficult to navigate along challenging terrains.

Expanding Into Zambia

The next investment destination was Zambia. In 2018, the FAO estimated that 32% of the country's 75-million hectare landmass had a medium-to-high potential for agriculture production (FAO, 2022). However, most Zambian farmers were small-scale, subsistence producers of staple foods, with an occasional marketable surplus. The government enacted several policies to promote agribusiness and diversify the economy, including bans on certain agricultural staples to protect domestic producers or ensure adequate local supplies of staple goods (Mofya-Mukuka & Chisanga, 2020). State-owned enterprises received preferential treatment when it came to agribusiness (Mofya-Mukuka & Chisanga, 2020). Investors reported cumbersome administrative procedures and unpredictable legal and regulatory changes that inhibited Zambia's immense private-sector investment potential (Manda, Tallontire, & Dougill, 2019). Nonetheless, most agriproducts from private-sector sources could freely enter the Zambian market if they complied with relevant standards.

Zambia's membership in COMESA, Southern Africa Development Community (SADC), EAC and World Trade Organization (WTO) greatly enhanced prospects for JR Farms' entry into agribusiness in Zambia. Implementing the Link Zambia 8,000 project, which sought to transform the country from land-locked to land-linked, paving 8,201 km of road, opened up more prospects for intra-continental travel. JR Farms' strategy was to make Zambia the southern African base where agricultural products like coffee could be moved by road to other countries. Two consultancy firms were engaged to gather data on Zambia before JR Farms committed to expansion into the country.

The opportunity to expand into Zambia came when a school feeding project sponsored by the World Food Programme included Garri, a Nigerian staple, on its menu. JR Farms wrote to the Zambian government and was lucky to be included as a partner in the project, which aimed to feed 2 million school children. An agreement was reached with the Zambia National Cassava Farmers' Association in 2019. JR Farms had an investment portfolio of half a million dollars for that project, and the government was willing to give support through the farmers' association. However, Wale did not follow through with that plan because their consultants advised them on the risks of a project whose primary market would be the government, citing future policy or political changes. Their decision to discontinue turned out to be a wise one. The government under whose watch the feeding project was initiated lost an election, and a new regime took over in 2021.

Instead, JR Farms set up a livestock feed factory in Zambia and explored opportunities for the sale of their coffee products. They produced livestock feeds from cassava peels and aimed to add value to the ecosystem by improving the productivity of livestock farmers. In addition, JR Farms also traded in agro-commodities and offered agro-consultancy services. The machines for their factory in Zambia were fabricated in Lagos, Nigeria and transported to Zambia (Fig. 7).

Nonetheless, JR Farms (n.d.) continued building relationships with business partners in the cassava value chain by committing to the commercial function and offering business and market linkages to the farmers belonging to Zambia National Cassava Association (ZANACA). In turn, ZANACA is committed to ensuring quality control, empowerment opportunities for women and youth, access to markets, training and land equity schemes (JR Farms, n.d.).

Fig. 7.   JR Farms Meeting With Cassava Farmers in Kawambwa,
Luapula Province, Zambia.

Rwanda Versus Zambia

With the free trade arrangements of the two countries facilitating international commercial activities of JR Farms, they could move coffee from Rwanda to Zambia without paying taxes since both countries belonged to COMESA. An African passport holder was allowed to stay in Rwanda for 30 days without a visa. They could also enjoy tax-free shipment of machines from Nigeria to Zambia, only paying import duty. Zambia is politically stable. Available security and infrastructure, such as electricity, water, and good roads, were relatively good for their business in Rwanda and Zambia.

Being both landlocked, Rwanda and Zambia brought additional logistics costs. To import machines, they passed it through South Africa and from there to Zambia by road. Wale also faced hurdles at the onset because he had to prove the honesty of his proposed business in Zambia because of stereotypes against his nationality caused by the criminal records of a few Nigerians in Lusaka.

In terms of size, Zambia had a more significant market for JR Farms but penetrating it was more difficult than in Rwanda. The latter was better organised and had greater accessibility. Registration and operational procedures were not fully digitalised in Zambia and were quite tasking due to the bureaucratic procedures involved, while in Rwanda, these services were seamless. Also, property costs were higher in Zambia, and JR Farms had to pay for business registration, unlike in Rwanda, where it was free.

Social Branding

Wale was sensitive to the fact that African governments made policies to protect their local industries. Consequently, JR Farms positioned itself as a socially responsible firm that sold impact rather than business ideas. They went into Rwanda and Zambia promising to create employment for young people and value for farmers, rather than to make money and share profits. They wanted to be seen not as a business, but as a development partner that was committed to adding value to the agribusiness ecosystem. Their business model which was built around this idea made it easy for government and other stakeholders to welcome them.

JR Farms believed that the organisation's contribution to the economy as well as the benefits of shareholders and the locals should be paramount and form the main thrust of communications, while that should be balanced with a lot of partnerships. He considered that the atmosphere of fear, lack of trust and unwillingness to share profits which is common with African businesses should be done away with as partnerships made each party achieve more:

> We value partnership. If a local can do something, why do we need to do it? It may be cheaper for us. Profit is not only money. sometimes profit could be money yet to come or bigger future projects.

This philosophy was evident in the type of projects incubated by JR Farms. For instance, before launching a seed project in Liberia, research was needed if a partnership with FAO was to be established. At the time, Wale reflected that it did not make sense to finance seed research as the cost of UN-standard research was high. However, he considered this cost insignificant compared to its impact value on future business. Designing such projects, pitching them to multilateral agencies and funding the research garnered the support and partnerships Wale wanted. The research project was eventually commissioned and financed by JR Farms across three countries. With the research findings, FAO came on board to facilitate the import and local population of seeds through the partnership with JR Farms. This project promoted JR Farms in the light of their social impact and further boosted their acceptability.

Shaping the JR Business Model

Wale's overall strategy for JR Farms was to achieve certain results before raising outside investment, keep within the law, engage competent lawyers and set up a proper governance structure. Fully family-owned, it operated as a holding company with subsidiaries. Different partners or shareholders owned each subsidiary. However, JR Farms maintained a position as the largest shareholder in all the subsidiaries.

Wale explained that this was his preferred model to preserve the company's vision. He learnt from experience that JR Farms worked better as a project-based shareholding company that had the freedom of decision-making and transparency along the entire supply chain. External shareholders were only allowed to invest in a specific subsidiary, not the holding company. In Zambia, for instance, shareholders of JR Livestock Feed Zambia were not shareholders of the coffee sales subsidiary.

JR Farms' model did not offer returns on investment (ROIs), only share-holding with the payment of dividends. After valuation, shareholders would buy shares in projects and share the risks. Wale was not surprised that this model was not attractive to many investors. He appreciated that people wanted to invest in a secure business and that the risks associated with start-ups were high. However, as results grew, interest in JR Farms also grew. All their shareholders were Africans. In Zambia, a single shareholder bought shares worth US$80,000. In addition, the company had a strict due diligence policy before anyone was allowed to buy shares in JR Farms. Wale explained that JR Farms did not engage investors whose values did not align with the firm's objective. He said theirs was a business model designed to add value to Africa rather than make money at all costs.

Indigenous Strategies

Wale reminisced that some of his biggest lessons about running an Indigenous agribusiness in Africa came from the failed farmers' cooperative in Nigeria. Wale acknowledged that he founded JR Farms when he had limited knowledge about agribusiness and so identified knowledge gaps as the predominant inhibitor of development for African agribusinesses. There were also faults in the imple-mentation process, which impacted the productivity and efficiency of operations.

He also learnt how the lack of local intelligence contributed to this failure as the company did not engage farmers properly, nor was there any due diligence in the process. For instance, they had discovered that many of those who enrolled with them as farmers were not farmers. This information could have been quickly garnered if stakeholder engagement within the local community had existed. Thus, there was a need to domesticate and deploy local intelligence, especially where readily available and verifiable data did not exist. The onus was on indi-vidual companies to generate the intelligence data they needed to add value to their operations.

Investing in human capital for growing the company became a fundamental strategy for JR Farms. It required significant investments in people as the business model thrived on engaged employees, who were the engine of innovation and creativity. Consequently, decisions were carefully curated to create a talent pipeline. Students were engaged as interns on a 3-month renewable contract and received a US$100 stipend. Only interns with the right values, work ethic and soft skills were retained. Those who had their contracts renewed thrice qualified to apply for a full-time role in the company. Full-time staff received a basic salary and transport allowance (in Nigeria) and monthly savings (social protection) of up to €10 in place of pensions. For senior staff, monthly savings was €10, which they could draw from during emergencies. Employees working in the coffee shops had a performance bonus aside from their salary. Managers went on sponsored training in business schools. There was no bias, anyone who could deliver exceptional value to the company was nominated. Wale learnt that in Africa, achieving goals took a long time, was painful and required proper planning. The goal posts changed continuously, making managing vendors, suppliers and con-tractors a hands-on activity. Young agricultural entrepreneurs needed to understand that experience in this sector was vital, and that perseverance was a necessity to succeed in agribusiness.

Mapping the Future

JR Farms' presence in Africa now spanned Rwanda, Kenya, Zambia, Nigeria and Liberia, with footprints in the Netherlands. So far, Nigeria and Zambia have proved to be the biggest markets for their coffee products. As shown in Table 2, by 2021, JR Farms generated approximately US$2 million in revenue, positioning it as a multi-million-dollar company.

In 2022, JR Farms had built a feeder network of over 4,000 coffee farmers across Rwanda; opened 11 coffee shops in corporate organisations in Nigeria; owned factory assets in Zambia valued at over US$700,000 (with the land) and ran an out-grower scheme for local farmers (Table 3).

However, Wale understood that diversification was one of the strategies to survive any upsets that could affect their agribusiness in these countries. JR Farms began exploring its options for expansion. These included extending their work in Kenya, penetrating the South African market, and scaling their production to open more coffee shops in Nigeria, Zambia, Cote D' Ivoire, Senegal and other East African countries. In the future, they planned to convert these coffee shops into a continental franchise and extend them into Europe and America.

Wale noted that their revenue growth has been organic, without exposure to grants or foreign aid. Their strategic goal was to become a listed company but only after attaining a specific level of growth. JR Farms intended to establish more African agribusinesses and employ a 1,000 people over the next five years.

Table 2. Excerpts from JR Farms' Financial Reports for the Year Ended December 2021.

	December 2021 US$	December 2020 US$
Revenue	1,808,222	1,477,232
Direct costs	1,049,410	1,181,786
Gross profit	*758,812*	*295,446*
Indirect/operating cost	163,454	117,123
Net profit before taxation	*595,358*	*178,323*
Net profit after taxation	*416,751*	*176,547*
Earnings at the beginning of the year	244,157	67,610
Earnings at the end of the year	*660,907*	*244,157*

Source: JR Farms.

Table 3. JR Farms Cassava and Coffee Export Data (2019–2021).

	2021	2020	2019
Coffee	65.07 tonnes	38.03 tonnes	19.8 tonnes
Cassava products	923.3 tonnes	668.9 tonnes	492.6 tonnes

Source: JR Farms.

Recommendations for Agribusiness in Africa

From the case, we make the following recommendations that we believe agribusiness in Africa will find useful in rethinking their strategies. Moreover, coming from an Indigenous agripreneur, the applicability of the business model to the experiences of other African agribusinesses is made more relevant.

(1) Knowing the local context in which one's business operates is essential for shaping strategies and making value-adding business decisions. The dearth of research reinforces the long-standing narrative about Africa's underdevelopment. There is a need to capture insights from business and development actors. JR Farms demonstrates the importance of research into the local market, the use of technology and stakeholder engagement in crafting a deeper understanding of the needs that an agribusiness intends to meet. This way, agribusiness's impact on local communities will become sustainable and profitable across the supply chain, a significant contributor to the development indices in Africa.

(2) The prospect of failure in business should be considered a necessary phase in the life cycle of any agribusiness. The agribusiness ecosystem in Africa is yet to reach its full potential due to the complex institutional and human factors. As seen with JR Farms, the opportunities to create value in almost any initiative stem from the fact that there is a significant gap to fill. A keen reflection on the factors that led to failure should constitute the experience that will help drive improvements in subsequent attempts. Piloting schemes ensure that all factors related to entering or expanding a market are considered to minimise losses from business failure.

(3) Agribusiness owners and investors should leverage AfCFTA and the regional economic markets like EAC and COMESA to facilitate intra-continental trade. Several concessions and tax breaks can be negotiated more easily through these trade agreements. JR Farms could expand in an organic and seamless manner through these markets. However, the value of growing social capital and informal networks should not be ignored. Likewise, adopting the JR Farms model of building relationships, partnering and collaborating with reliable actors should be considered.

(4) The role of government in driving opportunities for agribusiness growth in Africa cannot be ignored. Rwanda was a launching pad for JR Farms from its inception. In the long term, advocacy should be encouraged to influence

policymakers who need to shape policies that facilitate agribusiness growth on the continent. In the short term, agripreneurs should consider entering markets with conducive policies. Using consultants to provide market intelligence, especially in new and unfamiliar countries, minimises the negative impacts of policy reversals on budding businesses.

(5) JR Farms has demonstrated impact investing as a viable and profitable route in agribusiness growth. Development indices in Africa indicate the critical role of agribusinesses in maximising agriculture gains. Rwanda and Zambia have provided JR Farms with opportunities for growth in coffee, livestock feeds and other products. With the variety of agricultural products available, the agribusiness ecosystem in Africa is limitless. The dividends to be gained by the communities are immense. Agribusiness owners and investors with a developmental agenda are still well placed to make profits while also changing the lives of millions of Africans.

(6) Finally, the business model adopted by JR Farms commits to four key pillars – integrity, ethical conduct, good governance and competence. This attractive image projects agribusiness in a positive and attractive light. JR Farms produced, packaged and branded to global standards, raising the bar for Indigenous agribusinesses in the same field. This position also magnifies the potential to attract funding and investors. Being intentional about positioning one's agribusiness for sustainability depends on these pillars.

In summary, Fig. 8 outlines the emergent model of internationalisation of an Indigenous agribusiness in Rwanda and Zambia.

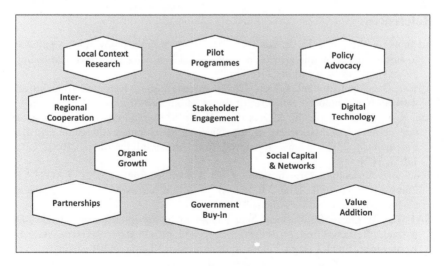

Fig. 8. Model of Industrialisation of JR Farms: An Indigenous
Agribusiness in Rwanda and Zambia.

Conclusion

Agribusiness in Africa is a huge untapped market. The continent has all the resources to become a leading supplier of agriproducts to the global market. Yet, there are still many gaps in knowledge about the workings of the agribusiness ecosystem and how to create a sustainable business. This case study has provided an overview of JR Farms and its journey from failure to becoming a major player in the agribusiness sector in Rwanda and Zambia. Recommendations for potential and existing agripreneurs based on the experiences of the founder are outlined.

Discussion Questions

(1) Suggest other agribusiness activities Wale can focus on as part of JR Farms' expansion plans and why.
(2) What measures could African manufacturers adopt to make products that compete effectively in global markets?
(3) Where financial institutions are unwilling to fund a business and family funding is insufficient, what other funding sources could African entrepreneurs access?
(4) In what ways could technology be deployed to scale up agribusiness in Africa?
(5) How can impediments to agribusiness and free trade in Zambia be overcome?

References

Ademola, A., Manning, L., & Azadi, H. (2017). Agribusiness innovation: A pathway to sustainable economic growth in Africa. *Trends in Food Science & Technology*, *59*, 88–104. doi:10.1016/j.tifs.2016.11.008

African Development Bank Group. (2022). *Investor report*. Retrieved from https://www.afdb.org/en/documents/investor-presentation-may-2022

Ani, K. J., Nnanwube, E. F., & Ojakorotu, V. (2018). Agriculture, oil-resource curse and conflict: An assessment of the Nigerian development quagmire. *African Renaissance*, *15*(3), 49–66. Retrieved from https://hdl.handle.net/10520/EJC-12b7723474

Food and Agriculture Organisation of the United Nations. (2022). FAOSTAT: Zambia agricultural land. Retrieved from https://www.fao.org/faostat/en/#country/251. Accessed on August 9, 2022.

GAF. (2020). Green Agribusiness fund targets young Agripreneurs in Nigeria and Rwanda. Retrieved from https://gafafrica.com/blogs/5/2020-07-17-21-46-22/Green-Agribusiness-Fund-Targets-Young-Agripreneurs-in-Nigeria-and-Rwanda

Gerard, A., Lopez, M. C., Kerr, J., & Bizoza, A. R. (2021). Relational contracts and value chain governance: Exporter approaches to overcoming transaction costs in Rwanda's coffee sector. *Journal of Agribusiness in Developing and Emerging Economies*. doi:10.1108/JADEE-07-2021-0176

Jongwe, A. I., & Sono, G. T. (2022). Exploring antecedents of international entrepreneurship: Focus on orientation perspectives in South Africa. In V. Jafari-Sadeghi & L. Dana (Eds.), *International entrepreneurship in emerging markets* (pp. 171–186). New York: Routledge.

JR Farms. (n.d.). Green Hangout. Retrieved from https://jrfarmsafrica.com/our-projects/green-hangout

JR Farms. (2020). Retrieved from https://jrfarmsafrica.com/blogs/4/2020-04-16-14-47-24/JR-Farms-Africa–Rwanda-Farmers-Coffee-Company-Renew-Partnership

JR Farms. (n.d.). Retrieved from https://jrfarmsafrica.com/blogs/6/2020-04-16-14-54-51/Zambia-National-Cassava-Association–JR-Farms-partner-on-commercial-cassava-processing-in-Zambia

Manda, S., Tallontire, A., & Dougill, A. J. (2019). Large-scale land acquisitions and institutions: Patterns, influence and barriers in Zambia. *The Geographical Journal*, *185*(2), 94–208. doi:10.1111/geoj.12291

Market Watch Inc. (2022). Zambeef products to expand business with $100 Mln investment Dow Jones Newswires June 16, 2022. Retrieved from https://www.marketwatch.com/story/zambeef-products-to-expand-business-with-100-mln-investment-271655369746. Accessed on August 9, 2022.

Mofya-Mukuka, R., & Chisanga, B. (2020). Agriculture and developmental regionalism in southern Africa. In S. Adejumobi & C. Obi (Eds.), *Developmental regionalism and economic transformation in southern Africa* (pp. 106–121). Routledge. doi:10.4324/9781351053570

Rwanda Development Board. (2022, August 13). Retrieved from https://rdb.rw/investment-opportunities/agriculture/

Rwanda Ministry of Finance and Economic Planning. (2015). Vision 2050. Retrieved from https://www.nirda.gov.rw/uploads/tx_dce/Vision_English_Version_2050_-31_Dec_2020.pdf. Accessed on August 9, 2022.

ZambiaInvest. (2022, August 13). Agriculture. Retrieved from https://www.zambiainvest.com/agriculture/

Chapter 12

Advancing Africa's Indigenous Business Practices: Recommendations for Educators and Business Actors

Ogechi Adeola

Abstract

Africa's diverse geographic regions are replete with indigenous business knowledge and practices embedded in the traditions, values and culture of the people. Many of these practices have been explored in the previous chapters of this book. This final chapter provides viable recommendations for adopting and improving Africa's indigenous business practices and methodologies. We expect that these observations and recommendations will support Africa's educators', business actors' and policymakers' efforts to draw from and apply rich insights from indigenous business knowledge and practices. However, beyond this, we hope that international enterprises operating in the continent can learn about the uniquely African business values and incorporate them appropriately into a context that fits. This concluding chapter, therefore, discusses how these objectives may be achieved.

Keywords: Indigenous business practice; business actors; Africa; educators; policymakers; theory

Introduction

African societies hold with high regard the values, practices and culture that have defined her identity. However, many of the continent's cultural values are losing ground as Western orientations become more prevalent. Traditional values and practices that have hitherto propelled the continent's socio-economic activities and cut through all institutional frameworks are gradually losing their essence. The theme that runs through the contributions of authors in this book is the

Casebook of Indigenous Business Practices in Africa, 225–243

Copyright © 2023 Ogechi Adeola

Published under exclusive licence by Emerald Publishing Limited

doi:10.1108/978-1-80455-762-420231022

restoration of business practices of indigenous enterprises and a re-look at their adaptation and adoption for sustainable growth in Africa.

This chapter extends the contributions of the authors in this book by proposing a theoretical framework that will contribute to the understanding of Africa's extant indigenous business traditions that sustain enterprise pathways, incubate entrepreneurs and practice economically sound models for providing products for market consumption. Examples of such enterprises/models are the Igbo business model in Nigeria, the Kente weaving in Ghana, the Ubuntu economics in South Africa, the cultural and creative industries in Ethiopia, the craft producers in Egypt and many more that raise the bar for Africa's indigenous business methodologies. The successes that have been achieved despite their unique challenges suggest that indigenous enterprises continue to be of relevance within Africa's socio-economic environment.

The qualitative case studies put forward by this book's authors include viable recommendations for business actors, i.e. business owners, entrepreneurs, consumers, government institutions/agencies and policymakers. These recommendations will provide enterprise stakeholders with the research-driven support needed to adopt practices that will appeal to the local communities in Africa and sustain the continent's social and cultural values. Indigenous methods and practices conform with the business sustainability literature that promotes sustainable economic, environmental and social outcomes.

The indigenous business practice and enterprise examples explored in this book have been drawn from North, West, East, Central and Southern Africa. The varied cultures and ethnic groups in these five regions have notable and unique indigenous business knowledge and practices that have existed for a considerably extended period. Throughout this book, the case studies portray a continent that is not bereft of local business knowledge and practices. That Africa is a resource-rich continent with abundant human and natural resources is not arguable. However, when it comes to business and management, the richness of Africa's indigenous knowledge and business practices is not yet well known or even acknowledged. Global management scholarship is dominated by research from the West (Boshoff, Adeola, Hinson, & Heinonen, 2022; Tsui, 2004). The search for solutions to Africa's many developmental challenges should not be limited to Western approaches. Indigenous developmental pathways may include unconventional solutions that differ from established global business and management practices derived from Western research and philosophies. Some leading economies of the world developed internally through indigenous approaches; it is time Africa started to look inward for African methods designed for Africans.

The sheer diversity of indigenous business practices in Africa is akin to the continent's diverse cultures. As many sometimes overlook the point that Africa is a continent of many countries, the point is also sometimes forgotten that Africa is a continent of many cultures (Ovadje, 2016; Oyewunmi, Esho, & Ukenna, 2021). Even within the same culture there may be huge variations in entrepreneurship and business practices (Igwe, 2021). Consequently, there is really no one culture-driven or indigenous business practice that can be regarded as being common to all African countries; each has its utility and can offer value in solving the economic, social, environmental and other developmental challenges of the continent. However, in their current state, these indigenous practices lie mostly dormant and are not offering the possible optimum utility.

This concluding chapter provides specific recommendations for prioritising Africa's indigenous business practices. The aim is not only to offer ways to advance knowledge and insights about these business practices but also to encourage their adoption locally and globally. One of the goals of the newly implemented African Continental Free Trade Area (AfCFTA) agreement is the promotion of intra-continental trade and cross-cultural adoption of Africa's many indigenous business practices.

A Theory for Business Practices and Management in Africa

Africa is replete with many indigenous business models and practices, many of which were portrayed in this book. Interest in these traditions is beginning to gain traction as more publications on the subject are gaining attention within business and management fields (e.g. Adeola, 2020; Amankwah-Amoah, Boso, & Debrah, 2018; Boso, Debrah, & Amankwah-Amoah, 2018; Igwe, 2021; Ingenbleek, 2019; Oyewunmi, Oyewunmi, & Moses, 2021; Uzo & Meru, 2018).

Various African tribes can be identified with traditional business practices embedded in their long-held cultural norms and values. From the *Igba-boi* apprenticeship system of the Igbos and *Osomalo* debt collection practice of the Ijesa tribe, both in Nigeria, to the agricultural practices of the Luba people in Central Africa and the Ubuntu economics of Southern African countries, unique indigenous business practices continue to thrive.

Though documented knowledge of these practices is only recently emerging and insights into the nature of their social and economic contributions are nascent, it is established that these practices are varied, can be linked to specific tribes and may be widely practised by businesses in the informal sector (Adeola, 2020; Boso et al., 2018). Documentation of the historical origins of the entrepreneurial nature of African tribes includes the categorisation of the different forms of indigenous entrepreneurship. Igwe (2021), for example, using four tribes in West Africa as a sample, created a taxonomy of the forms of entrepreneurship: clan-, kindred-, tribal-, community- and nomadic entrepreneurship. Surprisingly, much of the formal and organised private sector in Africa has not adopted or adapted portions of these well-known indigenous business practices. However, many Indigenous African Enterprises (IAEs) have evolved from these business practice models.

Ubuntu: Few indigenous business practices have birthed formal and well-recognised management theories; however, the concept of *ubuntu* promises to become a well-recognised management theory, in fact, the African concept of *ubuntu* has become one of the most popular management concepts attributable to Africa (Ibeh, Eyong, & Amaeshi, 2022). *Ubuntu* originated in Southern African countries and literally translates to 'I am because we are' or 'I am who I am because we are' (Paulson, 2020). *Ubuntu* emphasises compassion, consensus, cohesion and a collectivist rather than an individualistic orientation (Boshoff et al., 2022). The concept of *ubuntu* offers lessons to businesses within and outside Africa (Amankwah-Amoah et al., 2018) and could be a useful framework for furthering theoretical understanding of other indigenous business practices in Africa. With more robust empirical evidence of its efficacious business and societal outcomes, *ubuntu* bears significant promise of becoming as well known as Confucianism and Taoism (Ibeh et al., 2022). Consequently, the identified frameworks of the Igbo business model and *ubuntu* ideology contain elements that can serve as the building blocks of a theoretical view of indigenous business practice in Africa.

The Theory of Indigenous Business Practice

Leaning on the model of the Igbo Business and the *Ubuntu*, the Theory of Indigenous Business Practice (TIBP) proposes five themes that should be present in an indigenous business to assure its survival and performance: definitions, development, management, sustainability and performance.

Definition. For a business to be tagged as indigenous it must emanate from the sociocultural values of a specific set of people. Indigeneity is not external but internal and should therefore flow from the cultural orientation, beliefs, norms and values of a particular group, a characteristic of all indigenous businesses identified in this book. When a business is tagged as indigenous, it should be able to identify the cultural values that guided the business formation, and which cultural norms thrive through the business practices.

Development: An indigenous business will be able to trace its development from practices within a local community for several years. All indigenous businesses have aboriginal roots. Even when their practices extend beyond the shores of their locality, they are still traceable to an aboriginal community – for instance, the Igbo business model emerged from the South-eastern group of Nigeria.

Management: For an indigenous business to be successful, there must be an informal management structure that guides business practices that derive from the cultural ideology of the community, and they must offer a unique and idiosyncratic approach to business operations. For instance, the *ubuntu* ideology from South Africa emphasises a management practice ideology of togetherness, commitment to others and mindful of ways to ensure that the existence of another is not made difficult by one's own activities. A similar approach can be recorded in the Igbo people, who believe that a business must help others and that no one is left behind. The informality of the Igbo business model is embedded in all forms of managerial activities, including recruitment, conflict management, succession planning, negotiation and sales practices (Adeola, 2020b). Indigenous businesses will evince cultural ideologies and principles that exemplify orderliness and effectiveness.

Sustainability: Indigenous business practices are focused on efforts that will ensure that their business does not become obsolete. The Igbo apprenticeship system, for example, is a crucial aspect of their business model as an enterprise incubator. Through the apprenticeship model, entrepreneurs are trained and established in a manner that sustains the offerings of indigenous businesses, whilst contributing to the preservation of its cultural characteristics for successive generations. Many indigenous businesses in Africa have a family lineage and a system of succession that allows for continuity of the business practices.

Performance: Whether they are driven by indigenous or western ideologies, indigenous businesses must set their performance measures. For the Igbo business, successful performance is a reflection of incubating more entrepreneurs and empowering others. A similar outcome can be noted in the *Ubuntu* philosophy, as we have seen with the rotating contributory scheme described in Chapter 10, and the indigenous healing process featured in Volume 1. What will the indigenous business define as performance success: helping others, making a profit or incubating entrepreneurs?

The proposition of the Theory of Indigenous Business Practice has not been scientifically tested; however, the narratives offered by the authors in the book capture the five themes of definition, development, management, sustainability and performance. Each must be evident in every indigenous business practice.

To buttress some of the arguments proposed in the theory, the findings and suggestions from authors in the book are presented in the next section.

Summary of Findings

Chapter Titles	Chapter Authors	Findings and Recommendations for Business Actors
Chapter 2: Challenges of Indigenous Black Soap (Ọṣẹ Dúdú) Entrepreneurs in Southwest, Nigeria	Olayinka Akanle Adedeji Adewusi	• Challenges of indigenous black soap distribution are weather, finance, copyright, succession challenges, large competitive number of sellers, debt, lack of support, pricing and brand competition, • Business actors in the indigenous Ọṣẹ dúdú market must collaborate with black soap entrepreneurs to ameliorate challenges.
Chapter 3: Preparation for Business Negotiation at the Livestock Auction Market in Tanzania:	Felix Nandonde	• Understanding the significance of key stages in business negotiation within indigenous practices is crucial for achieving a successful outcome.

(Continued)

Chapter Titles	Chapter Authors	Findings and Recommendations for Business Actors
The Case of Maasai Livestock Traders		• Conduct research to understand the effect of goal setting on the behaviour of negotiating parties and how they set their goals, and the factors that influence them. • Business development services (BDS) and institutions that offer negotiation training can include lessons from the practice of negotiation in indigenous settings in related courses.
Chapter 4: Sustainability of Indigenous Butchery Business amongst Dagombas and Nanumbas in Ghana	Mohammed Majeed, Prince Gyimah and Adiza Sadik	• The results show that starting a butchery business depends on a person's tradition or cultural heritage, apprenticeship, training and skills or past experiences • Butchery businesses require prior training or some level of apprenticeship before starting and adequate capital to ensure sustainability. • Business actors must consider suggested recommendations to scale up the practice
Chapter 5: What is Peculiar in the Sustainability Practices of Indigenous Female Business Owners in Africa	Patricia Isabirye	• Business sustainability can essentially be a fulfiling process if done holistically and altruistically within female-owned indigenous businesses. • A range of interdependent variables that capture environmental, social and economic dimensions should be implemented.

(Continued)

Chapter Titles	Chapter Authors	Findings and Recommendations for Business Actors
Chapter 9: Financial Literacy of Chama Women's Groups in Rural Western Kenya	Lillian Zippora Omosa	• The study found community engagement, centred learning and discovery learning as relevant ways of engaging with women's groups. • The study suggests indigenous practices and values that educators can draw upon to support and enhance the teaching of financial literacy to African women based on the Chama women's group experience
Chapter 10: Traditional Rotating Stokvel Model for Entrepreneurial Success in South Africa: Analysis of the Building Constructs	Ishmael Obaeko Iwara Ogechi Adeola	• Formation, operation, financial segment and disciplinary measures are the building blocks for a Rotating Stokvel model • The step-by-step approach to setting up successful Rotating Credit Stokvel discussed in the chapter can provide entrepreneurs with an alternative informal and reliable capital mobilisation channel.
Chapter 11: Internationalisation of Indigenous Agribusiness In Africa: The Case Of Jr Farms In Rwanda And Zambia	Belinda Nwosu and Edidiong Esara	• Africa has significant and sufficient natural resources to become a leading supplier of agriproducts in the global market • Agribusiness entrepreneurs should leverage the opportunities in internationalisation to scale up their businesses.

Suggestions and Recommendations for Educators

Research and Scholarship: The first and foremost recommendation is to conduct more research into Africa's indigenous business knowledge and practices. Advocacy for acknowledgement and adoption of the many indigenous business practices explored in this book, and those beyond, require concerted scientific assessment generated by in-depth research and scholarship. Scientific evidence that emanates from econometric analysis of large systemic surveys and data gathered from empirical studies would validate the positive contributions and effects of Africa's indigenous practices. The positive performance implications of indigenous practices adopted by local business enterprises need to be documented.

Qualitative research has been able to establish the practice and structure of indigenous knowledge bases and ways of doing business. Qualitative research, such as case studies, has great utility and indeed can contribute to building theoretical frameworks (Eisenhardt, 1989; Eisenhardt & Graebner, 2007). However, much of the qualitative research that has been conducted on Africa's indigenous business knowledge and practices have been exploratory and lacking in theory building protocols. At this stage, large and rigorous quantitative empirical studies that can be easily replicated are required for the scientific support needed for advancing Africa's indigenous business practices.

Quantitative research into the prevalence and performance effects of the forms of indigenous entrepreneurship is enumerated by Igwe (2021) and others. Indeed, the exploratory qualitative research in this book and other publications could be a starting point for further data-driven research.

Another form of research that is urgently needed is in-depth qualitative research into the successful and sustainable businesses that emerged from Africa's indigenous business practices. Timberg (2014), for example, reports that the Marwaris in India own the majority of the country's private industrial enterprises, a result of indigenous trading and lending practices that had been practised for years. Without research highlighting successful African businesses that emanated from indigenous practices, those practices may not be tested and replicated by businesses in other parts of the world. For example, much has been said about the *Igba-boi*, the remarkable Igbo business school or the apprenticeship system practised by the indigenous Igbo ethnic group of Eastern Nigeria (Adeola, 2020), but case studies of successful and sustained businesses built on the *Igba-boi* model would provide further validation of this unique business practice.

Without the urgently needed research and applied scholarship, discussion of Africa's indigenous business practices may remain only rhetorical; continually yearning for recognition from 'non-indigenous' or 'mainstream' business practices whose viability has been established by extant management research. Indigenous business practices in Africa, like the widely accepted erudite advocacy for African management, must 'demonstrate its efficacy and impact on indices that really matter' (Ibeh et al., 2022, p. 188). This can be achieved by conducting systemic, rigorous quantitative and qualitative studies that would stand up to replication from outside of Africa and support confirmation of findings.

Numerous avenues exist for research that would support advancement of indigenous business practices in Africa (see Table 1). A veritable research area is an investigation into the sustainability of Africa's indigenous business models and practices. Research is also required to categorise the myriad of indigenous business practices and how their application in various areas of business and management can be integrated into the existing knowledge base. For example, the Savings Groups in the regions represented in this book can be classified as a form of business finance. The savings group phenomena, widely practised across many African countries, could also be categorised under personal finance. How categorisations of indigenous practices could be done effectively, how they fit into mainstream business knowledge and how they provide answers to some research gaps are exciting areas for research.

Comparative studies that aim to identify 'best performance' are also required. For example, how do indigenous business practices differ among and across different African cultures and regions. Also, apart from proffering definitions of Indigenous African Enterprises (IAEs), research would document how IAEs are different from other common domestic businesses and enterprises. Can differences be attributed to the founders' origins or the fact that they are, by birth, indigenous to Africa? Extant research has shown that IAEs are enterprises whose structure, modes of operations and practices emanate from *African* cultural expectations (Ojera, 2018). This seemingly simple matter of definition raises some pertinent questions: What about foreigners who start up or operate enterprises based on indigenous knowledge or cultural practices? Are such enterprises still IAEs? Lacking solid philosophical and theoretical underpinnings, questions such as these will receive contradictory responses; each with its convictions.

Apart from helping to validate these indigenous business practices for local and global adoption, one further reason to conduct research is to ensure the documentation of these practices and their historical origins. Otherwise, there is a tendency such indigenous business practices will be lost and irrecoverable. Africa has a rich economic history that dates back long before colonial times when businesses were conducted by families and clans rather than by firms as we know them today (Verhoef, 2017). However, lack of documentation has limited the knowledge of this business history, and sadly, the loss of significant business lessons.

Research will encourage the refinement of indigenous practices. Cultural influences that stand the test of time are not embedded in rigid traditions but are adaptable and open to change to meet the needs of the communities they serve (Varnum & Grossmann, 2017). Being rooted in culture does not preclude change and refinement.

Theoretical and conceptual explorations based on multi- and inter-disciplinary research beyond business and management are required. Much of the Africa-centric research has been based on application, context or country-specific exploration and replication studies (Bishoff et al., 2022; Tsui, 2004). Research into the Fulani and Hausa ethnic groups, for example, has found them to depend less on competition (Igwe, 2021); how could lessons learnt from their indigenous practices contribute to scholarship on the concept of competing and cooperating simultaneously (Brandenburger & Nalebuff, 1996, 2021). Research focussed on

Table 1. Summary of Possible Research Agendas.

Research	Type/Area	Focus	Broad Research Aim
Systemic surveys and large empirical studies	Quantitative and qualitative research	Rigorous econometric analysis	To establish positive effects and to aid validation and generalisation of findings to other businesses within and outside Africa
In-depth case studies	Qualitative research	Showcase Successful IAEs and Indigenous African practices	Theory Building (A knowledge gap addressed in this book)
Theoretical explorations	Qualitative and quantitative research	Sustainability of indigenous practices	Provide some form of philosophical underpinnings
Ethnographic studies	Qualitative research	Categorisation of practices into different indigenous themes	Promote adoption by non-indigenous businesses
Comparative studies	Mainly qualitative but could also be quantitative	Comparison of the various indigenous practices	Tease out similarities and differences

Source: Author.

theory building is necessary for providing philosophical comprehension and advancing the nature of entrenched business practices. For example, it has been purported in some literature that African cultures share attributes of communalism and collectivism (Hofstede, 2022; Igwe, 2021). It would therefore be profitable to understand how these specific attributes contribute to various indigenous business practices and the mechanisms. Theory-building research would help to enlighten these relationships.

Several management and international business scholars from Africa and other climes have been calling for more research about Africa because of the paucity of research generated from within or outside the continent (e.g. Barnard, 2020; Boshoff et al., 2022; Boso et al., 2018; George, 2015; George, Corbishley, Khayesi, Haas, & Tihanyi, 2016; Ibeh et al., 2022; Mol, Stadler, & Ariño, 2017). Interestingly, these calls for research coincide with the sprouting interest in African indigenous business practices, a topic that has not received as much attention as in other areas of the African economy. A perennial challenge to research in Africa is the availability and reliability of data (Boshoff et al., 2022). Though this may have affected research, the onus is on scholars from African countries to collaborate with foreign counterparts to forge means of conducting reliable research on the business models and practices embedded in many African cultures. This would help to create greater visibility and extend the adoption of these practices beyond the originating cultural and country contexts to international contexts.

Management Training and Consulting: Conducting the necessary research would be a great step towards advancing the cause of documenting business practices from African cultures. However, in order to advance the adoption of African indigenous practices, research findings need to be applied to practice. Dissemination through publications in journals, books and other outlets definitely has its utility. However, most published research is read by fellow researchers and scholars. Although practitioner-oriented publication outlets exist, few are read by people from the private sector. An initial step toward persuading the private sector to adopt Africa's indigenous business knowledge and practices is to create awareness through training, especially management training, and by offering management consulting services to companies and organisations.

Training: The management training and staff development opportunities available in African countries are largely based on western knowledge and methods. It is almost as if the continent's indigenous business knowledge and practices do not exist. Consequently, companies and organisations in the private and even public sectors are unaware of the valuable business practices endemic to their cultures. Hence, they do not, and indeed cannot, adopt these practices if they are not aware of them.

However, just as the private sector needs to be trained on these practices, IAEs also need training to advance their business practices. For example, the Fulani ethnic group found in many countries across Africa are well known for their nomadic lifestyle and livestock trade, especially in cattle. How can this trade of livestock be developed and expanded into successful and sustainable businesses? What type of training and development would advance their business practices but retain their cultural authenticity? How could lessons learnt drive similar initiatives in other contexts?

Management Consulting: Most organisations that conduct management and other forms of business training also offer management consulting. These organisations, many of whom offer a curriculum derived from western business practices, need to be sensitised on the value of incorporating indigenous business practices into their training programmes. Following an introduction to Western-oriented business practices, indigenous organisations tend to adopt the methods proffered by consultants with credentials authenticated by local and global experience. Business schools and management consultants in Africa can actively promote indigenous business practices by incorporating them into their academic and short-course programmes. Faculty and trainers can make purposeful efforts to demonstrate to students and business managers how indigenous practices have been validated and established throughout Africa.

Africa's business schools can aid in advancing the cause of indigenous business practices by writing and publishing relevant case studies of successful enterprises that emerged from indigenous African cultures or businesses that have success-fully adopted indigenous business practices. Because these teaching cases are sold and exchanged across business schools in other parts of the world, the teaching cases can also be used to extend awareness of these indigenous business practices around the globe.

Many business schools in Africa have struggled to gain a competitive edge among global institutions. African schools' unique opportunity to research and teach indigenous practices across various management specialties could serve as a form of competitive advantage that differentiates them from the rest. The responsibility lies with Africa's business schools to apply rigorous research stra-tegies to group these practices, extricate the fundamental theoretical and applied framework of the groups and communicate the lessons learned to managers and students. Optimal mixing and weaving of these business practices is another path business schools can take to advance the cause of culturally based business practices.

Although it has been previously stated that research outlets do not serve the primary purpose of communicating research information to practitioners, more quality journal outlets are also required in Africa for management consultants who regularly turn to journals in search of research results that support innovative ideas. Current management journals such as the *Africa Journal of Management* (AJOM) and the *Journal of African Business* are encouraged to take the initiative to project indigenous business practices from the continent to the global research space and the private sector. Journals dedicated to disseminating and advocating for Africa's indigenous business knowledge and practices to the private sector within and outside Africa are also needed.

Incorporation into Business Studies at all Education Levels: An important step towards promoting indigenous business practices in Africa would be to incor-porate knowledge of these practices into the curricula of primary to tertiary levels of education. It is unfortunate that many African students are not made aware of these business practices, especially those that exist within their own cultures. For example, as widely practised as savings groups are, many Africans are only aware of them from the informal society and not from educational institutions. Phe-nomena like this have led to the call for the decolonisation of education.

The argument for decolonisation of education in Africa has been more intense in countries in Southern Africa than those in other African regions. The assertion is that the education system inherited from colonisation was deliberately designed to undermine development in Africa (Mampane, Omidire, & Aluko, 2018; Musitha & Mafukata, 2018). Decolonisation of education would introduce inclusion of Africa's indigenous business practices into the curriculum at sec-ondary and tertiary educational institutions. The subtle notion that anything African is primitive, inferior and of less value than those of Western origin needs to be discarded. Incorporation of education regarding IAEs and indigenous business knowledge and practices does not mean the existing curriculum should be discarded entirely. What it requires is the application of what Mampane et al.

(2018) refer to as 'glocal initiatives' that emphasise the importance of business education that is 'foregrounded in indigenous knowledge, *and practices*, and integrated worldviews' (Mampane et al., 2018, p. 1; italics mine). Indigenous business models and practices can be included in the curriculum and taught alongside other aspects of business studies education influenced by Western cultures.

In addition, it is recommended that business history become a part of the curriculum. Interestingly, and rather unfortunately, many secondary or tertiary business schools in Africa do not offer business history courses. This is despite the long history of business in Africa that pre-dates precolonial years. The historical origins of Africa's diverse cultural business practices and how they may be adopted or reformed would constitute an important element of a business history course. This background may also help to spur interest in further research into the origins and the nature of local business practices across the continent.

Suggestions and Recommendations for Business Actors

Diverse indigenous African businesses are many and can be found in all African countries. However, the challenge is that majority are medium-, small-, and micro-enterprises (MSMEs) that operate within the informal sector. Even though some may have been in business for a number of years they remain small due to lack of modernisations that would enable them to compete with multinational companies' innovative methods, processes, products and services. Indigenous entrepreneurs could build capacity by forging partnerships with stakeholders such as financial institutions, education institutions and multilateral agencies such as non-governmental organisations. For many MSME businesses, it may be easier to enter into such strategic partnerships as a group rather than as individual enterprises. Fortunately, trade unions comprised of several small and micro IAEs exist to support various industries.

A lot has been written in this chapter on the forms of research and scholarships that may be required to document evidence of the efficacy of indigenous business practices. However, such research may be complex if not conducted with the full participation of the indigenous entrepreneurs themselves. Therefore, a vital form of partnership is that of business educators and indigenous entrepreneurs. The aim would be to not only build research capacity but also help in codifying processes that enable scalability and modernisation of these practices. The end goal is to build African businesses that are both successful and sustainable.

Emerging African entrepreneurs and those already in business need to begin to assess the many opportunities inherent in indigenous business practices across Africa. It is rare for start-ups in the 'tech' landscape to incorporate indigenous knowledge and practices, though a few are capitalising on the savings groups' practices in many African cultures to develop web and mobile applications. Entrepreneurs are encouraged to explore the viable opportunities embedded in indigenous business practices.

The Role of Government and the Third Sector

The implementation of some of the suggestions and recommendations mentioned in this chapter may be outside the purview of governments. However, some require institutional backing and policy interventions from governments. The inclusion of business history and indigenous business practices into the curriculum, for example, require a new look at instructional priorities. In an attempt to spur graduates to accept self-employment and gear up job creation, many universities and other higher educational institutes have included indigenous knowledge and business practices in their curricula as a way to fuel interest in entrepreneurship.

The search for growth solutions, means of job creation and support for indigenous businesses should become a priority for African governments. African governments can begin to set out strategic plans to support IAEs with policies and regulations that drive the creation of more indigenous businesses. Tax holidays and tax rebates could be established. These policies will also encourage their populations, especially young adults, to embrace and start up indigenous businesses within their cultures and societies. Indeed, the inclusion of indigenous businesses knowledge as part of entrepreneurship in higher education could be integrated into national strategic plans to bolster indigenous businesses. Local and regional governments should also develop strategic plans that may or may not be derived from the national strategic plan. Local government authorities are closer to the people and may be able to capitalise on the opportunities in indigenous business practices more directly than national governments.

Various local government agencies can provide easy access to advisory and other consulting services for indigenous businesses as part of a strategic plan that includes capacity building initiatives. Governments can forge partnerships with special training institutions and business schools to offer some of these services. Partnerships with local and international financial institutions that provide funding in the form of grants and loans with single-digit repayment agreements for start-ups and existing indigenous businesses could also be a great initiative, if carefully planned and executed. Capacity building initiatives could also include plans and frameworks for indigenous business personnel to be upskilled. This will transform the many IAEs' abilities to initiate scaling for both local and international markets.

The size of Africa's informal economy is huge. On average, the informal sector has been estimated at 42% of the population and accounts for between 76% and 80.8% of employment (Boso et al., 2018; Guven & Karlen, 2020; ILO, 2020). The spatial divide between the formal and informal economies in Africa has become generally accepted (Boso et al., 2018; Charman, Petersen, Piper, Liedeman, & Legg, 2017). It is also sometimes forgotten that some businesses in this huge informal sector may be utilising indigenous business models and practices. However, little has been done to uncover the theoretical conclusions that can be drawn from the intersection between indigenous businesses and Africa's large informal economy. Government research institutions can spearhead research in this direction and utilised the findings to create comprehensive strategic plans at the national and local levels.

An obvious role for African governments that cannot be overemphasised is the provision of infrastructure and a conducive business environment. No economy can truly grow and be competitive when the cost of doing business is high; it reduces the global competitiveness of the economy. Therefore, it is important to reiterate that indigenous businesses are particularly affected by the high costs of doing business. The provision of necessary infrastructure to aid transportation, logistics and production, to rural and semi-urban areas in Africa, where many IAEs are situated, is pertinent to their growth and development.

One form of a third-party organisation whose potential for development has been largely overlooked is religious organisations. Religion permeates the lives of many Africans. In a survey of African countries conducted by Pew Research Centre in the United States, a substantial percentage of Africans placed religion above their ethnicity and nationality (Adeleye, Fawehinmi, Adisa, Utam, & Ikechukwu-Ifudu, 2019). In Nigeria, for example, that percentage approaches 91% in some locales (Adeleye et al., 2019). In many African countries, religious institutions are a substitute institutional framework (Barnard & Mamabolo, 2022; Ibeh et al., 2022) that participate in many aspects of the continent's socio-economic development (Aziegbe-Esho & Anetor, 2020). African governments can leverage this resource by partnering with religious organisations to provide enlightenment campaigns, training and capacity building programmes, and other initiatives aimed at promoting indigenous businesses and adopting indigenous business practices.

Conclusion

To advance the cause of indigenous business practices and IAEs in Africa, Africans themselves will have to truly believe that the indigenous business models and practices inherent in their cultures offer great value. The general belief that anything indigenous to Africa is primitive and of less importance than derivatives of western cultures need to be discarded. Cross-fertilisation of indigenous business practices within Africa, that is, between African cultures and countries, needs to be encouraged by researchers, businesses, educational institutions, governments and also IAE practitioners.

The research agenda suggested in this chapter needs to be conducted scientifically and objectively to avoid any sense of bias or self-promotion of particular tribes. Collaborations across and within Africa, inter-continental collaborations and partnerships among African universities and international scholars should be encouraged. Research collaborations between scholars of African descent and non-African descent published in high-impact journals would elevate the conversation on African indigenous business practices and attract international attention.

Advancing the cause of indigenous business practices in Africa is one way of contributing to and encouraging entrepreneurial businesses to be essential participants in meeting Africa's true potential. To meet this end, Africa's indigenous business practices need further extensive and in-depth research. Borrowing the words of Ibeh et al. (2022), the indigenous business practice in Africa 'begs to be further conceptualised, evidenced, and advanced'.

References

Adeleye, I., Fawehinmi, A., Adisa, T., Utam, K., & Ikechukwu-Ifudu, V. (2019). Managing diversity in Nigeria: Competing logics of workplace diversity. In *Diversity within diversity management* (Vol. 21, pp. 21–40). Advanced Series in Management. Bingley: Emerald Publishing Limited. doi:10.1108/S1877-636120190000021002

Adeola, O. (2020). The Igbo traditional business school (I-TBS): An introduction. In O. Adeola (Ed.), *Indigenous African Enterprise: The Igbo traditional business school* (pp. 3–12). Bingley: Emerald Publishing Limited.

Adeola, O. (2020b). The Igbo business practice: Towards a model for Africa conclusion and recommendations. In O. Adeola (Ed.), *Indigenous African enterprise* (Vol. 26, pp. 235–245). Advanced Series in Management. Bingley: Emerald Publishing Limited. doi:10.1108/S1877-636120200000026016

Amankwah-Amoah, J., Boso, N., & Debrah, Y. A. (2018). Africa rising in an emerging world: An international marketing perspective. *International Marketing Review, 35*(4), 550–559.

Aziegbe-Esho, E., & Anetor, F. (2020). Religious organisations and quality education for African women: The case of Nigeria. In O. Adeola (Ed.), *Empowering African women for sustainable development*. Cham: Palgrave Macmillan. doi:10.1007/978-3-030-59102-1_7

Barnard, H. (2020). The Africa we want and the Africa we see: How scholarship from Africa stands to enrich global scholarship. *Africa Journal of Management, 6*(2), 132–143.

Barnard, H., & Mamabolo, A. (2022). On religion as an institution in international business: Executives' lived experience in four African countries. *Journal of World Business, 57*(1). doi:10.1016/j.jwb.2021.101262

Boshoff, C., Adeola, O., Hinson, R. E., & Heinonen, K. (2022). Viewpoint: Plotting a way forward for service research in and out of Africa. *Journal of Services Marketing*. doi:10.1108/JSM-07-2021-0258

Boso, N., Debrah, Y., & Amankwah-Amoah, J. (2018). (How) does Africa matter for international business scholarship? *AIB Insights, 18*(4), 6–9.

Brandenburger, A. M., & Nalebuff, B. J. (1996). *Coopetition*. New York, NY: Doubleday.

Brandenburger, A., & Nalebuff, B. (2021). The rules of co-opetition. *Harvard Business Review*. Retrieved from https://hbr.org/2021/01/the-rules-of-co-opetition

Charman, A. J., Petersen, L. M., Piper, L. E., Liedeman, R., & Legg, T. (2017). Small area census approach to measure the township informal economy in South Africa. *Journal of Mixed Methods Research, 11*, 36–58.

Eisenhardt, K. M. (1989). Building theories from case study research. *Academy of Management Review, 14*(4), 532–550.

Eisenhardt, K. M., & Graebner, M. E. (2007). Theory building from cases: Opportunities and challenges. *Academy of Management Journal, 50*(1), 25–32.

George, G. (2015). Expanding context to redefine theories: Africa in management research. *Management and Organization Review, 11*(1), 5–10.

George, G., Corbishley, C., Khayesi, J. N. O., Haas, M. R., & Tihanyi, L. (2016). Bringing Africa in: Promising directions for management research. *Academy of Management Journal, 59*(2), 377–393.

Guven, M., & Karlen, R. (2020). Supporting Africa's urban informal sector: Coordinated policies with social protection at the core. World Bank Blog. Retrieved from https://blogs.worldbank.org/africacan/supporting-africas-urban-informal-sector-coordinated-policies-social-protection-core

Hofstede-Insights. (2022). Compare countries. Retrieved from https://www.hofstede-insights.com/product/compare-countries/

Ibeh, K., Eyong, J. E., & Amaeshi, K. (2022). Towards advancing African management scholarship. *Journal of Management History, 28*(2), 187–198.

Igwe, P. A. (2021). Cross-cultural tribes, community and indigenous entrepreneurship. In A. Caputo, M. Pellegrini, M. Dabić, & L.-P. Dana (Eds.), *The international dimension of entrepreneurial decision-making, cultures, contexts, and behaviors.* Basel: Springer Nature.

ILO. (2020, December). *The transition from the informal to the formal economy in Africa.* Global Employment Policy Report, Background Paper N4.

Ingenbleek, P. T. M. (2019). The endogenous African business: Why and how it is different, why it is emerging now and why it matters. *Journal of African Business, 2,* 195–205.

Mampane, R. M., Omidire, M. F., & Aluko, F. R. (2018). Decolonising higher education in Africa: Arriving at a glocal solution. *South African Journal of Education, 38*(4). doi:10.15700/saje.v38n4a1636

Mol, M. J., Stadler, C., & Ariño, A. (2017). Africa: The new frontier for global strategy scholars. *Global Strategy Journal, 7,* 3–9.

Musitha, M. E., & Mafukata, M. A. (2018). Crisis of decolonising education: Curriculum implementation in Limpopo Province of South Africa. *Africa's Public Service Delivery and Performance Review, 6*(1), 1–8. doi:10.4102/apsdpr.V6i1.179

Ojera, P. (2018). Indigenous financial management practices in Africa: A guide for educators and practitioners. *Advanced Series in Management, 20,* 71–96.

Ovadje, F. (2016). The internationalisation of African firms: Effects of cultural differences on the management of subsidiaries. *Africa Journal of Management, 2*(2), 117–137.

Oyewunmi, A. E., Esho, E., & Ukenna, S. I. (2021). Navigating the realities of intercultural research in Sub-Saharan Africa: Insights from Nigeria. In D. S. A. Guttormsen, J. Lauring, & M. Chapman (Eds.), *Field guide to intercultural research* (pp. 256–269). Cheltenham: Edward Elgar Publishing.

Oyewunmi, A. E., Oyewunmi, O. A., & Moses, C. L. (2021). Igba-Boi: Historical transitions of the Igbo entrepreneurship model. In O. Adeola (Ed.), *Indigenous African enterprise: The Igbo traditional business school (I-TBS)* (pp. 13–26). Bingley: Emerald Publishing Limited.

Paulson, S. (2020). *I am because we are.* Retrieved from https://www.ttbook.org/interview/i-am-because-we-are-african-philosophy-ubuntu

Timberg, T. (2014). *The Marwaris: From Jagat Seth to the Birlas*. London: Penguin Books.

Tsui, A. S. (2004). Contributing to global management knowledge: A case for high quality indigenous research. *Asia Pacific Journal of Management, 21*(4), 491–513.

Uzo, U., & Meru, A. K. (Eds.). (2018). *Indigenous management practices in Africa: A guide for educators and practitioners*. Bingley: Emerald Group Publishing.

Varnum, M. E. W., & Grossmann, I. (2017). Cultural change: The how and the why. *Perspectives on Psychological Science, 12*(6), 956–972.

Verhoef, G. (2017). *The history of business in Africa: Complex discontinuity to emerging markets*. Cham: Springer.

Index